Guardians of the Grail

. . . and the men who plan to rule the world!

By J. R. Church

Editorial and Research
Ralph G. Griffin
G. G. Stearman

Guardians of the Grail
First Edition, 1989
Copyright © 1989 by **Prophecy Publications**
Oklahoma City, OK 73153

Printed in the United States of America

Published by:
Prophecy Publications
P. O. Box 7000
Oklahoma City, OK 73153

Library of Congress Catalog Card Number 89-91688
ISBN 0-941241-02-5

Foreword

My interest was first stirred in this subject when I read that Paramount Pictures planned to produce a movie in which Jesus Christ was to have a love affair with Mary Magdalene. I was angered by the prospect and began to research the history behind the myth. Over the next two years, I was able to uncover some startling facts, dating back as far as 1,500 years and weaving through European medieval history.

There is indeed a legend which proposes that Mary Magdalene bore sacred children — who in turn became the royalty of Europe. The documentation for the research is included in this volume.

This book deals with uncovered secrets, ancient mysteries and legends of long ago. Some of the legends are credible, others are not. Some of the sources utilized in gathering research for this book make a skillfully orchestrated attempt to deceive by carefully including false but easily believable lies. Such is a considerable amount of written history. We will discuss a few well-guarded secrets from the past as well as expose a few false myths which have been given credence by many.

It is not our interest to become involved with political issues, conservative or otherwise. The conspiracy we sometimes refer to in this book is not necessarily conservative versus liberal or capitalistic versus communistic. Our attention must not be diverted to political discussions of organizations whose ideologies are an outgrowth of European medieval knights, such as the Mormons, the Freemasons, etc. But our study deals principally with the biblical issue of the development of world government and the rise of the coming world dictator, who is called "the antichrist" in the Bible. I especially want to distance myself from anti-Semitic groups who tend to blame the Jews for the conspiracy.

The primary purpose of this book is to present a scenario showing that this world is now ready to be duped into the most outrageously deceptive scheme ever perpetrated on mankind. In short, the world is soon going to accept a man as its leader. He will not only be accepted, he will be idolized and worshiped. Many will believe he is God. Not just a god, but God Almighty!

Satan does not, in most cases, manipulate his devotees overtly. He operates in a subtle way, gradually seducing and deceiving, much of the time without his victim recognizing what is taking place. Each of us should realize that every day we are constantly being seduced and asked to make compromises in all areas of our lives. We are being systematically desensitized to vulgar, vile and even blasphemous activities that we would not have thought possible only a few years ago. Today we accept vulgarity through innuendo and even laugh at it. Satan is also laughing. What is watched on television and in movie theaters — and is listened to in so-called "music" — is in accordance with his plan.

Is it so difficult to imagine such a coming deception since we are unwilling to even alter our lifestyles? We are unwilling to eliminate the slightest degree of satanic influence. Would it not be likely that someday, we might be unwilling to deny that Lucifer is commanding our allegiance, as well as the worship of the entire world?

Someday, the Lord will allow his enemies to be controlled by "a reprobate mind." He will also "send them strong delusion, that they should believe a lie." Only those who have a very close relationship with the Lord will be able to resist the acceptance of "the lie." It is my deepest prayer that all who read this book will accept — or have already accepted — Jesus

Christ as their personal Savior so that they will not be among those who are deceived by "the lie."

Eschatology is the branch of theology dealing with the study of last things, or end-time events. To me, the study of Bible prophecy is fascinating. Possessing knowledge of what God's prophets had predicted thousands of years ago allows one the ability to perceive current events and issues with godly insight. Knowledge of prophetic scripture gives the capacity to observe events from their proper biblical perspective.

It is essential for us to recognize the times in which we live. We must comprehend what is happening in our world so that, in the short time we have left, we may be able to warn those who have not yet accepted salvation through Jesus Christ.

We may have heard those warnings before, but have not listened. We may have become desensitized to their importance. They may have ceased to make an impact on our sense of urgency. However, I believe the exhortation may be more valid at this time than in the past!

Not only do we currently see world events taking shape precisely in accordance with Bible prophecy, we are watching them occur in a very rapid manner. But what really makes these days more apocalyptic than days past is the prevailing mentality, or "mindset" of people. The mindset in the West seems to be almost identical with that in the East. The mindset of most Christians seems to be moving toward the same as that of non-Christians.

For example, the book, THE LAST TEMPTATION OF CHRIST, was written in the 1950's and translated into English and published in 1960. However, few knew of its existence until very recently when the movie was released. Its release was first planned in 1984, but "public outrage" canceled its production. What has changed since 1984? Today's "public outrage" seems only to be coming from a small group of

Christian "fundamentalists" or "evangelicals." Many liberal Christians as well as their pastors, priests and elders publically state they see nothing harmful with the story. The mindset of the modern citizen of the world, Christian or not, now passively accepts such blasphemy.

The mindset that helps make worthless and offensive theological garbage such as THE LAST TEMPTATION acceptable is the same mindset predicted to prevail in the last days by the prophets, as well as Jesus Himself:

"But evil men and seducers shall wax worse and worse, deceiving, and being deceived" (II Timothy 3:13).

"And many false prophets shall rise, and shall deceive many. And because iniquity shall abound, the love of many shall wax cold" (Matthew 24:11-12).

The days in which we are presently living are the LAST DAYS, believe it or not! But, is there some heretofore unrevealed truth, knowledge or ancient wisdom imparted from Nikos Kazantzakis and other writers? Have any of them actually stumbled onto some "truth" which has been hidden for centuries until today? Can we really know what is BEHIND the legend of the Holy Grail? What is the truth behind the story of the so-called "marriage," or the alleged affair between Jesus Christ and Mary Magdalene?

Was Jesus only a man who became a god?

Did He and Mary Magdalene produce sacred children — the royalty of Europe?

Will the coming antichrist claim descent from Jesus Christ and Mary Magdalene?

Will he be from European royalty?

I shall attempt to answer those questions.

Table of Contents

The Holy Grail

Chapter 1

Who Are the Guardians?

This book reveals the sordid story of a secret organization based in Europe, which, down through the centuries, has been the guardian of a so-called "holy bloodline." Participants in this clandestine group believe that members of this "sacred lineage" are descended from Mary Magdalene and Jesus Christ. Their ultimate goal is world government!

This mysterious group is presently made up of over 9,000 men, including Protestants, Roman Catholics, Jews, and Moslems. The members of this secret sect should be considered unfaithful to their respective beliefs, for in reality they are neither Christian nor Catholic, they are neither Jew nor Moslem. Their doctrine sidesteps the basic tenets of those beliefs and replaces them with the teachings of their greatest prophet — whom they believe to be Buddha.

Over the last three decades, stories have been surfacing in

France about the existence of such a group. Little by little, they have been preparing the political climate across the world for the emergence of a one-world government and the introduction of a global dictator. According to the tenets of the organization, Jesus Christ did not die on Calvary — but merely pretended to die, was taken from the cross, stolen from the tomb, and was believed to have married Mary Magdalene and even produced children.[1]

They claim that when the Romans destroyed the Temple at Jerusalem in 70 A. D., the Magdalene fled with her sacred children by boat across the Mediterranean to France. There she found refuge in a Jewish community. Future generations of her offspring were said to have married into the royal Frankish family and by the fifth century produced a king.[2]

His name was Merovee. He was the first in a series of kings called the Merovingian bloodline. It is said that the offspring of Merovee were noted for a birthmark above the heart — a small red cross. This symbol eventually became the emblem of the Guardians of the Grail. Furthermore, these kings claimed to have clairvoyant powers and the ability to heal the sick by the laying on of hands.[3]

Merovee, king of the Franks from 447 to 458 A.D., was an adherent of the religious cult of Diana. His son, Childeric I, (458 - 481 A.D.) practiced witchcraft. His son, Clovis I, (481 - 511 A.D.) adopted Christianity in 496 A.D.

The Roman emperor, Constantine, (307 - 337 A.D.) embraced Christianity in 324 A.D., divided the Roman empire, and eventually moved his throne to the city of Byzantium, the name of which he changed to Constantinople. It is called Istanbul, Turkey today. Constantine upset the political structure of the Imperial Roman empire and created a division in fourth century Christianity.

After the death of Constantine, the Roman empire split

between the east and the west. The Eastern Orthodox Church grew in power and influence, while the Roman church faltered. In 496 A.D., the Bishop of Rome made a pact with Clovis, the grandson of Merovee, and king of the Franks, calling him the "New Constantine," giving him authority to preside over a "Christianized" Roman empire. (The term "Holy Roman Empire" was not officially used until 962 A.D.) The pope did so to consolidate the power of the faltering Roman church.

The so-called offspring of Mary Magdalene were thus established as leaders of the empire. The authors of HOLY BLOOD, HOLY GRAIL even suggest that the French cathedrals, including Notre Dame, were built in honor of Mary, the Magdalene — rather than Mary, the mother of Jesus. [4]

When King Clovis died, his son, Clotaire I (558 - 562 A.D.) ascended the throne. After Clotaire came his son, Chilperic I (566 - 584 A.D.), followed by Clotaire II (584 - 628 A.D.), son of Chilperic I, and finally Dagobert I (628 - 637 A.D.), who was assassinated after becoming king of the Franks in 630 A.D.

Dagobert I fathered two sons who carried on the Merovingian bloodline. The first son was Clovis II (637 - 655 A.D.) and the succession continued to Childeric III, who, in turn, was deposed in 751 A.D. He was the last known Merovingian to sit upon the throne of France. [5] The other son was Sigisbert III (629 - 656 A.D.), from whom came "Godfroi de Bouillon and various other royal families — Blanchefort, Gisors, Saint-Clair (Sinclair in England), Montesquiou, Monpezat, Poher, Luisignan, Plantard, and Habsburg-Lorraine." [6]

Alex, sister of Godfroi de Bouillon and Baudouin, married Emperor Henry IV, of the Holy Roman Empire. The lineage continues to the Habsburg Dynasty. The following charts show the Habsburg connection to the Merovingian bloodline.

THE MEROVINGIAN BLOODLINE

(Dates represent dates of reign unless marked "b" for birth)
Merovee (Merovech or Meroveus) (447 - 458).
Some claim he was the offspring of Jesus Christ and
Mary Magdalene, though Merovee claimed descent
from Odin. (See Chapter 5).

I

Childeric I (458 - 481), son of Merovee.

I

Clovis I (481 - 511), son of Childeric I.

I

Clotaire I (558 - 562), son of Clovis I.

I

Chilperic I (566 - 584), son of Clotaire I.

I

Clotaire II (584 - 628), son of Chilperic I.

I

Dagobert I (628 - 637), son of Clotaire II.

I

Sigisbert III (629 - 656), son of Dagobert I.

I

Dagobert II (674 - 678), son of Sigisbert III.
He was assassinated on orders of Pepin the Fat
who placed his son, Charles Martel on the throne.
Charles Martel, also called Carl the Hammer, drove the
Moslems out of Europe. His grandson was Charlemagne.

I

Sigisbert IV (b676 - 758), son of Dagobert II.
He was the first to be called "Plant-Ard."

I

Sigisbert V (b695 - 768), son of Sigisbert IV.

I

Bera III (b715 - 770), son of Sigisbert V.

I

Guillame (? -?), son of Bera III.

I

Bera IV (b755 - 813), son of Guillame.

I

Argila (b775 - 836), son of Bera IV.

I

Bera V (b794 - 860), son of Argila.

Hilderic I (b? - 867), son of Bera V.

Sigisbert VI "Prince Ursus" (b? - 885), son of Hilderic I.

Guillame II (b? - 914), son of Sigisbert VI.

Guillame III (b874 - 936), son of Guillame II.

Arnaud (b? - 952), son of Guillame III.

Bera VI (b? - 975), son of Arnaud.

Sigisbert VII (b? - 982), son of Bera VI.

Hugues I (b951 - 971), son of Sigisbert VII.

Jean I (b? - 1020), son of Hugues I.

Hugues de Plantard (b? - 1015), son of Jean I.

Eustache I (b1010 - ?), son of Hugues de Plantard.

Eustache II (b? - 1081), son of Eustache I.

Godfroi de Bouillon (b1061 - 1100) son of Eustache II.
He was Duke of Lower Lorraine.
He was the Founder of the "Priory of Sion" in 1099.
He was offered title of King of Jerusalem,
but preferred to be called "Guardian of the Holy Sepulchre."

Alex, sister of Godfroi de Bouillon and Baudouin,
married **Henry IV,** emperor of the Holy Roman Empire.
(See pages 18-19 to continue the lineage of Alex and Henry IV.)

Baudouin (Baldwin) (b? - 1131) son of Eustache II.
He was the brother of Godfroi de Bouillon and accepted the title,
King of Jerusalem in 1100 upon Godfroi's death.
He was the First Grand Master of the "Knights Templar."
|

Fulk V, (b1092 - 1143).
He was the Count of Anjou who married Melisend,
daughter of Baudouin, and became King of Jerusalem upon
Baudouin's death in 1131.
|

Geoffrey Plantagenet (b1113 - 1151), son of Fulk V.
Geoffrey married Matilda, widow of
Holy Roman Emperor **Henry V.**
|

Henry II (b1133 - 1189), son of Geoffrey Plantagenet and
Eleanore of Aquitane, widow of Louis VII, King of France.
|

Philip II Augustus (b1165 - 1223), son of Henry II.
|

Louis VIII (b1187 - 1226), son of Philip II Augustus.
|

Louis IX (b1214 - 1270), son of Louis VIII.
|

Philip III (b1245 - 1285), son of Louis IX.
|

Philip IV (b1285 - 1314), son of Philip III.
|

Philip VI (1293 - 1350), son of Charles Valois.
He was the brother of Philip IV.
|

John II, the Good (b1319 - 1364), son of Philip VI.
|

Louis, Duke of Anjou (? - ?), son of John II.
|

Louis II (? - ?), son of Louis.
|

Rene I D'Anjou (b? - 1480), son of Louis II.
|

Iolande D'Anjou (b? - 1483), daughter of Rene I.
|
Rene II D'Anjou (b? - 1508), son of Iolande.
Rene II fathered two sons, Claude de Lorraine
and Antoine II de Lorraine. Claude's daughter, Marie,
married James V, and bore Mary, Queen of Scots.
Antoine II carries on the lineage in this chart.
|
Antoine II (b? - 1544), son of Rene II D'Anjou.
|
Francois de Lorraine (b? -1545), son of Antoine II.
|
Charles III de Lorraine (b? - 1608), son of Francois.
|
Henry II de Lorraine (b? - 1624), son of Charles III.
|
Nicolas-Francois de Lorraine(b? - 1670), son of Henry II.
|
Charles V de Lorraine (b? - 1765), son of Nicolas Francois.
Charles V married Eleonore Marie von Habsburg, daughter of
Ferdinand III, Emperor of the Holy Roman Empire.
The Merovingian bloodline is at this point intersected by
the Habsburg Dynasty, which continues to the present time.
|
Leopold de Lorraine (b? - 1729), son of Charles V.
|
Francois de Lorraine (**Francis I**) (1745 - 1765), son of Leopold.
Francis I married Maria Teresa von Habsburg, Empress
of Austria. Among their children was Marie Antoinette von
Habsburg, who married Louise XVI, king of France. The son who
carries the Habsburg lineage followed in this chart was Leopold II.
|
Leopold II (1790 - 1792), son of Francis I.
|
Francis II (1792 - 1806), son of Leopold II.
He abdicated the throne when Napoleon abolished
the Holy Roman Empire in 1806.
He was also called Francis I, Emperor of Austria.
|

Ferdinand I (1835 - 1848), son of Francis II.
Ferdinand fathered two sons:
Francis Joseph I,(who started World War I and died in 1916,
and Charles Louis, who continues this chart.
|
Charles Louis (b1833 - 1896), son of Ferdinand I.
|
Otto (b1865 - 1900), son of Charles Louis.
|
Charles I (1916 - 1918), son of Otto.
Charles I became Emperor of Austria in 1916,
upon the death of Francis Joseph I.
He abdicated the throne in 1918, having lost the war.
|
Otto von Habsburg (1912 -   ), son of Charles I.
Otto is a member of the European Parliament.
He and his son , Karl, have promoted the establishment
of the United States of Europe.
|
Karl von Habsburg (1961-), son of Otto.
Could he become the leader of the United States of Europe?

****

HEIRS OF THE HOLY ROMAN EMPIRE

The term "HOLY ROMAN EMPIRE" was introduced
in 962 A. D., when the concept of an empire was revived.
This chart shows how the Merovingian bloodline and the
Habsburg dynasty became heirs to the title, "Emperor of the Holy
Roman Empire." This is not a genealogical chart, but a partial
list of emperors of the Holy Roman Empire showing the bloodline
from the beginning of the Holy Roman Empire to the present.
Names of emperors will appear in **bold** type.

Otto I (962 - 973), son of Henry I, King of Germany.
He was the first "Holy" Roman Emperor.
|

Otto II (973 - 983), son of Otto I (Otto the Great).

|

Otto III (983 - 1002), son of Otto II.

|

Henry II (1003 - 1024), grandson of Henry I.

|

Conrad II (1024 - 1039), great-great-grandson of Otto I.

|

Henry III (1039 - 1056), son of Conrad II.

|

Henry IV (1056 - 1106), son of Henry III.
Alex, sister of Godfroi de Bouillon and Baudouin,
married **Henry IV**, emperor of the Holy Roman Empire.
At this point, the Merovingian bloodline was infused into
the throne of the Holy Roman Empire.
(See the chart on Page 15)

|

Henry V (1106 - 1125), son of Henry IV.

|

Frederick the One-eyed (? - ?), son of Henry V.

|

Frederick I (Barbarossa) (1152 - 1190),
son of Frederick the One-eyed. He was the nephew of
Conrad III, of the House of Hohenstaufen.
Frederick I followed **Conrad III** as Holy Roman Emperor.

|

Henry VI, King of England (1190 - 1197), son of Frederick I.

|

Frederick II (1215 - 1250), son of Henry VI.

|

Conrad IV (1250 - 1254), son of Frederick II.

****

The Great Interregnum (1254 -1272).
This was a transitional period of the Holy Roman Empire,
a time of decline. Two nominal emperors ruled,
William of Holland (1254 -1256) and
Richard, Earl of Cornwall, King of the Romans (1256 - 1272).

****

THE HABSBURG DYNASTY

Rudolf I of Habsburg (1273-1291).
The Habsburg dynasty has continued to the present.
The Habsburgs ruled the Holy Roman Empire until 1806,
when the throne was abolished by Napoleon.
Rudolf, like **Conrad III** and **Frederick I**
before him, was of the House of Hohenstaufen.
|
Albert I (1298-1308), son of Rudolf I.
|
Albert II, Emperor of Austria (1330 - 1358), son of Albert I.
|
Albert III, Emperor of Austria (1358 - 1397), son of Albert II.
|
Albert IV, Emperor of Austria (1397 - 1404), son of Albert III.
Albert IV fathered two sons, **Albert V** and **Frederick III**,
who both became Emperors of the Holy Roman Empire.
|
Albert V, Emperor of Austria (1404 - 1439),son of Albert IV.
He was also known as **Albert II** of Habsburg (1438-1439).
|
Frederick III (1440 - 1493), son of Albert IV.
|
Maximilian I (1493-1519), son of Frederick III.
|
Philip I (b1478 - 1506), son of Maximilian I.
Philip I had two sons, both becoming Emperors of
the Holy Roman Empire. **Charles V** (1519 - 1556)
also was King of Spain as Charles I (1516 - 1556).
He introduced the Habsburg Dynasty in Spain,
continuing to the present day in King Juan Carlos.
Philip's other son, **Ferdinand I** , continued the Austrian
line of emperors of the Holy Roman Empire.
|
Ferdinand I (1556 - 1564), son of Philip I.
|
Charles (b1540 - 1590), son of Ferdinand I.
|

Ferdinand II (1619 - 1637), son of Charles.
|
Ferdinand III (1637 - 1658), son of Ferdinand II.
Ferdinand III's daughter, Eleonore-Marie von Habsburg,
married Charles V of Lorraine. Charles V fathered
Leopold of Lorraine, who was the father of
Francis I, Holy Roman Emperor (1745-1765).
Ferdinand's son, **Leopold I** continued this line of
Holy Roman Emperors.
|
Leopold I (1658 - 1705), son of Ferdinand III.
|
Charles VI (1711 - 1740), son of Leopold I.
Charles VI's daughter, Marie-Teresa von Habsburg,
Empress of Austria, married Holy Roman Emperor **Francis I**,
thereby increasing the likelihood that future Emperors of the
Holy Roman Empire would continue from the Habsburg line.
|
Francis I (1745 - 1765), son of Charles VI.
|
Leopold II (1790 - 1792), son of Francis I.
|
Francis II (1792 - 1806), son of Leopold II.
The Holy Roman Empire was officially abolished in 1806 by
Napoleon. Francis II continued as Emperor of Austria until 1835.
****

THE SPANISH HABSBURGS

The Habsburg Dynasty ruled the Holy Roman Empire
continuously from 1438 until it was abolished by
Napoleon in 1806. The dynasty also began its rule
of Spain in 1519 and continues to this day.

Charles I (**Charles V** (1519 - 1556), son of Philip I.
He was the brother of **Ferdinand I** (1556 - 1564).
Charles was also the grandson of King Ferdinand and
Queen Isabella of Spain and ruled during the time Spanish
galleons were hauling gold and silver from the Americas.
|

Philip II (1556 - 1598), son of Charles I (**Charles V**).
|
Philip III (1598 - 1621), son of Philip II.
|
Philip IV (1621 - 1665), son of Philip III.
Philip IV's daughter, Marie-Therese, married Louis XIV,
King of France (1643 - 1715).
|
Philip V of Anjou (1701 - 1724), grandson of Louis XIV.
|
Ferdinand VI (1746 - 1759), son of Philip V.
|
Charles III (1759 - 1788), son of Philip V.
|
Charles IV (1788 - 1808), son of Charles III.
|
Ferdinand VII (1808 - 1808 and 1814 - 1833), son of Charles IV.
|
Isabella II (1833 -1868), daughter of Ferdinand VII.
|
Alfonso XII (1874 - 1886), son of Isabella II.
|
Alfonso XIII (1886-1931), son of Alfonso XII
|
Don Juan de Borbon Battenberg (1913 -   ),
son of Alfonso XIII
|
Juan Carlos I (January 5, 1938 -   ),
King of Spain (1975 -   ), son of Don Juan.
|
Felipe Juan (January 30, 1968 -   ), son of Juan Carlos.
**Could Juan Carlos (or perhaps his son) become the
ruler of the United States of Europe?**

The European Currency Unit (ECU), the official coin of
the European Economic Community, which is destined
to become the "United States of Europe" by 1992,
displays the bust of **Charles V**, progenitor of
the "Spanish" Habsburgs.

It is said that the Merovingian bloodline found its way to most of the thrones of Europe — an incredible story which may not be altogether true, but that is beside the point. The fact is, there exists a secret organization in Europe today which believes it is true.

From the Merovingian bloodline has come most, if not all, the ruling families of Europe and, believe it or not, has even included some of the popes of the Roman Catholic Church. Among them was Pope Stephen IX, leader of the church in the 11th century — during the years of the Crusades.

The Crusades, by the way, played an important part in the promotion of the Merovingian bloodline. Many of the Crusaders were French who went to Palestine to liberate the Holy Land from the Moslems. By 1061 A.D., the Catholic Crusaders had conquered the city of Jerusalem and established Godfroi de Bouillon (of the Merovingian bloodline) on the throne of Jerusalem. Claiming to be of the lineage of David, Godfroi de Bouillon organized a secret society called the Ordre de Sion — today called Prieure (Priory) de Sion — in 1099 A.D. The clandestine Priory of Sion still exists after almost 900 years. It is very much alive today.

In the years that followed, Godfroi de Bouillon and his secret group, the Priory of Sion, began to lay plans for a front organization to carry out their goals. In 1118 A.D., Hugues de Payen organized the Knights Templar and made Baudouin, the brother of Godfroi de Bouillon, its first Grand Master. They adopted the Merovingian birthmark as their emblem — a red cross!

The stated purpose of the Knights Templar were to guard the highways around Jerusalem to protect the pilgrims coming for worship. Those nine men supposedly gave of themselves to go to Jerusalem and become the "poor knights of the Temple." They pledged themselves to be subject only to the pope and to no other political or ecclesiastical authority.

Upon their arrival in Jerusalem, they were given living quarters in the palace of King Baudouin on the Temple site. Though there is no historical proof, it is believed that they spent the next nine years digging — digging up the buried treasure of the ancient Jewish Temple. [7]

In 1953 a copper scroll was found in a cave near the Dead Sea which told of a fabulous Temple treasure — estimated at more than 138 tons of gold and silver which had been buried by the Jewish priesthood in 64 locations before the Romans destroyed the Temple in 70 A.D. Twenty-four of those hordes of gold and silver were buried under the Temple mountain. [8] It is believed that the Knights Templar plundered the treasure of the Temple and took it back to Europe. After nine years in Jerusalem, the Templars returned to Europe wealthy beyond belief.

In the years following they built castles all over Europe and became famous as the guardians of the Holy Grail. It is believed that the Priory of Sion organized the Knights Templar to excavate the Temple site in hopes of finding the fabulous treasure of the Temple. Evidently they were successful, for they instituted an international banking system across Europe and had the resources to loan gold to kings and governments. [9]

The Knights Templar soon broke away from their allegiance to the Bishop of Rome and became an arrogant organization aloof from all recognized authority. They refused to be subject to kings or popes. Those international bankers also invented a method by which they could transfer gold from one city to another or from one bank to another simply by writing a note on a piece of paper. Today we call it writing checks. [10]

The secret purpose for the Knights Templar, however, was to preserve the Merovingian bloodline in hopes of one day establishing a world government and putting their king upon the throne — a king who could claim to be the offspring of Jesus Christ and Mary Magdalene.

The Knights Templar wore white uniforms, each having a large red cross on the mantle. Legends were told of their exploits. They were the guardians of the Holy Grail, the so-called cup from which Jesus drank at the last supper, and of the Grail family, the bloodline of the Magdalene.

In 1188 there was a split between the Ordre de Sion and the Knights Templar. Only the year before, the Knights had lost a battle over Jerusalem and their Grand Master was accused of treason. From that time the days of the Knights Templar were numbered.

The king of France tried to destroy the Knights Templar and confiscate their treasure in the early 1300's. Between 1303 and 1305 Philip IV, king of France, engineered the kidnapping and death of Pope Boniface VIII and the murder by poison of his successor, Pope Benedict XI. In 1305 King Philip managed to secure the election of his own candidate, the Archbishop of Bordeaux, to the vacant papal throne.[11]

The new pontiff took the name Clement V and together with Philip organized the infamous Inquisition in an effort to destroy the power and influence of the Knights Templar — and especially the Merovingian bloodline that hung like a cloud over the Roman church. Another main objective was to confiscate the treasures of the Temple.

On October 13, 1307, all the Templars in France were arrested — including their Grand Master, Jacques de Molay. The king also tried to locate the treasure of the Templars, but the treasure could not be found. In March, 1314 A.D., Jacques de Molay, the Grand Master of the Knights Templar, and Geoffrey de Charney (owner of the shroud, today called The Shroud of Turin) were burned at the stake.[12] From that point on, the Knights seemed to vanish from the stage of history. Nevertheless, the order continued to exist.

The French Templars found a refuge in Scotland, where the group maintained itself as a coherent body for at least the next 400 years. They eventually developed into an organization called the Scottish Rite.

By 1789 the legends surrounding the ancient Knights Templar pictured them as illumined alchemists, magi, and sages — veritable supermen endowed with an awesome arsenal of arcane power and knowledge. They were regarded as heroes and martyrs.

The death of Jacques de Molay at the hands of King Philip was never forgotten. During the French Revolution, as the head of King Louis XVI fell beneath the guillotine, a man leaped onto the scaffold, dipped his hand in the monarch's blood, flung it out over the surrounding throng, and cried, "Jacques de Molay, thou art avenged!"[3]

The mystique surrounding the Knights Templar has not diminished. There have been a few contemporary organizations which claimed to possess a pedigree from the ancient organization. Certain Masonic lodges have adopted the grade of Templar, as well as rituals supposedly descended from the original order. In the United States, young men are admitted into the De Molay Society — a fraternal organization — most without adaquate knowledge of the origin of the name. It was taken from Jacques De Molay, the 14th century Grand Master of the Knights Templar.

In the Mormon temple, certain rites are performed which are identical to Masonic rites. Mormonism also has a philosophical connection to the order of the ancient Templars.

In the last century, Helena Blavatsky, founder of theosophy, spoke of an esoteric wisdom tradition running back through the Rosicrucians to the Knights Templar. The teachings of

Helena Blavatsky can best be seen in the New Age Movement today.

Toward the end of the 19th century a sinister Order of Templars was established in Germany and Austria employing the swastika as one of its emblems. At first it was known as the Thule Society but later changed its name to the Nazi party.

But let us not forget that the Order of the Knights Templar was, at first, only a front organization for a more secretive group known as the Priory of Sion, whose real purpose was to capture the wealth of the world, establish their own world government, and introduce a Merovingian king to sit upon a throne in Jerusalem. They are said to be the true possessors of the Temple treasury and the behind-the-scenes controllers of the world's currencies.

In 1979 Mr. Pierre Plantard de Saint-Clair, the present Secretary General of the Priory of Sion, was interviewed in Paris, France by reporters from the BBC. When asked the question, "Does the Priory of Sion possess the treasures of the ancient Jewish Temple?", he said, "Yes." He added, "They will be returned to Jerusalem when the time is right."[14] Pierre Plantard is himself a descendant of the Merovingian bloodline.

Pierre Plantard de Saint-Clair

In 1903 the Russian czar was presented with a highly controversial document called the "Protocols of the Learned Elders of Zion." The publisher of the manuscript, a Russian Orthodox priest named Sergei Nilus, claimed that it was the work of a Jewish conspiracy to take over the governments of the world. The document had obviously been altered to make it look like a Jewish conspiracy.

The czar declared the document to be an outrageous fabri-
cation and ordered all copies of it destroyed. However, some
copies survived and in the following years was used by a great
many anti-Semitics as convincing proof of an international
Jewish conspiracy. In 1919, for example, it was distributed to
troops of the White Russian army. Over the next two years
some 60,000 Jews were massacred. They were blamed for the
1917 Russian revolution.

Adolf Hitler even used the "Protocols" to fuel his own
fanatical prejudices which led to the murder of six million
Jews. In the "Protocols" the so-called Learned Elders of Zion
speak of a Masonic kingdom and of a king of the blood of Zion
who will preside over this world kingdom.

It asserts that the future king will be of the dynastic roots of
King David. The "Protocols" also say that the king of the Jews
will be the real pope and the patriarch of an international
church. It concludes in a most cryptic fashion, "Certain
members of the seed of David will prepare the kings and their
heirs ... Only the king and the three who stood sponsor for him
will know what is coming." [15]

It is absurd to think that these "Protocols" could be the work
of traditional Judaism. These plans for world government are
no more Jewish than they are Christian. It has been suggested
that they are the work of the ancient Priory of Sion, established
by Godfroi de Bouillon in 1099. This Priory of Sion may be the
group who plan to introduce the so-called "offspring of Jesus
and Mary Magdalene" to sit upon the throne of a world
government.

The Priory of Sion appears to be the guardians of a "holy
bloodline" and the Holy Grail — the holy bloodline being the
lineage of Mary Magdalene and the Holy Grail being the cup
from which Jesus drank the Last Supper.

The Holy Grail, therefore, was believed to contain the holy blood, or in a mystical sense, the holy bloodline from the "harlot," Magdalene. (See page 75.) We are told in Revelation 17 of a woman guiding the governments of the world — and in her hand was seen a golden cup. It may well represent what I consider to be the UNholy blood and the UNholy grail.

Now all of this, it seems, has a French connection. The legend began with the Frankish king, Merovee, and continued with the French Crusaders, who captured Jerusalem in the 11th century. Also, the Knights Templar had their headquarters in France.

I do not wish to sound unpatriotic, but a century ago the Frenchman, Auguste Bartholdi, built a statue and placed it in New York harbor. Its construction was funded in large part by the Freemasons in France and America.[16] The figure stands dressed in a Roman toga — and in her hand, a golden cup-like torch. Could it represent the Grail? Does it symbolize the Magdalene bloodline enlightening the world?

The official name is "Liberty Enlightening the World." But, doesn't that sound a bit like blasphemy? Jesus Christ is the Light of the world — not Liberty. Could the statue really be that of Mary, the Magdalene? The statue was renovated in 1986-87, and was reopened to the public on July 4, 1987, with a spectacular celebration. I wonder if that is why the psalmist wrote in Psalm 87:

"I will make mention of Rahab and Babylon to them that know me ..." (Psalm 87:4).

Rahab was a notorious harlot in the days of Joshua, and the verse appears to be a reference to the harlot Babylon. According to Psalm 87, the harlot will one day be revealed. At this point we can only pose the question. We can only say that her name is "Mystery."

Chapter Notes

CHAPTER 1

1. Michael Baigent, Richard Leigh, and Henry Lincoln, HOLY BLOOD, HOLY GRAIL (New York: Dell, 1983), p. 358.
2. Ibid., p. 313.
3. Ibid., p. 236.
4. Ibid., pp. 102-103.
5. Gene Gurney, KINGDOMS OF EUROPE (New York: Crown, 1982), p. 124.
6. Michael Baigent, et al, HOLY BLOOD, p. 107.
7. Ibid., p. 91.
8. Ibid., p. 88, quoting J.M. Allegro, THE TREASURE OF THE COPPER SCROLL (London: 1960), p. 107ff.
9. "Knights Templars," WORLD BOOK ENCYCLOPEDIA, Vol. 11, 1973, p. 279.
10. Baigent, HOLY BLOOD, p. 71.
11. Ibid., p. 75.
12. Ibid., p. 76.
13. Ibid., p. 80.
14. Ibid., p. 225.
15. THE PROTOCOLS OF THE MEETINGS OF THE LEARNED ELDERS OF ZION, trans. Victor E. Marsden (Sudbury, Suffolk, England: Bloomfield Books, 1920), pp. 123-124.
16. Christian Blanchet and Bertrand Dard, STATUE OF LIBERTY, THE FIRST HUNDRED YEARS, trans. by Bernard A. Weisberger (New York: Houghton-Mifflin, 1985), p. 44.

Merovee (458)

Dagobert I (638)

Baptism of Clovis (496)

Rudolf of Habsburg (1273)　　　**Godfrol de Bouillon (1099)**

The traditional site of the Upper Room is located in the Jewish Quarter of Old Jerusalem, just above the site of David's tomb. Its architecture dates back to Crusader times and was revered by the Knights Templar as the place where Jesus drank the cup of the Last Supper. It is reported that many ceremonies were conducted here by the Templars. Out of this site grew the legend of the Holy Grail.

Chapter 2

What Is the Grail?

In 1910, a team of archaeologists, digging at the site of the ancient ruins of Antioch, Syria, uncovered a beautiful chalice made of silver.[1] The intricate design work around it revealed pictures of Jesus Christ with the 12 disciples. The goblet sparked the imaginations of adherents to the legends of the so-called Holy Grail, reputed to be the cup out of which Jesus drank at the Last Supper. It was suggested that the chalice could have been made to contain the Grail. The Silver Chalice resides today in the Metropolitan Museum of Art in New York City. If it is the Silver Chalice, then where is the so-called golden cup? It should have been inside.

In the previous chapter, we considered a cup in the hand of Babylon, the Great and suggested the possibility that it may have a connection with the legend of the Grail. In Revelation 17, the harlot was seen holding a golden cup in her hand:

"And the woman was arrayed in purple and scarlet colour, and decked with gold and precious stones and pearls, having a golden cup in her hand full of abominations and filthiness of her fornication:" (Revelation 17:4-5).

Could the golden cup in her hand be a prophetic reference to the Grail? There are many be-

The Silver Chalice

liefs for precisely what was the Grail. The word "grail" may have derived from "graal," meaning cup, or shallow dish. Also, it may have come from the word "gredalis," which means gradually. The legendary search for the Grail was accomplished degree by degree, or gradually. The origin of the word in many of the early manuscripts was "Sang raal." "Sang," meaning "blood" and "raal," meaning "royal." This may be the key to the genealogy of the royalty of Europe. Reportedly, they are the family of the Holy Grail.

There is yet another possibility. The Grail may originally have been considered a "stone of light." According to Trevor Ravenscroft, in his book, THE CUP OF DESTINY, there is a Manichaean origin for the legend of the Grail. Supposedly, in the eons of eternity past, Lucifer rebelled against his Creator. In the legend, the "lightbearer" wore a crown of sparkling beauty, in the center of which was a magnificent stone — called the "stone of light." [2]

During a monumental conflict the archangel Michael struck the stone from Lucifer's crown. Some accounts say that the stone was transformed into a golden cup, while others say that Michael incarnated himself into the Grail and descended to earth to prepare the way of redemption — not only for a fallen

Lucifer, the so-called "Light Bearer" lost his "stone of light" during a battle with the archangel, Michael.

human race, but also for Lucifer as well.

The legendary capstone of the great Giza pyramid was suggested to be a clear crystal — a candidate for the so-called "stone of light" knocked from the crown of Lucifer by the mighty Michael.

Also, in the darkened room of the seance, the crystal ball of European witchcraft also represents that "stone of light." It becomes the catalyst for clairvoyant powers.

This concept, however, predates medieval European witchcraft. It may have been incorporated into Christianity by a man named Mani, the founder of Manichaeanism. Born around the year 242 A.D., Mani worked as a slave in the home of a man who traded in art treasures and antiquities. The man also kept an archive of the initiation cults of ancient civilizations. Not long after the boy came to live in the house, the old man died. Ravenscroft wrote that he continued to inspire the youth from beyond the grave. As a young man, Mani angered

The capstone of the pyramid of Giza was believed to be a large crystal. The legend of a capstone has become a symbol for the belief in the so-called "All-Seeing Eye."

the Zoroastrian priests by proclaiming that Jesus Christ was the incarnation of their sun god. His teachings were condemned as heresy and he was executed in Baghdad by being skinned alive. [3]

His teachings, however, were eventually carried into Europe and can be seen in the legend of the Grail. Mani combined the Christian teaching of salvation with the Zoroastrian belief that two opposing principles govern the universe — a mixture of light and darkness, representing good and evil.

Manichaeanism taught that man's soul, which rose from the kingdom of light, wants to escape from the body, which represents the kingdom of darkness. It was believed that the soul could find release only through wisdom — obtained through a series of initiations. A Master Teacher was to provide that wisdom necessary for release. Sounds like New Age thinking, doesn't it? The New Age Movement is nothing more than the worship of an ancient mystery cult.

The Last Supper

The conviction of many is that the Grail is a golden vessel. The cup was said to be used by Melchizedek as he offered the bread and wine to Abraham on Mount Moriah. Over the years it was also said to be preserved in the mystery cult of Hercules, a platonic sun hero. It was guarded in a Phoenician temple in Tyre, the city of Hiram, the king who designed and built the Temple for Solomon.

Eventually, it passed into the hands of the Queen of Sheba, the so-called queen of star wisdom — who brought it to King Solomon. Preserved down through the centuries, the cup was supposedly used by Christ as He partook of the Last Supper with His disciples. It is said that a Jew brought it to Pilate when Christ was led before him. And when, after the crucifixion, Joseph of Arimathaea begged the body of Jesus from Pilate, the Roman potentate committed to him that golden Grail.[4]

According to legend, either Mary Magdalene, or Joseph of Arimathaea, caught the blood of Jesus with the golden Grail as the soldier pierced His side. Joseph, the Magdalene, Martha and Lazarus later took the Grail to France (some say as far as

The cup with the sun-host above it depicting the rays of the sun. The window overlooks the Moslem Dome of the Rock in Jerusalem.

Scotland). Over the centuries, however, it disappeared. A vision of the Grail was supposedly seen by a nun, sister to one of the Knights of King Arthur's Round Table. This vision was so inspiring that all the knights vowed to search for the Grail. According to the legend, only three finally got to see it — Galahad, Percival, and Bors.

It is said that Joseph of Arimathaea was present when Longinus, the Roman centurion, pierced the side of Christ with a likewise legendary spear. That spear, by the way, resides today in a museum in Vienna, Austria, but that's another story which we shall review in chapter 3. Joseph of Arimathaea and his descendants supposedly became the guardians of the Grail. It is a ridiculous story, but that is only the beginning.

Over the years the Grail was depicted as a cup holding the

so-called sun host, a small round wafer that represented not only the body of Christ, but the disk of the sun as well. According to the mystery cult, Jesus was the sun god who left the heavenly sphere to prepare a pathway for the evolution of human consciousness.

The idea that the Grail contained the glowing rays of the sun god was preserved in a series of Eastern mystery cults dating back through the centuries with roots in ancient Persia — perhaps at the Tower of Babel.

The concept of the descent of the sun god was taught by Zarathustra, the founder of both Persia and a religion called Zoroastrianism. Ravenscroft wrote, "When the ancient Persian looked up to the heavens, he knew that behind the surface of the sky, hidden by the darkness, shines the spiritual sun. It becomes visible only at one spot where the sun's disk appears.... The sun spirit, behind the glowing disk ... was experienced by the ancient Persians as far away in cosmic space. By steps, he descended then to earth, and his descent is the descent of the world savior...." [5]

In Greek mythology, the sun god was called Apollo, who supposedly descended to earth to prepare this so-called pathway. The concept was also promoted 2,600 years ago in the teachings of Buddha. Buddha talked about the fate of man — which he called, "karma." He also taught that through a series of "chakras," known in the Orient as "lotus flowers," or "whirling wheels ... spiritual energy located at various points along the spinal column," [6] man could eventually become a part of the great cosmic mind — which he called god.

Sometime between 1195 and 1216 A.D., Wolfram von Eschenbach published PARZIVAL, a poem about the quest for the Holy Grail. [7] The poem was no ordinary work. Ravenscroft suggests that it is an initiation document of the highest order. It is the story of Percival, a young man who

Percival holds the Holy Grail -- the cup of the Last Supper

desired to become one of the knights of King Arthur's Round
Table.

Through a series of adventures he was initiated to become
the Guardian of the Grail. In the poem, the pathway to the
Grail was to be accomplished degree by degree. The term
grail, according to Ravenscroft, was derived from the word
"gradual." The search and ultimate attainment of the Grail
was thought to represent a gradual development in the inner
life of the soul from a state of dullness to a positive spiritual

Modern adepts (students) sit in the "lotus" position to meditate.

awakening. This compares significantly with the goal of the New Age Movement today.

Wolfram Von Eschenbach began his poem by describing a city under siege — Petalamund — a mystical city in medieval times located somewhere in the middle ground between East and West. A battle takes place at each of its 16 gates. Around the city a fierce conflict is waged — by a black army and a white army, each laying siege to eight gates of the city.

The city called Petalamund is, of course, fictitious. The word actually represents the petals of a lotus flower, the symbol used in Buddhism. It is also used by the New Age Movement today. It is said to represent the battle between good and evil taking place within a person who is trying to work out his karma. While practicing Transcendental Meditation, the adherent of the mystery cult sits in a so-called lotus position, symbolic of the battle of Petalamund, found in the legend of the Grail.

The hero, Percival, is said to be the incarnation of the sun god. The name Percival is suggested to have emerged from the term, "pierce the veil." This is what the light of the sun does, shining in the heavens from beyond the veil, which we call a blue oxygen atmosphere.

Although the Grail narratives were not published until sometime after 1195, Wolfram Von Eschenbach wrote of knight Percival as if he were alive in the ninth century — around the year 870. It was in the ninth century that most of the European nations took shape. Harald Fairhair became the first recognized king of Norway in 872; the Danes were for the first time united under one sovereign, King Gorm the Old, in 883; and Burik, the Swedish Norseman, became the founder of Russia in 862. The rise of the Polish dukes can be traced back to this time and Bulgaria had its first csar, Boris I, who began his reign in 852.

In England, Alfred the Great (871-901)laid the Saxon foundation for what later was to become Britain. Through the partition of the Carolingian empire near the end of the century, the kingdoms of France and Germany came into existence; and Italy, though still joined to Burgundy in 899, had its own ruler, Louis III. Thus, in the ninth century, Europe was formed into the embryonic shape of the continent that we recognize today.[8]

The legend of the Grail seems to reflect upon events in the ninth century, which were to determine the future kingdoms of Europe. It was thought to be a time when the Merovingian bloodline found its way, through intermarriage, to the establishment of the thrones of Europe.

Percival, the hero of the poem, starts out as a naive young man who desires to become a knight of King Arthur's Round Table. Through a series of adventures, he finds the castle of the Holy Grail, at none other than the Rennes-le-Chateau, in the south of France, the reputed home of Mary Magdalene,

Pictured above is the Church of St. Mary Magdalene at the hilltop village of Rennes-le-Chateau in the south of France, which was the reputed home of Mary Magdalene, castle of Merovee, and scene of the legend of the Holy Grail.

and later, of Merovee and his dynasty. Eventually, Percival becomes the possessor of the Grail, the king of the Grail castle, and protector of the Grail family — the Merovingian bloodline.

According to Adolf Hitler, an avid adherent to the mysteries of the Grail, the characters in the story represent the potentates of ninth century Europe. He also believed the story was in reality a prophecy to be replayed on the stage of world history a thousand years later, in the twentieth century.

According to the testimony of Dr. Walter Stein, a close acquaintance of Hitler, the German Fuehrer believed himself to be the reincarnation of the Grail's Landulph of Capua and ninth-century Lord of Terra di Labur, possessor of the "spirit of antichrist."[9]

Trevor Ravenscroft writes in THE CUP OF DESTINY that

Percival rides through the constellations of the zodiac in his quest for the golden cup. His destination is Aries, where lies the castle of the Holy Grail. According to the doctrine of the ancient mystery cult, as he enters the Grail castle, he is entering the mystery world of the human body, the brain. It is there that "the stone of light" resides.[10] The stone is supposedly the pineal gland, located at the base of the brain. It is at the so-called "center of a man's consciousness."

When Percival enters the castle of the Grail, he steps into a large room where hundreds of people are gathered, observing a mystical ceremony. He looks across the great hall and sees a group of Knights Templar. A squire enters the room carrying a bleeding spear. It is the spear of Longinus, which pierced the side of Christ.[11]

In a strange ceremony, the squire carries the spear around the room touching each of the four walls. Everyone weeps as if heartbroken. When he leaves, everyone is happy again.

The spear in the story resides today at the Hofburg, the Habsburg family museum in Vienna, Austria. It is reported that Adolf Hitler learned the legend of the spear four years prior to the outbreak of World War I.

In 1938, Hitler stole the spear. The Nazis buried the relic beneath the city of Nuremberg. It was retrieved by American soldiers on the very day Adolf Hitler took his own life in his Berlin bunker, April 30, 1945.

General Dwight Eisenhower ordered the spear returned to the treasure house of the Habsburgs in Vienna.[12] According to the legend, whoever possesses the spear should be able to rule the world. But, beware, says the legend; whoever loses the spear, loses both his throne and his life. Adolf Hitler lost possession of the spear within the hour of his death. We'll take a closer look at the legendary spear in the next chapter, but now, let's return to the story:

The king Anfortas sits in the center of the room. As the squire comes in with the spear, we notice that the king is sick. As Percival watches, the queen enters the room holding the Grail. It has healing qualities for the king. The purpose of the story is to save the king and preserve his kingdom. This, by the way, has been the goal of the Guardians of the Grail — down through the centuries. Eventually, they hope to restore the European monarchy and enlarge the kingdom to include the whole world.

A knight called Gawain later entered the castle of the Grail to gaze upon "the stone of light." When he did so, the stone opened up his clairvoyant powers of perception. It was as if he had a third eye — the mind's eye. He saw the knight, Percival, doing battle with another knight named Feirifis.

According to the ancient mystery cult, at the moment of body-free consciousness, which can be attained through Transcendental Meditation, a man perceives the birth of light forces within his own skeleton. His whole physical body becomes penetrated by a new force, opening a third eye, the eye of perception. That is the concept of the Grail. It is said to be an enlightenment of the human karma.

As one gazes upon "the stone of light," a mystical light arises from the blood in the human heart to initiate a transformation of the brain in the pineal gland. This so-called transformation passes through the equivalent of seven phases of the moon and becomes the very highest organ of clairvoyant perception — the Third Eye. Ravenscroft says it occurs at the moment when the human soul becomes the living vessel of the Christ-consciousness — which, by the way, is another one of those terms used by the New Age Movement. As long as one gazes on the "stone of light," he cannot die. His hair may turn a little gray, but he does not grow old. [13]

Such a "stone of light" stands today in the Meditation Room

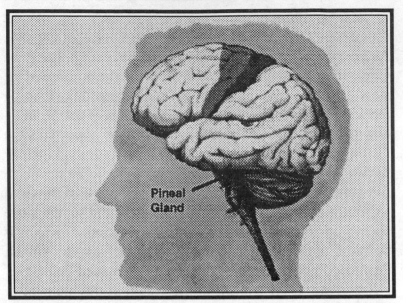

The pineal gland at the base of the brain is supposed to be the center for the Third Eye, allowing clairvoyant perception.

at the United Nations. In the center of the room stands a six and one-half ton lodestone altar. It is a natural magnet emitting magnetic waves. It may not give off light in the visible spectrum, but is, nevertheless, a "stone of light." Those who use the room for meditation can look beyond the stone to a three dimensional mural at the front of the room. The painting contains a circle depicting the sun, half of which is black. It represents the Manichaean concept of the conflict between light and darkness. [14]

According to the legend, there are two ways to learn the ABC's of the Grail. Learning the ABC's "without black magic," involves the use of Transcendental Meditation. Learning the ABC's "with black magic" involves the use of mind expanding drugs. This could be at least one of the underlying reasons why drugs are being distributed to young people. The adherents of the "Age of Enlightenment" seem to be deter-

The Meditation Room at the United Nations

mined to speed up the process of capturing the souls of a new generation in order to introduce the worship of their great light-bearer, Lucifer.

Actually, there are three heroes in the legend of the Grail — Percival, who represents the spirit of man; Gawain, who represents the soul of man; and Feirifis, who represents the body of man. They are all Percival. It is said that Percival has the steadfastness of Saturn. Feirifis calls his god by the name of Jupiter. And, Gawain's planet is Mars, transformed by the healing powers of Mercury. As king of the Grail, Percival possesses those forces which gradually unfold in the human being from birth to death. When these three stop fighting each other and get together in love, they become possessors of the Grail.[15]

Thus, in accordance with the Manichaean tradition, the Holy Ghost is actually believed to be the transformed Lucifer.[16] And the dove is the transformed serpent. Carrying this perverted belief system forward, good becomes evil; and evil becomes good. For example, it is the same concept taught in the movie, "Star Wars," when Darth Vader turns out to be the father of Luke Skywalker.[17] It is a major heresy of the New Age Movement.

This concept may be difficult for some to comprehend. However, be assured of this: there is a group of people who believe this heresy. According to their astrological projections, the Age of Aquarius is about to bring on a New World Order. To introduce this "New Age of Enlightenment," every person on the face of the earth will be forced to accept a "Luciferic initiation."

According to the cult, Percival becomes the king of the Grail when the planets Saturn, Jupiter, Mars and Mercury get together. For this reason, adherents of the New Age Movement expected their utopia to emerge in the years following the alignment of the planets in 1981-82 which included the conjunctions of Jupiter, Saturn and Mars.

Ravenscroft, in his book, THE CUP OF DESTINY, reported, "At the end of this century the Order of the Knights Templar will re-emerge to change the whole existing social order. This will take place in the period immediately following the coming world catastrophies, which will commence in 1982 and continue in three terrible waves of destruction up to the year 2001 on an apocalyptic scale. During the struggle to rebuild the civilized world, the anti-Christ and the great dictator will attempt to seize world power. Their adversaries will be the reborn Templars and the souls they shall choose to join them in rebuilding a new world order in which the freedom of the individual spirit will find its true place. Throughout this period, that ... spirit behind the figure of Parzival [Percival] will be their heroic and beloved leader."[18]

That is precisely the teaching of The New Age Movement. Ravenscroft's "anti-Christ" and "great dictator" are to be overthrown by "reborn Templars." His "anti-Christ," however, in my opinion, will not be the predicted man of sin. Instead the Templars may introduce that great world dictator. Bear in mind, Benjamin Creme tried to introduce his so-called Christ in April 1982,[19] and again in January 1987.[20] The adherents of the mystery cult intend to establish their religious beliefs worldwide, while eradicating all other religions. They are attempting to eliminate each opposing religion by incorporating it into their own system of doctrine.

In the Christian religion, for example, New Agers claim that Jesus was just another one of their Masters of Wisdom, that He was the incarnation of the sun god, to provide a pathway for the evolution of human consciousness, that He merely contained the reincarnation of the Christ spirit, and that the coming Lord Maitreya will be the ultimate answer for world peace.

Well, when the true antichrist finally does emerge to establish a one-world government, he just might be of the Merovingian bloodline, claiming descent from the lineage of Mary Magdalene and Jesus Christ.

Chapter Notes

CHAPTER 2

1. "The Gifts of Golden Byzantium," NATIONAL GEOGRAPHIC, Vol. 164, No. 6, December, 1983, p. 733.
2. Trevor Ravenscroft, THE CUP OF DESTINY (York Beach, Maine: Samuel Weiser, 1982), p. 36.
3. Ibid., p. 39.
4. Ibid., p. 36.
5. Ibid., p. 34.
6. Manly P. Hall, THE SECRET TEACHINGS OF ALL AGES (Los Angeles: The Philosophical Research Society, Inc., 1977), p. XCIII.
7. Wolfram von Eschenbach, PARZIVAL, trans. Helen M. Mustard and Charles E. Passage (New York, 1961).
8. Ravenscroft, CUP OF DESTINY, op. cit., p. 46.
9. Trevor Ravenscroft, THE SPEAR OF DESTINY (York Beach, Maine: Samuel Weiser, 1982), p. 186.
10. Ravenscroft, CUP OF DESTINY, op. cit., p. 85.
11. Ibid., p. 88.
12. Ravenscroft, SPEAR OF DESTINY, op. cit., pp. 352-353.
13. Ravenscroft, CUP OF DESTINY, op. cit. p. 149.
14. Robert Keith Spenser, THE CULT OF THE ALL-SEEING EYE (Hawthorne, CA: Omni Publications, 1968), pp. 8-17.
15. Ravenscroft, CUP OF DESTINY, op. cit., p. 186.
16. Ibid., p. 193.
17. STAR WARS, Twentieth Century Fox Studios, 1977.
18. Ravenscroft, CUP OF DESTINY, op. cit., pp. 143-144.
19. LOS ANGELES TIMES, April 25, 1982. Also NEW YORK TIMES, April 25, 1982.
20. USA TODAY, January 12, 1987.

Chapter 3

The Legend
of the Spear

In the legend of the Holy Grail, the hero, Percival, finds the Grail castle and enters a huge banquet hall to observe a mystical ceremony. Across the room sits a group of Knights Templar. Near the center of the room the king, Anfortas, appears to be quite ill. From one end of the banquet hall a squire enters holding a bleeding Spear. In a ritual-type ceremony he walks around the room touching each of the four walls. While the Spear is present everyone weeps. When the ceremony is concluded and the squire leaves the room, everyone appears to be happy again. It is an unusual story — but then, it is an unusual Spear.

According to the legend, it was the Spear of Gaius Cassius who became known as Longinus, the Spearman — the Roman soldier who pierced the side of Christ at Calvary. Today that Spear resides in a museum in Vienna, Austria. The legendary

Spear has an incredible history and is reputed to possess magical powers. According to the legend, whoever owns it can rule the world. For that reason, Adolf Hitler became the possessor of the Spear in 1938 — one year before he launched

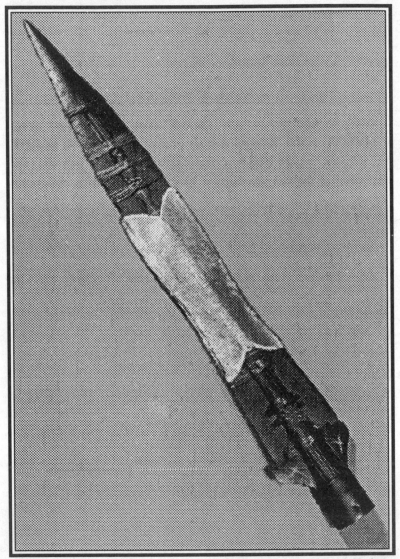

The legendary Spear reputed to have pierced the side of Christ

World War II.

The legendary Spear is made of iron. The long tapering point is supported by a wide base with metal flanges depicting the wings of a dove. Within a central aperture in the blade, a hammer-headed nail (thought to be from the cross) has been secured by a cuff threaded with metal wire. On the side of the lowest portion of the base, golden crosses have been embossed.

For over a thousand years the Spear was the symbol of power to the emperors of the Holy Roman Empire — an incredible history. According to the legend, Joseph of Arimathaea took the cup from which Christ drank at the Last Supper and brought it to the cross at Calvary. When Gaius Cassius, a Roman centurion, took his Spear and pierced the side of Christ, Joseph of Arimathaea caught His blood in the golden Cup. The Cup has now come to be known as the Holy Grail. At this point, we have the Spear and the Cup together, which appear to represent the contrast between good and evil. In the years that followed, Joseph of Arimathaea was said to have taken the Holy Cup to England, where he and his offspring became the Guardians of the Grail.

The Spear, on the other hand, eventually passed from the possession of the Roman centurion. Down through the years it fell into the hands of Mauritius, the head of a 3rd century garrison of Roman soldiers, called the Theban Legion. Mauritius and his men were stationed in Egypt in the year 285 A.D., when word came from Rome for him and his men to attend a mass assembly of the Roman Army for a pagan festival — where sacrifices would be made to the pantheon of Roman gods.

Mauritius and his men had become Christians, and therefore refused to worship the pagan gods of Rome. His commanding officer was a tyrant named Maximian, who demanded that

Mauritius and his men obey the orders to worship the Roman gods. When Mauritius refused, Maximian threatened to kill the entire garrison. As a final gesture of passive resistance, Mauritius knelt down in front of the ranks of his own soldiers and bared his neck to offer himself for decapitation in their stead. As his head rolled from his shoulders, Mauritius grasped within his hands the Spear which had pierced the side of Christ, the Spear of Longinus.

His men were so inspired by his example of faith in Christ that they elected to die with their leader rather than worship the Roman gods in whom they no longer believed. At first, Maximian cut off the heads of every 10th man, but the others would not recant their faith in Christ. Eventually, 6,666 Legionnaires — the most disciplined force in Roman military history — laid aside their weapons and knelt to bare their necks for slaughter. Maximian made a dreadful decision to massacre the whole legion as an offering of sacrifice to his gods.[1]

Such a barbaric massacre remained unequaled until the 14th century when the Roman Church launched the Inquisition to destroy the Knights Templar and other dissident groups. During the Inquisition, 60,000 men, women, and children were slaughtered in a single day. Such savagery again remained unequaled until the Holocaust of Hitler and the massacre of six million Jews.

In the years that followed, Mauritius' Spear and sword passed into the hands of Constantine (307-337 A.D.), who wielded the "serpent powers" of the Spear to rise to the throne of the Roman Empire. Constantine held it to his breast before the assembled Church Fathers when he declared himself to be the "Thirteenth Apostle." He also carried the Spear with him when he staked out the boundaries of Constantinople, his new capital city. When he moved his throne from Rome in 324

Constantine conquers under the sign of the cross .

A.D., he split the Roman Empire. In the years that followed, the Eastern Orthodox Church became strong while the Roman Church faltered.

In 496 A.D., the Roman Church made a pact with Clovis, the King of the Franks and grandson of Merovee, to be the new Constantine and emperor of the Holy Roman Empire. Keep in mind that Merovee, the father of the Merovingian dynasty was purported to be a descendant of Mary Magdalene and Jesus. It is also said that the Merovingian kings used an ancient spear as a symbol of their power, but it cannot be proven to be the Spear of Longinus.

However, with the assassination of Dagobert II in 679 A.D., the Merovingians were replaced by the Carolingian dynasty as rulers of the Franks. Pepin II (Pepin the Fat), the mayor of the palace, engineered the death of Dagobert and passed the political power of the kingdom on to his son, the famous Charles Martel. Charles was also known as Carl the Hammer, from whom the Carolingian dynasty derived its name.

Charlemagne

Charles Martel

Charles Martel is considered to be one of the most heroic figures in French history. He assembled a great army of all the kingdoms of Europe and led the armies against the Arabs in the battle of Tours in 752 A.D., one of the great battles to decide the fate of the world. It was this battle that determined whether Europe would be Christian or Moslem. By virtue of Charles' victory, he has become known as the "savior of Christendom."[2]

It was said that the new ruler possessed the Spear of Longinus and used it as a symbol of his power when he drove the invading Moslems from the continent of Europe. His grandson, the famous Charlemagne, used the Spear as a symbol of his political power. He kept it with him night and day, for he believed it to have magical powers.[3]

Charlemagne, known as the father of the Holy Roman Empire, came to the throne in 800 A.D. He was not only the king of France, but also the crowned emperor of the Roman Empire. He founded his whole dynasty on the possession of the Spear and its legend of world-historic destiny — a legend which attracted the greatest scholars in all Europe to serve the power of the Holy Roman Empire. Charlemagne fought 47 campaigns with assurance of victory through the power of the Spear.

The legendary Spear was said to have given him clairvoyant faculties through which he discovered the burial place of Saint James in Spain, and uncanny powers to anticipate future events. Throughout his life, Charlemagne lived and slept within reach of the Spear. After the victory of his last campaign, he accidentally let the Spear fall from his hands. His soldiers believed that the dropping of the Spear was an omen of his impending death. Such was said to be the occult powers of the Spear. In the years that followed it was passed from one emperor of the Holy Roman Empire to another.

Frederick Barbarossa, who ruled from 1152 to 1190, knelt in Venice with the Spear in his hands as he kissed the feet of the Pope. He died in 1190, while crossing a stream. At that very moment, the Spear had fallen from his hands.[4]

Frederick II, who ruled from 1215 to 1250, prized the Spear beyond all things. He made it the focal point of his whole life — especially calling on its powers during his Crusades (in which Francis of Assisi once carried the Spear on an errand of mercy). Frederick II also believed in astrology and practiced alchemy.[5]

In the year 1273, Rudolf I of the Habsburg dynasty became emperor of the Holy Roman Empire. Until 1806, all succeeding emperors were Habsburgs. Altogether forty-five emperors claimed the Spear of Destiny from the coronation of Charlemagne to the fall of the Holy Roman Empire in 1806.

Napoleon abolished the throne of the Holy Roman Empire in 1806, but his second marriage was to a Habsburg princess, Marie Louise of Austria, perhaps in hopes of carrying on the Merovingian bloodline. Napoleon wanted to become emperor of the world and may have planned to provide a Merovingian son to succeed him, but the child, Napoleon Charles, King of

Marie Louise (Habsburg) with Merovingian Bees on her robe.

Napoleon Bonaparte in his coronation robe displaying the Bees.

Kaiser Wilhelm of Germany and Franz Josef of Austria were allied against the rest of Europe in World War I.

Rome, died at an early age. [6]

Napoleon felt that his rise to world power was dependent upon his possession of the Spear, but before he could get to it, the Spear disappeared. It had been intentionally hidden so that he could not find it.

After 1806, the Habsburg dynasty continued as emperors of Austria and after 1867, they provided the kings of Hungary. The last Habsburg to hold a throne was Charles I. He ruled the combined empire of Austria-Hungary and lost his title at the end of World War I. His son, Otto von Habsburg, tried to regain the throne during the second World War, but was unsuccessful. Today, the crown of the Holy Roman Empire and the Spear of Longinus remain in the Habsburg Treasure House in Vienna, Austria.

In 1913 Kaiser Wilhelm, ruler of Germany, wanted to

launch a war, but he felt that first he must become the possessor of the Spear of Longinus. He sent a letter to the aged Emperor Franz Joseph of the Habsburg dynasty in Vienna on the pretense that he wanted to borrow the historic crown along with the legendary Spear and royal jewels of the emperors of the Holy Roman Empire for a special exhibition in Berlin. But General Helmuth von Moltke sent a secret note to the

Helmuth von Moltke

emperor, warning him not to loan those items to the Kaiser, for, he said, the Kaiser would keep them and never give them back. Kaiser Wilhelm was surprised when the request was denied, but never realized that one of his trusted officers was the reason for the denial. [7]

On June 28, 1914, Archduke Francis Ferdinand and his wife Sophie of the Habsburg Dynasty (heir to the throne of Austria as nephew of Franz Joseph) were assassinated. They had boarded their royal touring car for a trip through the streets of Sarajevo, capital of the Austrian province of Bosnia. Suddenly, a man jumped onto the running board of their touring car and shot both of them point-blank. The death of a Habsburg (of Merovingian bloodline) caused the outbreak of World War I. [8] His great-nephew, Otto von Habsburg, tried unsuccessfully to regain the throne in World War II. [9]

Think of it! It is believed that Otto von Habsburg is of the lineage of David, offspring of Jesus Christ and Mary Magdalene! As late as the 16th century it is reported that a Habsburg, Henry of Lorraine, upon entering the town of

Archduke Francis Ferdinand and his wife, Sofie, enter their touring car for a fateful ride through the streets of Sarajevo.

Joinville in Champagne was received by exuberant crowds. Among them certain individuals are reported to have chanted, "Hosannah, filio David!" (Hosannah to the son of David!).

That bit of history comes from a book about the modern history of Lorraine, printed in 1966.[10] Furthermore, the book contains a special introduction by Otto von Habsburg — who today holds the royal title, "Duke of Lorraine and King of Jerusalem."

Otto von Habsburg

But that's not all. There are at least a dozen royal families across Europe with Merovingian backgrounds. Among

them is the Luxembourg dynasty — where the giant computer has been built to control the coming "one-world" monetary system. This three-story high computer, housed in a building over a half block square, is located in Luxembourg, approximately 100 miles from Brussels, Belgium. Brussels, of course, is the headquarters of the European Common Market and NATO. The huge computer, called Euronet, also known affectionately as "the Beast," was activated in November, 1979, and has the capability of keeping detailed facts and information on every person in the world!

Currently, all banking systems throughout Europe and America are connected to the giant computer system. Since its inception, all Social Security records and all military records have been entered into it. Its secret, but likely, purpose is to help implement the new one-world monetary system, which will one day soon be a reality by the merging of European and United States currency into a common currency. How simple it would be for the coming world dictator to be able to enslave and control earth's billions through a sophisticated computer fashioned in his likeness. He would have all the facts at his fingertips on every member of the human race and know who receives his orders, obeys his commands and honors his laws. I'll discuss the coming world monetary system in more detail in Chapters 10-13.

The crown of the Holy Roman Emperor, the royal jewels and the legendary Spear — are all kept today in the Hofburg, the Treasure House of the Habsburgs in Vienna, Austria. The Treasure House is a museum where royal items are on display to this very day.

In 1909, Adolf Hitler was 21 years old. He lived in Vienna, where he was a student at the university. He became intrigued by the legend of the Spear and believed that the destiny of the world lay in its magical powers. He frequently went to the

Adolf Hitler

Hofburg, where he would stand for hours at a time gazing at the Spear. The young Hitler became obsessed with the idea that if he possessed the Spear, he could rule the world.[11]

According to the book, THE SPEAR OF DESTINY, by Trevor Ravenscroft, Adolf Hitler became involved with an occult group called the "Thule Gesellschaft," which, as we have previously observed, claimed descent from the Knights Templar — guardians of the Grail. They worshiped Lucifer and were involved in the art and practice of black magic. They used a swastika for their insignia. This was the group which eventually became known as the Nazi Party.[12]

During this time, Adolf Hitler lived in a flop house as a tramp. It was said that he seldom took a bath. The other unfortunate patrons of poverty couldn't stand the smell of him. During this time, Hitler was on drugs. He tried to learn the so-called "ABC's of the Grail" by the use of the mind expanding drug, mescalin, found in peyote. The "ABC's" refer to the development of a "higher consciousness" or transcendent awareness" that permits one to communicate with the spirit world.

It is said there are two ways to learn the ABC's of the Grail. The "proper route," is to learn "without black magic" — through the process of Yoga or Transcendental Meditation. But it is a slow process of initiation and requires a devoted, personal quest for the mystical "Grail." The other way is to learn by the use of "black arts" or "black magic" — through the use of mind expanding drugs, which short-circuits the arduous process of attaining the level of spirituality supposedly needed to cope with the reality of the spirit world. Hitler and the other members of his satanic group chose the "advantages" of the drug shortcut to attaining higher consciousness in their quest for the Grail. [13] But Hitler was more than a mere novice initiate into the occult. He had actively sought and discovered elements of the secret knowledge of occultism and thereby became a functioning agent of satan.

One day Hitler went to the Treasure House to study the Spear of Longinus. Hour after hour he gazed upon the relic, as if in Transcendental Meditation. According to his own testimony he went into a trance:

"The air became stifling so that I could barely breathe. The noisy scene of the Treasure House seemed to melt away before my eyes. I stood alone and trembling before the hovering form of the Superman — a Spirit sublime and fearful, a countenance intrepid and cruel. In holy awe, I offered my soul as a vessel of his Will." [14]

Before him stood a mighty spirit — the power behind the Spear. He gave himself that day to the spiritual hierarchies of darkness. He yielded himself to become the vessel of the spirit of antichrist.

Adolf Hitler rose to power in 1933. His satanic group, which claimed descent from the ancient Knights Templar, became the Nazi Party. During those years, Adolf Hitler had one obsession — to possess the Spear of Longinus. Finally, in April of 1938, Hitler's army entered Austria under the guise of annexing the nation and incorporating it into the Third Reich. Crowds gathered to welcome the German Fuehrer to Vienna. They did not realize at the time what utter contempt Hitler had for the city and its inhabitants because of the days he spent there as a vagabond.

His real purpose for entering Vienna, however, was to take possession of the legendary Spear of Destiny. It must be his, he thought, so that with it he could rule the world. On October 13, the Spear, along with the crown of the Holy Roman Empire, was taken to Nuremberg, the center for the Nazi movement, and placed in the Hall of St. Katherine's Church.

Listed among the treasures was the crown which had been worn for over 1,000 years by the emperors of the Holy Roman Empire, the royal jewels, a piece of wood said to be from the

J. R. Church views the Spear in Vienna, Austria.

cross of Calvary, the Sword of St. Mauritius, and the legendary Spear of Longinus — the Spear which pierced the side of Christ.

Hitler claimed that the Imperial Regalia had always belonged in Nuremberg and had been taken from the city in 1796 to keep Napoleon from getting the legendary Spear. When it arrived in Vienna, however, the Habsburgs decided to keep it. Hitler, "the hero," was just bringing it back home. According to Hitler's view of history, Charlemagne was a German, as were all the great Emperors of the Holy Roman Empire. [15]

It seems that Germany plays a far more important role in the fulfillment of Bible prophecy than one might think at first glance. The thought that the future antichrist could have his roots in Germany becomes more plausible when one considers the historical roots of the empire. I have long believed that the prophecy of Daniel's leopard represented a German influence in world history. The rise of the European Common Market under the influence of Germany may be a modern consolidation of the various branches of the Merovingian bloodline in an attempt to fulfill their ancient dream to establish a world kingdom in this generation.

Adolf Hitler gained possession of the Spear in 1938, and one year later, invaded Poland and ignited the Second World War. When the Royal Air Force of Great Britain began to devastate Nuremberg, the Nazis decided to find a hiding place for the Spear of Destiny. An ancient tunnel was opened up beneath the historic Nuremberg Fortress. The tunnel was cleared, widened, and extended some 900 feet into the rock — where, at its furthest end, an air conditioned bunker was erected. Massive steel doors, embedded in concrete, guarded the entrance to the vault where the treasures were deposited.

Innocent looking double garage doors and a gabled house disguised the tunnel entrance. A false back wall of the garage noiselessly slid sideways for the truck carrying the treasure to move down the secret passage to the huge iron doors of the vault 900 feet below the eleventh century fortress. Only three men knew how to gain entrance into the vault. To one was given a five digit combination; to another was given a key; and to the third was given both the combination and a key.

It was quite by accident that American bombs blew away the camouflage, leaving a gaping hole in the ground. On March 30, 1945, the Nazi high command ordered the treasure to be moved again before the expected Americans invaded the city. The treasure was moved, but the Spear was inadvertantly left behind in an apparent oversight. [16]

Around 2:00 on the afternoon of April 30, 1945, a party of American soldiers were searching out the area when one of the men found himself looking down into the wide tunnel. It was not long until the United States of America became the new owners of the Spear of Destiny. At that same hour, Adolf Hitler ended his own life in another bunker 50 feet below Berlin. Perhaps it is merely a coincidence that he died in the same hour in which he lost possession of the Spear. [17]

In the months that followed, the United States, possessor of the legendary Spear of Destiny, unleashed the most hideous monster of destructive power ever imagined — the atomic bomb! While in possession of the Spear, America was the undisputed master of the world. However, none of the American senators who went to Nuremberg to see the Nazi loot showed the least interest in the age-old legend of the Spear of Longinus.

General Patton was the only one who appeared to be totally fascinated at the sight of the Spear of Destiny. General Dwight Eisenhower, commander of the Allied Armies in Europe, made the final decision. He said bluntly: "Return the Habsburg Regalia to Austria." [18]

On January 4th, 1946, the Imperial treasures were loaded aboard a convoy of jeeps. Two days later, they arrived in Vienna.

Today, the Spear of Longinus is back in the Treasure House of the Habsburgs. The talisman of world historic destiny stands on a base of faded red velvet in the same spot where Adolf Hitler first beheld it in 1909. It is on view to the public from Monday to Saturday from 9 A.M. to 6 P.M. Admission is free.

According to the legend, whoever owns the Spear can rule the world. It is presently in the possession of Austria, in the Treasure House of the Habsburgs. And members of the royal family of the Habsburg dynasty are today among the prime movers and shakers behind the unification of Europe.

American tanks from Company B move into the devastated city of Nuremberg. It was here that American soldiers found the infamous Spear, reputed to have pierced the side of Christ. It had been hidden by the Nazis.

Chapter Notes

CHAPTER 3

1. Ravenscroft, SPEAR OF DESTINY, op. cit., pp. 13-14.
2. Gurney, KINGDOMS OF EUROPE, op. cit., pp. 59-60.
3. Ravenscroft, SPEAR, op. cit., pp. 15-16.
4. Ibid., p.17.
5. Ibid., p. 18.
6. Gurney, KINGDOMS OF EUROPE, op. cit.
7. Ravenscroft, SPEAR, op. cit., pp. 122-123.
8. C. A. Macartney, THE HABSBURG EMPIRE, 1790-1918 (New York: Macmillan, 1969), pp. 806ff.
9. Charles Fenyvesi, SPLENDOR IN EXILE, The Ex-Majesties of Europe (Washington: New Republic Books, 1979), p. 53.
10. J. de Pange, L'AUGUSTE MAISON de LORRAINE (Lyons, France, 1966), p. 60.
11. Ravenscroft, SPEAR, op. cit., pp. 61-62, 87, 287, 318.
12. Ibid., pp. 59, 91-92, 161.
13. Ibid., pp. 74-83.
14. Ibid., p. 38.
15. Ibid., p. 217.
16. Ibid., p. 335.
17. Joseph J. Carr, THE TWISTED CROSS (Shreveport, LA: Huntington House, 1985), p.228.
18. Ibid., p. 228-229.

Chapter 4

The Myth of Mary Magdalene

What is the origin of the infamous skull and crossbones? The symbol was used hundreds of years ago by the pirates on the high seas. In more recent times it became a symbol of warning used on bottles of poison. But where did it originate?

The story goes back to at least the year 1307 — to Paris, France, and the overthrow of the Knights Templar by the French King Philip and his puppet pope, Clement V.

Philip, king of France, hated the Templars and wanted to confiscate their treasure. The king's men surprised the knights, broke into their castle at Paris, arrested them, and searched the place in hopes of finding their magnificent treasure. But, alas, the gold was nowhere to be found. However, they did find a large, silver bust in the shape of a woman's head. It was hinged on top, and inside were two head bones wrapped in a cloth of white linen, with another red cloth around it. The bones were those of a rather small woman.[1] They were evidently worshiped by the Knights Templar and were thought to be the skeletal remains of Mary Magdalene.

Some of the Templars who were interrogated told of a strange ritual wherein the Templars worshiped something called "Baphomet." The word seemed to be associated with an apparition of a bearded head. Some of the knights told of seance-type rituals in which the bearded head would appear out of nowhere and give instructions to the secret worshipers.

The word Baphomet likely came from an Arabic word meaning "father of wisdom." The existence of these secret ceremonies involving a head of some kind became the dominant theme running through the records of the Inquisition. According to one account, the mysterious head was that of Hugues de Payen, the founder of the Knights Templar.[2]

Perhaps Templar worship of a head was connected with the famous Turin Shroud, which was in the possession of the Templars between the years 1201 and 1307. The crusader knights invaded Constantinople in 1201, sacked the city, and reportedly stole the shroud. The ancient relic had been in Constantinople for several centuries — displayed in such a manner that only the face was visible. During those years, the shroud was called the Mandylion,[3][4] which, by the way, could have been a corruption of the name Magdalene. The owner of the shroud, Geoffrey de Charnay, was burned at the stake alongside Jacques de Molay, the Grand Master of the Templars, in 1314.

The Templars seemed to have a preoccupation with the

skulls of those considered to be guardians of the Grail. For example, the skull of Lazarus is kept in the Chapel of the Holy Grail in Ansbach, Germany. Lazarus, you may recall, was the brother of Mary and Martha. According to the guardians of the Grail, Jesus was supposed to have married both Mary (who eventually became associated with the title, Magdalene) and her sister, Martha. Evidently, their so-called offspring down through the centuries have had a special affection for uncle Lazarus, so they keep his skull in one of the family chapels.

The Knights Templar also kept the skull of Dagobert II, one of the last Merovingians to sit upon the throne of France. His skull is kept in a silver cup, reminiscent of the Grail. It resides at a convent in the village of Mons, France. The severed head of John the Baptist, part of which is kept at the Vatican in Rome, has also been linked to the bizarre religious fervor of the Knights Templar.

The skull and crossbones is also connected to another mysterious story traditionally linked with the Templars. It was reported that a great lady of Maraclea was loved by a Templar, a lord of Sidon, but she died in her youth. On the night of her burial, this wicked lover crept to the grave, dug up her body, and violated it. A voice from the void bade him return to the tomb after a given period of time, and he obeyed.

When he came back several months later and opened the grave again, he found only the skull and crossbones. The same voice spoke again from the void of the tomb and said, "Guard it well, for it will be the giver of all good things." And so he carried it away with him. It became his protective talisman. He was able to defeat his enemies by merely showing them the magic skull and crossbones.[5] According to the legend, the skull and crossbones eventually passed into the possession of the Knights Templar. It is a bizarre story. It is said that the name of the woman in the story was Isis. This name also became associated with Mary Magdalene. A few years ago a booklet was published in France entitled LE SERPENT ROUGE (The Red Serpent). It contained 13 prose poems, each corresponding with a sign of the zodiac — "a zodiac of thirteen signs, with the thirteenth, Ophiuchus or the Serpent Holder, inserted between Scorpio and Sagittarius." [6] Under the astrological sign of Leo was this paragraph:

"From she whom I desire to liberate, there wafts towards me the fragrance of the perfume which impregnates the sepulchre. Formerly, some named her: Isis, queen of all sources, benevolent. Come unto me all

**St. Mary Magdalene with a skull in her lap
by Georges de La Tour**

ye who suffer and are afflicted, and I shall give ye rest. To others, she is Magdalene, of the celebrated vase, filled with healing balm. The initiated know her true name: Notre Dame des Cross." [7]

The implications of this paragraph are extremely interesting. Mary Magdalene is linked with the Egyptian goddess of fertility, Isis, whose Babylonian name was Ishtar. In the paragraph she is also affiliated with the words "Notre Dame," a French term meaning "our lady," which down through the centuries was considered to be Mary, the mother of Christ. The authors of HOLY BLOOD, HOLY GRAIL, however, speculate that the Cathedral of Notre Dame was built in the honor of Mary Magdalene, who, according to the guardians of the Grail, became the so-called wife of Jesus Christ. [8]

I have concluded that Mary Magdalene had nothing to do with the legendary bit of blasphemy that she became one of the wives of Jesus. Furthermore, there is no place in our Bible which states that she was an harlot. All we know of Mary Magdalene is that our Savior cast seven devils out of her. Neither are we told the nature of her sins.

We are not told in the Scripture that she was the one caught in the act of adultery and brought before Christ for stoning when He stooped down and wrote in the sand and said, *"He that is without sin among you, let him first cast a stone at her"* (John 8:7).

We are not told that she was the sister of Martha and Lazarus. And we are certainly not told that she was one of the wives of Jesus. That hoax was perpetrated hundreds of years later by the so-called guardians of the Grail. Poor Mary has been victimized by a wicked and perverted legend.

Over the centuries, the symbol of the skull and crossbones has been connected with the Knights Templar. In fact, many European tombs of the Templars contain the symbol of the skull and crossbones. It has been suggested that the original skull and crossbones may have been those of Mary Magdalene.

The series of 13 poems published under the title LE SER-
PENT ROUGE (The Red Serpent), dated January 17, 1967,
contains a Merovingian genealogy and two maps of France in
Merovingian times, in addition to a commentary on the
Merovingian bloodline. The poems represent a symbolic or
allegorical pilgrimage through the signs of the zodiac, beginning with Aquarius and ending with Capricorn. They appear
to be the story of a red snake representing a bloodline or
lineage uncoiling across the centuries —the bloodline of the
Grail family.

According to the document, Mary Magdalene possessed the
"celebrated vase filled with healing balm." This could be a
reference to the alabaster box of ointment with which she
supposedly anointed the feet of Jesus — or could it be a
reference to the Grail?

Mary Magdalene reportedly fled Jerusalem in A.D. 70, with
her "sacred" children. She sailed across the Mediterranean to
France, bringing the cup from which Christ drank the Last
Supper and in which her alleged uncle, Joseph of Arimathaea,
had caught the blood of Christ. Some accounts say that Joseph
took the Grail on to England, while other accounts hold that
Mary Magdalene kept the Grail in France.

The question remains, what was the Holy Grail? In Wolfram von Eschenbach's epic poem on the subject, published
around 1200, [9] the Grail represents a "stone of light" (similar
to a crystal ball). Eschenbach said the "stone is the Grail,"
while other authors of the period refer to the cup of the Last
Supper as the Grail. [10] But the cup and the stone appear to be
only symbolic of a deeper esoteric meaning. Now, take a deep
breath and consider what I believe to be the greatest heresy of
history. These so-called guardians of the Grail have made the
cup to become symbolic of another "vessel" which supposedly contained and preserved the bloodline of Christ —

namely the body (or perhaps I should say the womb) of Mary Magdalene! This age-old worship of the Magdalene appears to be the result of an esoteric mystery religion, which I believe is described in Revelation 17 as "Mystery, Babylon the Great."

This undue preoccupation with "goddess worship" is also a motivating force for women's movements (women's liberation, feminism, and the New Age Movement) who are seeking to replace Christ with a woman. The women's movement is an important aspect of the New Age Movement. It is at the heart of the consciousness revolution presently sweeping our Western culture. In universities across America a new group of courses called "women's studies" have come into existence within the past two decades. There are now centers for feminist therapy and political groups which promote a feminist agenda. National attention was given a decade ago to their so-called Equal Rights Amendment.

Many of those involved in the feminist movement may sincerely believe it to be a political crusade to gain equality with men, when in fact, it is more than that. It is also a spiritual movement based partly upon a reawakening of the "goddess consciousness." Its real goal is "matriarchy," not equality.

The major spiritual force behind some aspects of the feminist movement is witchcraft — based upon the power of female sexuality derived from a mystical relationship with "Mother Nature" and "Mother Earth." Goddess worship, Wicca, and witchcraft are all names for a form of so-called "natural" religion centered around the mystery, sexuality, and psychic abilities of the female.

In May, 1984, a four foot bronze statue of the Crucifixion was unveiled at the Episcopal Cathedral of St. John the Divine in Manhattan. The figure on the cross was that of a naked woman — complete with undraped breasts and rounded hips.

The work was created by sculptress Edwina Sandys for the United Nations "Decade for Women." She is the granddaughter of Winston Churchill. The Cathedral of St. John the Divine is a center for New Age Movement activity. It appears to be yet another symbol in what I call the myth of Mary Magdalene. James Parks Morton, who is the Cathedral Dean, organized the display and said that it sends a positive message to women. He and his followers thought it reflected a "mystic Christian view that sees Christ as our mother." It is the same pagan concept that promotes Mary Magdalene as the wife of Jesus — and vessel bearing the bloodline of Christ. "

In an esoteric sense, the womb of Mary Magdalene becomes the Grail — preserving the bloodline or lineage of Jesus. Her offspring supposedly married into the royal family of the Franks, eventually producing a king to sit upon the throne — Merovee, from whom has come the so-called sacred Merovingian bloodline.

Chapter Notes

CHAPTER 4

1. Baigent, Leigh, and Lincoln, HOLY BLOOD, HOLY GRAIL, op. cit., p. 83.
2. Ibid., p. 82.
3. Ian Wilson, THE SHROUD OF TURIN (Garden City, NY: Doubleday, 1979), p. 106ff.
4. Kenneth E. Stevenson and Gary R. Habermas, VERDICT ON THE SHROUD (Ann Arbor, Michigan, Servant Books, 1981), pp. 17-26.
5. Baigent, et al., HOLY BLOOD, op. cit., p. 84.
6. Ibid., p. 102.
7. Ibid., p. 102, quoting Pierre Feugere, Louis Saint-Maxent, and Gaston de Koker, LE SERPENT ROUGE (Pontoise, France, 1967), p. 4.
8. Ibid., p. 103.
9. von Eschenbach, PARZIVAL, op. cit.
10. Ibid., p. 297.
11. "Vexing Christa," TIME, May 7, 1984, p. 94.

The Cathedral of Notre Dame in Paris, France, was built to honor Mary Magdalene rather than the mother of Christ, says authors of HOLY BLOOD, HOLY GRAIL. The architectural design is fashioned after a womb — not the womb that bore Christ, but the womb that supposedly bore the bloodline of Jesus — the Merovingian Dynasty!

Chapter 5

The Merovingian Bloodline

Merovee died in 458 A.D., leaving the throne to his son, Childeric I. Though the grave of Merovee has never been found, the grave of Childeric I was discovered in 1653. "The tomb contained arms, treasures, and regalia such as one would expect to find in a royal tomb. It also contained items less characteristic of kingship than of magic, sorcery, and divination — a severed horse's head, a bull's head made of gold, and a crystal ball!"[1] Childeric I was the father of Clovis, the most famous and influential of all the Merovingian rulers. In 496, Clovis adopted the Christianity of Rome, but his father before him used a crystal ball!

There were other items of interest also found in the tomb of King Childeric I, son of Merovee and father of Clovis — a special set of 300 miniature solid gold bees! It is not known what kind of significance was attached to the bees, but they were given to Leopold Wilhelm von Habsburg, military governor of the Austrian Netherlands, who was considered to be a descendant of the Merovingian dynasty. By 1804,  when Napoleon was crowned emperor, those 300 golden bees had been returned to France. Having special importance to Napoleon, he had them affixed to his coronation robes. Napoleon, of course, had a special interest in the Merovingian dynasty. In 1810, Napoleon married Marie-Louise, the daughter of Francis II, the last Habsburg to sit upon the throne of the Holy Roman Empire.

The symbol of the bee is also used in Mormon temples today. The bee is the state symbol for Utah. Furthermore, Mormon doctrine teaches that Mary Magdalene was the wife of Jesus Christ. The religion of the Mormon Church of the Latter Day Saints is replete with Merovingian ideology.

There were 21 kings of the Merovingian dynasty reigning over a Germanic tribe known as the Franks, from 447 to 751 — 304 years. They were called "the long-haired kings." In the tradition of Samson, they thought their hair was the source of their power. During those years, however, the kingdom became fragmented due to political assassinations, kidnappings, and intrigues. The later Merovingian rulers were politically weak and were often called "the enfeebled kings." Many of the Merovingian princes were placed upon the throne at an extremely youthful age and were easily manipulated by their advisors. But those who did attain manhood proved as strong and decisive as any of their predecessors. This was the case with Dagobert II.[2]

Dagobert was born in 651. His father, the king of Austrasia

(now Eastern France), died when Dagobert was only five years old. Grimoald, the mayor of the palace, kidnapped the young Dagobert and took him to a monastery. He was able to convince Dagobert's mother that her son was dead and that the king had given him permission to put his own son upon the throne. In secret, Dagobert had been given to the Bishop of Poitiers, who was supposed to murder the child. However, he couldn't bring himself to do it. Instead, he sent Dagobert to Ireland, where he grew to manhood in an Irish monastery not far from Dublin.

In 666 A.D., Dagobert moved to England and established a residence at York, in the kingdom of Northumbria. He became acquainted with Bishop Wilfrid, who helped him to regain his throne in the French province of Austrasia. In 671, Dagobert married Giselle de Razes, the daughter of the Count of Razes and niece of the King of the Visigoths. The Merovingian bloodline was now allied to the royal bloodline of the Spanish Visigoths. Dagobert and his new wife settled in southern France at the Merovingian castle called the Rennes-le-Chateau. Their marriage was celebrated in the Church of Mary Magdalene. According to the legend, Dagobert was alleged to be of the lineage of Mary Magdalene (600 years removed). The Rennes-le-Chateau was thought to be the home of Mary Magdalene in the latter years of her life.

Over the next few years Dagobert restored the authority of his throne. His wife bore him an infant son, Sigisbert IV. By 679, after three years on the throne, Dagobert had made a number of powerful enemies, one of which was the king's own mayor of the palace, Pepin the Fat.

On December 23, 679, Dagobert went hunting. Toward mid-day the king laid down to rest beside a stream at the foot of a tree. While he slept, one of his servants, acting under Pepin's orders, thrust a spear through his eye and into his brain. The murderers then tried to find the rest of the royal family in order to kill them, but his wife got away, carrying with her Dagobert's three-year-old son, Sigisbert IV. For the next 75 years other Merovingians ascended the throne, but they were not of the main lineage of Dagobert. To all intents and purposes, Dagobert's assassination may be regarded as signaling the end of the Merovingian dynasty. Pepin stayed on as mayor of the palace and later turned that office over to his son, the famous Charles Martel (also called Carl the Hammer), who drove the Moslems out of Europe.

In 751 Pepin, the son of Charles Martel, deposed Childeric III, considered by most historians to be the last Merovingian king. He confined the young king to a monastery. To humiliate him and to deprive him of his so-called "magical powers," Pepin had Childeric's long hair cut off. This, of course, was the same kind of humiliation inflicted upon Samson in the Old Testament. Four years later, Childeric died, and Pepin's claim to the throne was undisputed. In 800, the famous Charlemagne, the son of Pepin, grandson of Charles Martel, ascended the throne of France and became the Emperor of the "Christianized" Roman Empire.

Presumably, history would hear no more from the Merovingian bloodline after the death of Dagobert. The story of the infant son of Dagobert faded from history after the death of his father. For many hundreds of years, the genealogy of Sigisbert IV could not be proven. But keep in mind, King Dagobert lived in a royal castle in the south of France called Rennes-le-Chateau.

The year of Dagobert's death was 679. However, 1,206 years later, something of historical importance took place in the tiny French village of Rennes-le-Chateau. It was on June 1, 1885, that a new parish priest, Berenger Sauniere, came to work in the village church of St. Mary Magdalene. In 1891,

Sauniere started a restoration program. While doing repair work, the workers removed the stone altar which rested on two archaic Visigoth columns. One of these columns proved to be hollow. Inside were found four parchments preserved in sealed wooden tubes. Two of these parchments are said to have contained genealogies. One dated from the year 1244 and the other from 1644. They followed the genealogy of Dagobert's son, Sigisbert IV, down through the centuries to a point where the Merovingian bloodline could be traced to modern times. (See the chart in Chapter One.)

Is it possible for the Merovingian bloodline to have continued to this day? Let's take a look at the role the Priory of Sion played.

According to the authors of HOLY BLOOD, HOLY GRAIL, there seem to be several key points now regarded as indisputable historical facts concerning the Priory of Sion:

1. There was a secret order behind the Knights Templar, which created the Templars as its military and administrative arm. This order functioned under the name of the Prieure de Sion (Priory of Sion).

2. Though the Knights Templar were thought to be destroyed and dissolved between 1307 and 1314, the Priory of Sion has continued to function through the centuries. It has orchestrated certain critical events in Western history.

3. The Priory of Sion exists today and is still operative. It plays an influential role in high-level international affairs as well as in the domestic affairs of certain European countries.

4. The avowed objective of the Priory of Sion is the restoration of the Merovingian dynasty and bloodline to the thrones of certain European nations. The restoration of the rule of the Merovingians is considered "justifiable, both legally and morally."[3] Although it was deposed in the eighth century, it did not become extinct, but perpetuated itself in a

direct line from Dagobert II and his son, Sigisbert IV —
through Godfroi de Bouillon, who captured Jerusalem in 1099
— and through various other noble and royal families. Some
of those family names include Saint Clair (Sinclair), Montesquiou, Plantard, and Habsburg. The Merovingian bloodline presently claims a so-called "legitimate claim to its
rightful heritage."[4]

The Order of Sion was founded in 1099 by Godfroi de
Bouillon just after his conquest of Jerusalem. Its official
headquarters was the Abbey of Notre Dame du Mont de Sion.
Mount Sion (Zion) is the famous "high hill" upon which the
city of Jerusalem is built. Godfroi was offered the title, "King
of Jerusalem," but declined, asking to be known only as "De-
fender of the Holy Sepulchre." Godfroi was of Merovingian
blood, directly descended from Dagobert II, Sigisbert IV, and
the line of Merovingian "lost kings." He was a king without a
kingdom — until he became ruler of the most coveted kingdom in the world — Jerusalem and the Holy Land.

In 1118 the Knights Templar were organized by Hugues de
Payen, perhaps as the Order of Sion's military and administra-
tive arm. In 1188 a formal separation occurred between the
institutions, commonly referred to as the "cutting of the elm."
At that time, the Order of Sion modified its name to the Prieure
(Priory) of Sion. As a subtitle, the name "Ormus" was adopted.

"According to esoteric teaching, Ormus was the name of an
Egyptian sage and mystic, a Gnostic 'adept' of Alexandria....
In A.D. 46, he and six of his followers were supposedly
converted to a form of Christianity.... From this conversion a
new sect or order is said to have been born, which fused the
tenets of early Christianity with the teachings of other, even
older mystery schools."[5]

Ormus and his new initiates took as their identifying symbol, a red, or rose colored cross. As already discussed, the red

cross on a white tunic had already been adopted as the symbol of the Knights Templar. From this, a second subtitle adopted by the Priory of Sion in 1188 came to be known as the Rose-Croix, or Rosicrucians.

One of the first Grand Masters of the Priory of Sion, Guillaume de Gisors (1266-1307), was said to have organized the body into an "Hermetic Freemasonry."[6] Hermetic thought, esoteric tradition and involvement in "secret societies" apparently began to control the Grand Masters of the organization from that time forward. The meaning of "hermetic" indicates an involvement in the mystical, magical or occult sciences. The word evolved from the Greek god, Hermes, who was called Mercury by the Romans. Mercury, by the way, bore the two symbols of the Israelite tribe of Dan — the eagle and serpent. He was also called Odin (a form of the word Dan) by the Merovingians who claimed ancestry from him. He was considered to be the god of science, eloquence and cunning, and also the guide of departed souls to Hades.

Written by a purported current member of the Priory of Sion is the following statement, "Without the Merovingians, the Prieure de Sion would not exist, and without the Prieure de Sion, the Merovingian dynasty would be extinct."[7]

The following chart lists the alleged Grand Masters of the Priory of Sion, — from founder of the Knights Templar, Hugues de Payen in 1118; to "the cutting of the elm" (the separation from the Knights Templar) in 1188; to the present Grand Master of the Priory of Sion, Pierre Plantard de St. Clair. This is not a genealogical chart, but does include some relevant ancestry, weaved and connected by a "royal bloodline."

Grand Masters of the Priory of Sion
(The names of Grand Masters appear in **bold** type.)

Tibaud de Payen (b1012-1064).

|

Tibaud had two children — Tibaud (b1035 - 1094),
who fathered Hugues de Payen (b1070-1131),
founder of the Knights Templar;
and Adelaide, who married Hugues de Chaumont
(b1032-1075), who was the father of Tibaud I.
The genealogical portion of this chart continues with Tibaud I.

|

Tibaud I (b1055-1130), son of Hugues de Chaumont.

|

Hugues II (b1090-1142), son of Tibaud I.

|

Jean de Gisors (1188-1220), 1st Grand Master - Priory of Sion.
Also, he was the founder of Rosicrucians in 1188.
He married **Marie de Saint-Clair**.
She was the 2nd Grand Master (1220 - 1266).

|

Hugues III (b1181-1225), son of Jean de Gisors.

|

Guillaume de Gisors (1266-1307), son of Hugues III.
Guillame married Iolande de Bar.

|

Edouard de Bar (1307-1336), grandnephew of Iolande.

|

Jeanne de Bar (1336-1351), sister of Edouard.

|

Jean de Saint-Clair (1351-1366), nephew of Jeanne.

Blanche d'Evreux (1366-1398), no known relation to
Jean de Saint-Clair. Blanche was daughter of King of Navarre
and married Philippe VI, King of France.

Nicolas Flamel (1398-1418), alchemist, Cabalist, steeped in Hermetic and esoteric thought, and "secret societies."

Rene d'Anjou (1418-1480) of the Merovingian bloodline, also carried title, King of Jerusalem.
|
Iolande de Bar (1480-1483), daughter of Rene d'Anjou.

Sandro Filipepi (1483-1510), developed tarot cards.

Leonardo da Vinci (1510-1519), an early Rosicrucian.

Connetable de Bourbon (1519-1527).
His sister married the great-grandson of Rene d'Anjou.
He was also a close friend of Holy Roman Emperor, Charles V.

Ferdinand de Gonzague (1527-1575), cousin of Connetable de Bourbon. He was a devotee of esoteric thought.

Louis de Nevers (1575-1595),
nephew of Ferdinand de Gonzague.
He was deeply versed in esoteric tradition.

Robert Fludd (1595-1637).
He was England's leading exponent of Rosicrucian thought.

J. Valentin Andrea (1637-1654)
He wrote the Rosicrucian manifestos, which promised
a transformation of the world and human knowledge
in accordance with esoteric and Hermetic principles.
He also created a network of secret societies.

Robert Boyle (1654-1691),
was deeply involved with demonology and
taught Isaac Newton the secrets of alchemy.
He closely studied the alleged connection
of Mary Magdalene to the Holy Grail.

Isaac Newton (1691-1727), was warden of the Royal Mint,
president of the Royal Society.

Charles Radclyffe (1727-1746),
grandson of Charles II, King of England.

Charles de Lorraine (1746-1780), married Eleonore Marie von
Habsburg, daughter of Holy Roman Emperor, Ferdinand III.
|
Maximilian de Lorraine (1780-1801).
Also known as Maximilian von Habsburg.
He was the nephew of Charles de Lorraine.

Charles Nodier (1801-1844),
father of the"occult revival" of the nineteenth century.
He was deeply involved in many secret societies.

Victor Hugo (1844-1885), chief disciple of Charles Nodier.

Claude Debussy (1885-1918).
He was steeped in esoterica, and consorted with all the
prominent names of the French occult revival.

Jean Cocteau (1918-1963).
He was a close friend of Jean, great-grandson of Victor Hugo.
Both became heavily involved in spiritualism and the occult.

(Names of Grand Masters were not published after 1956.)

Pierre Plantard de St. Clair (1981-   ).
Current Grand Master of the Priory of Sion.
He has stated that the Priory of Sion does in fact
hold the lost treasure of the Temple of Jerusalem,
plundered by Titus' Roman legions in 70 A.D.
He has said these items would be returned to Jerusalem
"when the time is right." He has also said that the true treasure
was "spiritual" and it consisted of a "secret." The "secret"
would cause a major social change which would involve
the restoration of a monarchy.

The Priory of Sion were the "kingmakers" from Godfroi's reign forward, and provided the "connection" between his family and the lineage of royalty through Rudolf I of Habsburg —to the present, which includes the current House of Habsburg. The Habsburg dynasty, which ruled the Holy Roman Empire since the 13th century, is the direct lineage of the Merovingian bloodline. The Habsburgs are reputed to be the family of the Holy Grail, offspring of Mary Magdalene. Franz Joseph, of the Merovingian Habsburg dynasty, launched World War I. He declared war against Serbia to avenge the assassination of his nephew, Francis Ferdinand, in 1914. Franz Joseph died in 1916, after 68 years on the throne, while World War I was raging. He did not live to see the disintegration of the Habsburg empire.

Charles I succeeded Franz Joseph in 1916. Two years later he lost the war and had to abdicate the throne. Germany had joined the war on the side of Austria, but Western Allies defeated the two armies, making the final catastrophe inevitable. Charles I was formally deposed by the Austrian parliament in April, 1919. After two unsuccessful attempts to regain the crown of Hungary, Charles retired to the island of Madeira, where he died of pneumonia in 1922.

His wife, the Empress Zita, then 29 years old, went into mourning and never relinquished the widow's black garb. She and their eight children lived for a while in Spain and finally settled in the Belgian countryside. She spent her life trying to regain the throne for her son, Otto. She spent World War II in Canada and Tuxedo Park, N.Y., then returned to Europe, taking up residence in the convent home in Zizers, Switzerland, in 1962. She did not return to Austria until May of 1982, at the age of 90. She died of natural causes on March 14, 1989, and was returned to Vienna for burial. 8000 mourners filed out of Vienna's St. Stephen's Cathedral to follow the catafalque drawn by six black horses. "Two hours later the procession ended at the Capuchin Church, where in keeping with tradition, a member of the funeral party knocked on the door and a priest asked, 'Who goes there?'

"The titles were read aloud: 'Queen of Bohemia, Dalmatia, Croatia, Slavonia, Galicia, **Queen of Jerusalem**, Grand Duchess of Tuscany and Cracow ...'

" 'I do not know her,' said the father.

"A second knock and 'Who goes there?' brought the response, 'Zita, Empress of Austria and Queen of Hungary.' Again the reply, 'I do not know her.'

"When the inevitable question was put a third time, the answer was simply, 'Zita, a sinning mortal.'

" 'Come in,' said the priest, opening wide the door not for royalty, but for a faithful member of the Church, whose life had finally reached its end." [8]

Her title, "Queen of Jerusalem," dates back to 1099, and the Crusader kingdom established by Godfroi de Bouillon.

The following chart is not genealogical, but lists the Merovingian "Kings of Jerusalem" from the founding of the Priory of Sion until today:

Empress Zita as she appeared in 1983 and in 1911.

KINGS OF JERUSALEM

Godfroi de Bouillon (1099).
|
Baudouin (1100-1131).
|
Fulk V (1131-1143), Count of Anjou.
|
Louis VII (1143-1180), King of France.
|
Philip II Augustus (1180-1223), King of France.
|
Louis VIII (1223-1226), King of France.
|
Louis IX (Saint Louis) (1226-1270), King of France.
|
Philip III (1270-1285), King of France.
|
Philip IV (1285-1314), King of France.
|
Louis X (1314-1316), King of France.
|
John I (1316-1316), King of France.
|
Philip V (1316-1322), King of France.
|
Charles IV (1322-1328), King of France.
|
Philip VI (1328-1350), King of France.
|
John II (1350-1364), King of France.
|
Louis II (1364-1418), Duke of Anjou.
|
Rene D'Anjou (1418-1480),
Grand Master, Priory of Sion.
|

Iolande D'Anjou (1480-1483),
Grand Master, Priory of Sion.
|
Rene II D'Anjou (?-1508), Duke of Lorraine and Bar.
|
Antoine II de Lorraine (?-1544).
|
Francois de Lorraine (?-1545).
|
Charles III de Lorraine (?-1608).
|
Henry II de Lorraine (?-1624).
|
Nicolas-Francois de Lorraine (?-1670).
|
Charles V de Lorraine (?-1765).
Charles married Eleonore-Marie von Habsburg,
daughter of Holy Roman Emperor, Ferdinand III.
The Habsburg dynasty became heirs to the title,
King of Jerusalem, from this point forward.
|
Leopold de Lorraine (?-1729).
|
Francois de Lorraine (1745-1765).
Francois married Marie-Teresa von Habsburg,
Empress of Austria
|
Joseph II (1765-1790)
& brother Leopold II (1790-1792).
|
Francis II (1792-1806), Holy Roman Emperor.
Empire abolished under Napoleon in 1806).
|
Ferdinand I (1835-1848), Emperor of Austria.
|
Francis Joseph I (1848-1916), Emperor of Austria.
|

Charles I (1916-1918), Emperor of Austria,
abdicated in 1918 when Austria became a republic.
|
Otto von Habsburg (1912-   ), Archduke of Austria
Otto currently holds the title, "King of Jerusalem."
|
Karl von Habsburg (1961-   ).
Karl will become heir to the title
upon the death of Otto.

(Juan Carlos, present King of Spain,
also claims the title, "King of Jerusalem."
His royal lineage also extends back to
Charles V, Holy Roman Emperor.)

Left to right, Karl, his mother, and Otto von Habsburg at Zita's funeral.

Although the Habsburg empire is gone, the spirit of the Habsburg dynasty is not extinct. In fact, when the first parliament of the European Economic Community convened in 1979, one of the important delegates and guiding forces was Dr. Otto von Habsburg, the eldest son of the last Habsburg emperor, Charles I.

In recent years, Archduke Otto von Habsburg and his son, Karl, have been spearheading the movement to unify Europe. The announcement was made in June, 1988, that the European Economic Community will indeed become a "United States of Europe" by December 31, 1992. [9] [10]

Otto von Habsburg wrote in his book entitled, CHARLES V, "Together with ecumenicity, European unity has become the major issue of our time...." [11] He also stated, "... it might be possible to establish a united Europe and world peace, together with a Christian community and harmony between all believers.... Our survival will depend upon a spiritual revival...." [12]

Other authors who write about the House of Habsburg, know the one burning wish in their hearts, "... to unite Europe in a supernational state. Thus, the ancient desire of the Habsburgs to unite Europe into another Holy Roman Empire has come full circle with one important exception — the Europe Otto von Habsburg wants to see rise from the multinational jigsaw puzzle it now represents is a continent without hatred and without political boundaries." [13]

Otto is currently a delegate to the Common Market's European Parliament, headquartered in Strasbourg, France. In a February 8, 1987, interview in Columbus, Ohio, the then 26-year old Karl von Habsburg was quoted as saying that the United States of Europe will become a reality because "history shows that power flows toward that which controls the purse strings." [14] (See page 230 for more details.)

Karl von Habsburg is the heir apparent to the Habsburg heritage. It may also be interesting to note that he was born in 1961 and will be 31 years old when Europe is scheduled for unification in 1992. It appears very likely that this European unification could well be the predicted "revived Roman Empire" which will produce the coming world ruler.

It may be coincidental, but if the system of "occult numerology" used by medieval witchcraft and the New Age Movement is applied to the name Karl von Habsburg, the numerical value just happens to equal 6-6-6!

Matthew Goodwin, author of NUMEROLOGY, THE COMPLETE GUIDE, a definitive work (two volume set) on numerology says, "Numerology is the study of the occult significance of numbers. It's probably the simplest of the occult fields to learn and master." When asked how and why numerology works, the author states, "Frankly, I don't know ... psychic energy, the God force, the vibratory effect of numbers."[15]

Basically, the system used by the occultists is simple. Each letter in a name is assigned a number based on its location in the twenty-six letter English alphabet. In assigning number values to letters, all numbers are reduced to a single digit. A, the first letter = 1. B, the second letter = 2, and so on down to I = 9. J, the tenth letter = 1 because all letters and numbers must reduce down to a single digit. Thus, 10 reduces to (1+0) = 1. K, the eleventh letter = 2, and so on. An explanatory chart follows:

1	2	3	4	5	6	7	8	9
A	B	C	D	E	F	G	H	I
J	K	L	M	N	O	P	Q	R
S	T	U	V	W	X	Y	Z	

The value of all letters are then added together. For example:

J E R R Y
—————————
1 5 9 9 7 = 31

As all double digit numbers are combined into a single digit number, 31 becomes 4.

31 reduces to $(3 + 1) = 4$

Below is the equivalent value of the name of Karl von Habsburg:

K	A	R	L	v	o	n	H	A	B	S	B	U	R	G
2	1	9	3	4	6	5	8	1	2	1	2	3	9	7

15	15	33
6	6	6

It is also interesting to note that if you add the three sixes together, the sum is 18; then reduce by combining:

$(1 + 8) = 9.$

According to Gesenius' HEBREW AND CHALDEE LEXICON to the Old Testament Scriptures, the number 9 comes from Tet, the ninth letter of the Hebrew alphabet, which means "a serpent."[16]

The number 9 also has a sacred meaning to cabalists — mystics who practice a religious philosophy developed centuries ago by Jewish rabbis. Cabalists base their beliefs on a mystical interpretation of the Scriptures. To them, the number 9 represents "the symbol of man in his unregenerate state and also the path of his resurrection." [17]

According to E. W. Bullinger, author of NUMBER IN SCRIPTURE, the number nine is "significant of the end of man, and the summation of all man's works. Nine is, therefore, *The Number of Finality or Judgment.*" [18]

In addition, if you combine the above sums: $15 + 15 + 33$, the total is 63, which reduces to 9. Also, adding $2193 + 465 + 81212397$, the sum is 81215055, which reduces to 27, which reduces to 9!

Add the three 9's together and it is 27, which reduces to 9.

Or, add the columns down: $2193 + 15 + 6 = 2214 = 9$; and $465 + 15 + 6 = 486 = 18 = 9$; and $81212397 + 33 + 6 = 81212436 = 27 = 9$.

Again add the three 9's. It equals 27, which reduces to 9!

Just coincidence?... perhaps ... perhaps not!

Chapter Notes

CHAPTER 5

1. Baigent, et al., op. cit., p. 237.
2. Ibid., p. 247.
3. Baigent, et al. op. cit., pp. 106-107.
4. Ibid.
5. Ibid., pp. 122-123.
6. Ibid., p. 133.
7. Ibid., p. 206.
8. "Europe's Heads, Crowned and Otherwise, Bury Zita, the Last Habsburg Empress," PEOPLE, April 17, 1989, p. 50.
9. "Europe's Internal Market," THE ECONOMIST, July 9, 1988.
10. Danielle Pletka, "Community's Goal: A State of Oneness," INSIGHT ON THE NEWS, June 20, 1988.
11. Otto von Habsburg, CHARLES V (New York: Praeger Publishers, 1970), p. xiii.
12. Ibid., pp. xiii-xiv.
13. Hans Holzer, THE HABSBURG CURSE (Garden City, NY: Doubleday, 1973), p. 139.
14. Martin Yant, "Archduke Says Unified Europe Is A Certainty," COLUMBUS DISPATCH, February 8, 1987, p. 1D.
15. Matthew Oliver Goodwin, NUMEROLOGY: THE COMPLETE GUIDE (North Hollywood, CA: Newcastle Publishing Co., 1981).
16. William Gesenius, GESENIUS' HEBREW-CHALDEE LEXICON OF THE OLD TESTAMENT, Trans. Samuel Prideaux Tregelles (USA: Baker Book House, 1979), p. 316.
17. Manly P. Hall, THE SECRET TEACHINGS, op. cit., p. CLXXXVIII.
18. E. W. Bullinger, D.D., NUMBER IN SCRIPTURE (Grand Rapids, MI: Kregel Publications, 1981), p. 235.

Chapter 6

The Roots of the Merovingians

The Merovingian dynasty ruled France for 300 years — from the 5th to the 8th centuries. It is also true that most of Europe's monarchs have been from the Merovingian lineage from the Middle Ages until today. We have discussed at length the ancient heresy which considered the Merovingian bloodline to be the descendants of Jesus Christ and Mary Magdalene. But, who really were the Merovingians? Where did they actually come from? Can we trace their history back to Mary Magdalene? Or does it go back further, to the days of the Old Testament?

To find the answer, we must research ancient history and trace the migration of nomadic tribes. Merovee was king of a Germanic tribe called Franks. His name "echoes the French word for 'mother' as well as both the French and Latin words for 'sea'."[1]

According to the legend reported in HOLY BLOOD, HOLY GRAIL, Merovee was born of two fathers. It was said that his expectant mother went swimming one day in the Mediterranean Sea and was attacked by a dreadful sea creature who impregnated her with a divine seed. Not only was Merovee the son of Clodio, King of the Franks, he was also supposedly the son of a beast of Neptune. It was believed that in his veins flowed a co-mingling of two different bloods; the blood of a Frankish ruler and the blood of a mysterious aquatic creature. Since that, of course is not possible, it was suggested that the story of the sea creature may have been symbolic of his lineage, leading to the development of the legend that he was of the offspring of Mary Magdalene.

It is believed to this day by the people in Provence, a district in southern France, that Lazarus and his two sisters, Mary Magdalene and Martha, landed there when they sailed across the Mediterranean to France, escaping the Roman destruction of Jerusalem in A.D. 70.[2] So, the belief that the mother of the Merovingian dynasty came from the Mediterranean Sea (or from across the sea) may have originated from this symbolic fairy tale. She is still considered today, by those who ascribe to the belief of the "holy bloodline," to be the progenitor of Merovee — 400 years removed.

A clue to where the Merovingians possibly originated is found in ancient Norse mythology. Merovee claimed to be descended from Odin, one of the gods worshiped by the Teutonic people of northern Europe — after whom Odin's Day (also called Woden's Day), or Wednesday, was named. Note the spelling of the word "Odin." Is it possible — could this be another way of spelling Dan, or could the name have evolved from the Israelite Lost Tribe of Dan? We shall analyze the possible Merovingian/Israelite connection in this chapter.

In order to explore that premise, perhaps we should begin with a story from Greece — of the battle between the Spartans and the Trojans. Keep in mind, the kings of the Merovingian dynasty claimed to be descendants from those ancient tribes.

According to the ancient Greek treatise, THE ILIAD, by Homer, the founder of Troy was named *Dar-dan-us*. [3] The name is strikingly familiar. It contains the name of Dan! It was said that Dardanus was the son of Zeus. Dardanus had a son named Erichthonius, who had a son named Tros, who was the namesake of the ancient Trojans and of their capital city, Troy.

Tros had three sons, Ilus, Ganymede, and Assaracus. Priam, the reigning king of the Trojans, was of the line of Ilus. Aeneas, founder of the Roman Empire, was a prince of the royal house of Assaracus. Ganymede was the great-grandson of Dardanus, the founder of Troy. According to Homer's ILIAD (Book V), [4] Zeus kidnapped the prince, Ganymede. Zeus wanted Ganymede to be a special cup-bearer to the gods (which may be a clue to the origin of the legend of the so-called Holy Grail).

The ILIAD does not relate how Zeus carried off Ganymede, but there is an ancient Roman mosaic showing Ganymede, the Trojan prince, being carried off by Zeus, who had taken the form of an eagle! Here is a possible clue to connect the progenitors of the ancient Trojans with the tribe of Dan, who had adopted the eagle as their insignia.

Zeus was sometimes pictured as an eagle, but at other times he was pictured as a serpent to whom offerings of honey were made. Here appears yet another clue. We have the symbol of a snake (the first insignia of Dan) to whom offerings of honey were made! The honey could be a reference to the bees in Samson's riddle — again, it smacks of the tribe of Dan.

According to Greek mythology, Zeus was the son of Cronus,

Ganymede, the Trojan prince, being carried off by Zeus (as an eagle) who wanted him to be a cup-bearer for the gods. Roman mosaic.

the sun god. It was said that Zeus was born in Arcadia (Spartan territory). When he reached manhood he overthrew his father Cronus and won the universe. He then divided it with his brothers according to lots: Hades drew the nether world, Poseidon the sea and the waters, and Zeus the heavens.

The Spartans also lived in the southern Greek peninsula called Arcadia. Over the centuries some of the group migrated northeast across the Aegean Sea to build the ancient city of Troy. There came a time when Paris, the Trojan prince, fell in love with Helen, wife of the Spartan king, kidnapped her and

The Trojan Horse brought the downfall of Troy. Trojan royalty scattered throughout Europe.

removed her to the city of Troy. By the way, Paris was the one after whom the capital of France was named. There is also a city in France named Troyes, after the ancient Trojan capital — for the Merovingian French royalty claimed descent from the Trojans.

According to the legend, the battle between the Spartans and the Trojans raged for 10 years. Then the Spartans hit upon an idea. They built a huge hollow horse, left it outside the walls of Troy, boarded their ships and pushed off into the Aegean sea. As they sailed out of sight, the people of Troy emerged to inspect the horse. They were warned that it might be a trick, but they wouldn't listen. They pulled the Trojan horse inside their city, and that night celebrated their victory over the Spartans. However, inside the horse, Spartan soldiers had been hidden, and under the cover of darkness, the Spartan ships returned.

While the people of Troy celebrated, the Spartan warriors crept out of their hiding place and opened the gates of the city allowing their army to enter. According to the account, the Spartans rescued Helen, killed many of the Trojans, and set fire to the city. Here's a side note: Aeneas, a Trojan prince, escaped the city and went to central Italy, where his offspring bore the twin boys Romulus and Remus, the founders of Rome.

Over the centuries some of the Spartans migrated into southern France, and some of the surviving Trojans moved north and west into Germany, Belgium and northern France, following the Danube River, and eventually settled in the region that became known as Austrasia in the province of Lorraine.[5] The lineage of the Merovingian kings, therefore, may have been rooted in the Trojans.

In the apocryphal book of I Maccabees there is an account about the Spartans of southern Greece — claiming that they were related to the Jewish people and were, in fact, of the stock of Abraham. A letter from the king of the Spartans to the Jewish high priest in Jerusalem is most revealing:

"Areus, king of the Spartans, to Onias, the high priest, greetings.

"It has been discovered in a document concerning the Spartans and Jews that they are brothers, and are of the race of Abraham" (I Maccabees 12:20-21).

Unfortunately, the "document" referred to in the letter does not exist today. If it did, however, it might have provided the missing link necessary to connect the Spartans to the tribe of Dan. However, Flavius Josephus also records the letter in his writings:

"We have met with a certain writing, whereby we have discovered that both the Jews and the Spartans are of one stock, and are derived from the kindred of Abraham. It is but just, therefore, that you, who are our brethren, should send to us about any of your concerns as you please. We will also do the same thing, and esteem your concerns as our own, and will look upon our concerns as in common with yours. Demotoles, who brings you this letter, will bring your answer back to us. This letter is foursquare; and the symbol is an eagle, with a dragon in his claws." [6]

The Spartan letter followed the invasion of Jerusalem by Antiochus Epiphanes, the Syrian general who sacrificed a sow upon the brazen altar of the Temple. In the course of events, Onias died, but his successor, Jonathan, wrote a letter of reply to the Spartans of southern Greece:

"Jonathan the high priest, the senate of the nation, the priests, and the rest of the Jewish people, to the Spartans their brothers send greetings.

"In the past a letter was sent to Onias, the high priest from Areus, one of your kings, stating that you are indeed our brothers, as the copy subjoined attests.

"Onias received the envoy with honor, and accepted the letter, in which a clear reference was made to friendship and alliance.

"For our part, though we have no need of these, having the consolation of the holy books in our possession.

"We venture to send, to renew our fraternal friendship with you, so that we may not become strangers to you, for a long time has elapsed since you sent us the letter.

"We may say that constantly on every occasion, at our

festivals and on other appointed days, we make a remembrance of you in the sacrifices we offer and in our prayers, as it is right and fitting to remember brothers."[7]

What relation the Spartans were to the Jews is not given. We can only surmise the possibility that they could have been from the tribe of Dan.

King Merovee supposedly possessed magical powers. He and his royal offspring wore their hair long as a symbol of their magic (similar to Samson). It was also said that they had the power to heal by the laying on of hands and that such power could be found in the tassels that hung as fringes on the bottom of their garments. This indicates a possible Hebrew heritage, for such power was believed to be in the fringes of the talliths worn by Israelites. You may recall the woman at Capernaum who touched the hem (fringes) of our Savior's garment and was healed of a 12-year infirmity.

Thus, we may consider not only a so-called Christian connection, but we are told of a more significant Israelite custom as well. These are two important clues: One, he wore his hair long like Samson, the Danite, with the belief that it gave him magical power; and two, he wore a tallith as did the ancient religious Israelite people. Is it possible that Merovee's forefathers were Israelites, of the stock of Abraham — perhaps even from the tribe of Dan? That brings us to another clue.

When the tomb of Childeric I, son of Merovee, was discovered and opened in 1653, there were found among the items in his tomb, 300 miniature bees made of solid gold. In Chapters 3 and 5 we mentioned the bees. We said that Napoleon had these 300 golden bees sewn onto his coronation robe — worn when he crowned himself Emperor of France. When he married Marie-Louise (Habsburg) of Austria, she wore a royal robe with the bees interwoven throughout. The bees may well represent a very important clue as to the lineage of the Merovingian dynasty. (See pages 58-59.)

Four symbols are used in the Bible concerning the Danites — a serpent, an eagle, a lion, and the bees. In the story of Samson, we find the famous riddle of the bees who made honey in the carcass of a lion which had been killed by Samson.* The symbolic nature of the bees could represent the concept that the descendants of the tribe of Dan would one day try to bring about the destruction of the tribe of Judah, whose symbol was the lion, and from the carcass of the lion the tribe of Dan would attempt to produce the golden age of a world empire, symbolized by the honey. The Merovingians claim of coming from the tribe of Judah (through Mary Magdalene and Jesus Christ) is not true. The lie may have been advanced because the symbol of Judah was the lion. However, I believe the Merovingians were from the tribe of Dan.

The eagle's wings detached from the back of the lion in the 7th chapter of Daniel may also be an ancient symbol for the tribe of Dan, which broke away from the tribe of Judah in the last chapters of the book of Judges:

"The first was like a lion, and had eagle's wings: I beheld till the wings thereof were plucked, and it was lifted up from the earth, and made stand upon the feet as a man, and a man's heart was given to it" (Daniel 7:4).

On a map of ancient Israel, the territory of Dan appears like a wing attached to the shoulder of the territory of Judah. Among the possible interpretations of Daniel's vision one must consider the story of Dan leaving its original territory and moving north into Lebanon.

When Moses gave his prophecies of the 12 tribes, he said that Benjamin would *"dwell between the shoulders of Judah"* (Deuteronomy 33:12), and that Dan, *"as a lion's whelp, would leap from Bashan"* (Deuteronomy 33:22). Bashan was located in ancient Lebanon. That Mosaic prediction came to pass when the tribe of Dan was deprived of its territory adjacent to Judah, moved north to Lebanon, and established its territory in Bashan. From there the Danites made a symbolic leap into obscurity. It is my opinion that they could have landed in Europe.

To follow the possible migration of the Danites, we must go back to the early pages of the Bible to the days following the death of Samson. [9] During those days, the tribe of Dan lived in the territory west of Jerusalem, over toward the coast of the Mediterranean Sea and down through the valley of Sorek to the borders of the Philistines. After the death of Samson, the men of Dan were deprived of their territory. Not only did Samson's death create a possible difficulty for the Danites, but the sin of the tribe of Benjamin at about that time also created a precarious situation for the tribe.

The story is given of the wife of a Levite who had been molested by the Benjaminites. When her husband discovered her corpse, he cut it into pieces and sent it to the other tribes demanding that they avenge the rape of his wife. The battle that followed almost annihilated the Benjaminites. In the war, however, the tribe of Dan also suffered. Flavius Josephus, a first century Jewish historian, described it:

"Now it happened that the tribe of Dan suffered in like manner with the tribe of Benjamin; and it came to do so on the occasion following: — When the Israelites had already left off the exercise of their arms for war, and were intent upon their husbandry, the Canaanites despised them, and brought together an army, not because they expected to suffer by them, but because they had a mind to have a sure prospect of treating the Hebrews ill when they pleased, and might thereby for the time to come dwell in their own cities the more securely; they prepared therefore their chariots, and gathered their soldiery together, their cities also combined together, and drew over to them Ashkelon and Ekron, which were within the tribe of Judah, and many more of those that lay in the plain. They also forced the Danites to fly into the mountainous country, and left them not the least portion of the plain country to set their foot on. Since then, these Danites were not able to fight them, and had not land enough to sustain them, they sent five of their men into the midland country to seek for a land to which they might remove their habitation. So these men went as far as the neighborhood of Mount Libanus, and the fountains of the Lesser Jordan, at the great plain of Sidon...." [10]

Thus, we have the migration of the tribe of Dan. Having been pushed out of their territory west of Jerusalem, they went north into Lebanon. The story is found in Judges 18. According to the chapter, the tribe of Dan established an idolatrous religion — the worship of the sun and moon. The summation of their move is given in the book of Judges:

"And they called the name of the city Dan, after the name of Dan, their father, who was born unto Israel; howbeit, the name of the city was Laish at the first.

"And the children of Dan set up the graven image; and Jonathan, the son of Gershom, the son of Manasseh, he and his sons were priests to the tribe of Dan until the day of the captivity of the land" (Judges 29-30).

According to the story, the tribe of Dan moved into Lebanon, where they lived for at least the next 600 years. In the year 721 B.C., the Assyrians took the northern ten tribes captive. Though there are no historical documents to prove that the tribe moved westward into Europe, the question remains: What happened to the tribe of Dan?

According to THE WORLD BOOK ENCYCLOPEDIA, the Celts, in 400 B.C., divided Ireland into small kingdoms called tuatha. [11] Celtic mythology claims that the most important race was the "Tuatha de Danann, or People of the Goddess Danu." Some have suggested that this name may refer to a connection to the ancient tribe of Dan. The Tuatha de Danann was "the source of most of the divinities that the Irish people worshiped before they became Christians in the A.D. 400's." [12]

Now, I am not an adherent of "British Israelism." It is not my purpose to try to promote the idea that the Europeans were the lost ten tribes of Israel. However, it is not impossible that at least the tribe of Dan could have migrated northwest — to eventually establish the thrones of Europe. I have no hard evidence that the name Denmark comes from Dan or that the Danube River is so named after the ancient tribe. I am simply pointing out the possibility, for the tribe of Dan is considered by Jewish rabbis to be a lost tribe.

The lineage of the Merovingian kings has not been historically established. But, we are relating in this chapter why we believe they probably descended from the early Spartans, which, according to the apocryphal book of I Maccabees, claimed to be of the stock of Abraham, father of Israel. Could they have come from the tribe of Dan? Could the name of the Danube River be derived from that ancient tribe? And could the country of Denmark also be so named?

Why should we be so interested in the tribe of Dan? What part would that ancient tribe have to play in the fulfillment of prophecy? For the answer, we must go to the 49th chapter of Genesis and consider the story of the dying Jacob, who gathered his 12 sons around his bed to give prophecies of that which would befall each of them in the last days. He spoke of Judah as a lion and said that the scepter shall not depart from Judah until Shiloh come — which is taken to be a prediction of the coming Messiah. But then he spoke of Dan:

"Dan shall judge his people, as one of the tribes of Israel.

"Dan shall be a serpent by the way, an adder in the path, that biteth the horse heels, so that his rider shall fall backward" (Genesis 16-17).

Here we see the trail of the serpent and are reminded of the prophecy to Adam and Eve that the serpent shall bruise the heel of the Messiah — the seed of the woman. The dying Jacob referred to Dan under the insignia of the serpent.

These symbols take us back to the ancient zodiac. To Judah was given the insignia of Leo, the Lion, and to Dan was given the insignia of Scorpio, the seed of the serpent. The reference by the dying Jacob could be a prediction that the offspring of Dan may one day produce Mr. 666, who will attempt to sit upon the throne of this world.

In Revelation 7 the 144,000 Israelites are listed. All of the tribes are given but the tribe of Dan. By the time we reach that point in world history (the time of Revelation 7), the tribe of Dan is missing. The implication is that Dan will produce the great usurper, the antichrist.

I have long believed that the tribe of Dan would somehow be involved with the rise of the antichrist — even while other theologians were suggesting that the future man of sin would be a Gentile — perhaps from Syria, Egypt, or even Rome.

I had no concrete proof to support my theory. I could not pinpoint the whereabouts of the offspring of Dan, for the ancient tribe slipped into obscurity some 3,000 years ago. Further, there is no scripture which specifically states that the future world ruler will be from that ancient Israelite tribe. I based my theory upon the implications of a few prophetic Scriptures.

The prophet Daniel predicted the coming of a future usurper, indicating that he could be an apostate Israelite, who would forsake the traditional religion of his forefathers:

"Neither shall he regard the God of his fathers, nor the

desire of women, nor regard any god: for he shall magnify himself above all" (Daniel 11:37).

Daniel indicated that the future world ruler would not regard the God of his fathers. That may be a reference to his lineage. He will have no regard for the God of the rabbis. Furthermore, it may be more than a coincidence that the Lord chose a man named Daniel to write one of the greatest prophetic books in the Bible. His very name, Dan-i-el, may, in itself, be a clue concerning this one about whom Daniel wrote. More than any other Old Testament Book, Daniel describes the coming world ruler who will persecute the Jewish people with a vengeance. It just might be a man from the tribe of Dan who will try to eliminate the Lion of the tribe of Judah.

If the predictions that *"Dan shall judge his people"* and *"Dan shall be a serpent"* are accurate, most of the suffering of Israel down through the centuries has been plotted and perpetrated by the lost tribe of Dan. The question is, can we prove it? Were the leaders of imperial Rome the offspring of the tribe of Dan? Was the Syrian general, Antiochus Epiphanes, who sacrificed a pig upon the brazen altar (168 B.C.) an offshoot from the tribe of Dan? Was Alexander the Great a Danite? And what about the thrones of Europe who persecuted the Jewish people over the past 1,600 years? Do they belong to that ancient tribe?

In these prophecies of the dying Jacob we can see the trail of the serpent who beguiled Eve in the Garden of Eden. God placed a curse upon the serpent and his seed. He said:

"I will put enmity between thee and the woman, and between thy seed and her seed; it shall bruise thy head, and thou shalt bruise his heel" (Genesis 3:15).

It is quite remarkable that the dying Jacob gave the symbol of the serpent to Dan and declared that he would judge his people.

There is an ancient apocryphal writing called the "Testaments of the Twelve Patriarchs" in which Dan was supposed to have made certain predictions concerning his offspring. The writing is apocryphal, and has been dated by scholars to have been written around 150 B.C. Fragments of the apocryphal writing were found in the Qumran caves, and are a part of the famous Dead Sea Scrolls.

The "Testaments of the Twelve Patriarchs" are purported to be the final utterances of the twelve sons of Jacob — modeled after Jacob's last words in Genesis 49. Just prior to death, each of the sons is depicted as gathering his offspring around him and prophesying those things which would befall each tribe in the future. According to the testament of Dan, he gathered his sons around him when he was 125 years old. Among the many things he had to say were these startling words:

"I read in the Book of Enoch, the Righteous, that your prince is Satan...." [13]

Because of this statement, Jewish scholars, some 150 years before Christ, linked the tribe of Dan with the antichrist — "your prince is Satan." Furthermore, in the apocryphal writing, Dan was made to say, "I know that in the last days you will defect from the Lord, you will be offended at Levi, and revolt against Judah; but you will not prevail over them." [14]

Finally, upon Dan's death, the writer concluded, "Dan prophesied to them ... that they would go astray from God's law, that they would be estranged from their inheritance, from the race of Israel, and from their patrimony; and that is what occurred." [15]

As the ancient writing indicated, the Danites lost their inheritance of territory after the death of Samson. Migrating north into Lebanon, they eventually lost their identity. Dan became a lost tribe.

When Moses built the Tabernacle, he was instructed to

choose two men to head up the project. They were Bezaleel of the tribe of Judah and Aholiab of the tribe of Dan (Exodus 31:1-6). These two men were chosen to do the design work with the gold, silver, brass, stone, wood, and fabric. In choosing these two men, I believe God was laying out a prophecy of those two tribes who would eventually fight over the possession and disposition of the sanctuary. Just as the Messiah has His roots in the tribe of Judah, the antichrist may have his roots in the tribe of Dan.

When the Tabernacle was completed, it was placed in the center of the camp. Each of the tribes were positioned around it — three to the east, three to the south, three to the west, and three to the north. Furthermore, each tribe was instructed to display their insignia:

"Now the Lord spake unto Moses and unto Aaron saying,

"Every man of the children of Israel shall pitch by his own standard, with the ensign of their father's house; far off about the tabernacle of the congregation shall they pitch" (Numbers 2:1,2).

The symbols of the tribes were given according to the constellations in the ancient Egyptian zodiac. The tents of the tribe of Judah were pitched to the east of the Tabernacle under the symbol of the lion. Alongside Judah were the tribes of Issachar and Zebulon. On the south side lay the tents of Reuben, Simeon and Gad. On the west side Ephraim, Manasseh, and Benjamin pitched their tents. And on the north side were Asher, Naphtali, and Dan:

"The standard of the camp of Dan shall be on the north side by their armies, and the captain of the children of Dan shall be Ahiezer" (Numbers 2:25).

This specific position of the Danites on the north side of the camp may be prophetic of their eventual location at the extreme north end of the nation — at the Lebanon border. It may also be connected to the prophecy given by Isaiah concerning the fall of Lucifer:

"How art thou fallen from heaven, O Lucifer, son of the morning! how art thou cut down to the ground, which didst weaken the nations!

"For thou hast said in thine heart, I will ascend into heaven, I will exalt my throne above the stars of God: I will sit also upon the mount of the congregation, in the sides of the north" (Isaiah 14:12-13).

The notes of the Open Bible say the north side means, "in the place of control." Could it be that the tribe of Dan, who was situated on the north side of the congregation was the target of Lucifer?

To Dan was given the symbol of Scorpio, which, in the ancient Egyptian zodiac was a snake. However, when the time came to hoist the symbol of the snake, Ahiezer refused and chose instead the symbol of an eagle. According to Unger's Bible Dictionary:

"Dan's position in the journey was on the north of the Tabernacle, with Asher and Naphtali. The standard of the tribe was of white and red, and the crest upon it, an eagle, the great foe to serpents, which had been chosen by the leader instead of a serpent, because Jacob had compared Dan to a serpent. Ahiezer substituted the eagle, the destroyer of serpents, as he shrank from carrying an adder upon his flag."[16] It may prove worthwhile to consider the possible connection to the tribe of Dan whenever an eagle is used as the symbol of subsequent leaders or nations.

Here are the clues which could connect the tribe of Dan with the political leaders of the Greeks, the Romans, the Germans, the French — all of the thrones of Europe, including the leaders of ancient Czarist Russia. Not only have those nations displayed the symbol of the eagle, but their colors have primarily been white and red, the colors of the Danites. It may be more than coincidence that the Knights Templar wore white uniforms displaying a red cross on the chest.

Dan was the largest tribe in Israel in the days of the Tabernacle. Their population numbered 157,600. After conquering Canaan, Dan was the last tribe to receive any land. Though they were the largest tribe, they received the smallest amount of territory — west of Jerusalem, down to the Mediterranean coast. After the death of Samson, however, they were deprived even of that, and had to migrate north into southern Lebanon. There, they captured the city of Laish and changed its name to Dan. Thus, we have the term in the Old Testament — *"from Dan to Beersheba."*

The ancient name "Laish" means "a lion,"which fulfills the prophecy of Moses in Deuteronomy 33:22 when he said:

"Dan is a lion's whelp: he shall leap from Bashan."

The city of the lion (Laish) was located in the ancient province of Bashan, in the territory of Lebanon. From there, however, according to the prediction of Moses, Dan was to make a historic leap. In fact, the tribe vanished over the next 400 years.

In I Chronicles 1-8, the Israelite tribes are listed — all, that is, but the tribe of Dan. The date for writing the first eight chapters of the Chronicles has been placed at 1056 B.C. By then, Dan had become a lost tribe. They were not listed among the tribes of Israel. We do not have to wait until we get to Revelation 7 to eliminate the tribe of Dan. It was apparent in the first of the Chronicles. The big question remains, what happened to the tribe of Dan? Where did they go with their symbol of an eagle as a killer of snakes?

We previously mentioned a letter, written by the king of the Spartans to the high priest in Jerusalem, wherein he claimed to be of the "stock of Abraham." We also related a similar statement written by the historian, Flavius Josephus.

According to Josephus, the symbol of the ancient Spartans was an eagle with a dragon in his claws. The dragon, by the way, was synonymous with the snake among the early cultures. This is an incredible clue linking the tribe of Dan with the Spartans of southern Greece. It is curious to note that the Spartans claimed to be brothers to the tribes of Israel, of the stock of Abraham — displaying the symbol of an eagle and its enemy, the snake.

When Herod the Great built the magnificent temple in the years before the birth of Christ, he placed a huge eagle above the gate. Flavius Josephus wrote of it:

"Herod had caused such things to be made, which were contrary to the law, of which he was accused by Judas and Mathias; for the king had erected over the great gate of the temple, a large golden eagle, of great value, and had dedicated it to the temple." [17]

Herod the Great had placed an eagle (a symbol of the tribe of Dan) above the temple in the years just prior to the birth of Christ. How significant! For the mysterious tribe of Dan appears to have laid claim to the temple, just as they may again, someday, when the antichrist commits the abomination of desolation.

When Herod the Great became extremely ill, a group of patriotic Jews pulled down the golden eagle. Josephus wrote:

"And with such discourses, as this did these men excite the young men to this action; and a report being come to them that the king was dead, this was an addition to the wise men's persuasions, so, in the very middle of the day they got up on the place, they pulled down the eagle, and cut it into pieces with axes, while a great number of the people were in the temple." [18] Needless to say, they were arrested and executed for destroying what may have been a Spartan eagle.

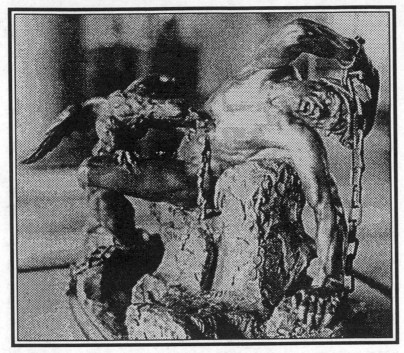

Legends similar to the one about an eagle eating Aqhat, found engraved upon a cuneiform tablet at the dig of Ugarit, have survived in Greek mythology.

Now, the question remains, how do we know the Spartans were the offspring of the tribe of Dan? Even though they admitted to being brothers to the children of Israel, of the stock of Abraham, what further clues can we gather to help determine their lineage?

Aside from the fact that the Spartans wore long hair as a symbol of their power (like Samson) there is a legend written about the son of Belus, king of the Spartans — in which is given the story of one named "Danaus," who arrived in Greece with his daughters by ship. According to the legend, his daughters called themselves Danades. They introduced the cult of the mother goddess, which became the established religion of the Arcadians and developed over the years into the worship of Diana. (Diana may be another form of Dan.) The Spartans so loved their king that they called themselves Danaans — long before they adopted the name of Spartans.

Also in the legend is a record of the arrival of "colonists from Palestine." Please note, the man who headed the expedition was named Danaus. He may well have been of the tribe of Dan, and thus would have been the progenitor of the ancient Spartans.

In 1928, the ancient Canaanite city of Ugarit was discovered in northern Syria, about a half-mile inland from the coast of the Mediterranean. In the years following, a team of archaeologists, digging at the site, uncovered hundreds of cuneiform tablets dating from about 1200 B.C. One of the tablets recorded a legend. It told of a king called Aqhat, the son of a man named Danel and his wife Donatiya. The names of these two parents may well be a clue to the ancient tribe of Dan which lived in the area in the 12th century B.C.

According to the legend, Kothar-wa-Khasis (the god of crafts) made a beautiful bow for Aqhat, which drew the attention of Anath, the goddess of war. Anath desired the bow for her arsenal, but Aqhat rejected her offers for it. In the story, Anath had Aqhat killed by one of her cohorts, Yatpan, who assumed the form of an eagle. In the ancient legend, the eagle ate Aqhat. His father, Danel, retrieved Aqhat's remains from the stomach of the eagle, and buried his son. Aqhat's sister, Pigat, then went to Yatpan the eagle to revenge her brother's death. Meanwhile, Danel entered a seven year period of mourning for Aqhat.[19] In the cuneiform text, the story ends here, but many scholars feel there is probably more to the legend.

And why was the legend written? No one is certain. But it could possibly be symbolic of the tribe of Dan, consumed by

the eagle, who sets out to get revenge, looking forward to that future day when they will enter a seven year period of mourning. The overtones are apocalyptic. The story seems somewhat prophetic of that future seven year period when the tribe of Dan will seek revenge upon the children of Israel for letting them be driven from their land.

Is it possible that the Danel of the Canaanite legend is the same as Danaus in the ancient Spartan legend? If they are not the same man, they may still be of the same tribe.

By the way, not only did the Spartans wear their hair long like Samson, ascribing a special magical significance to it, but even Alexander the Great, the youthful king of Macedonia, wore his hair long. When Alexander approached the city of Jerusalem with his army, the Jewish high priest welcomed him with open arms. Jerusalem was the only capital city which did not come under the sword of Alexander. Is it possible that Alexander the Great was of the tribe of Dan? Was he perhaps an Israelite of the stock of Abraham?

After the death of Alexander, his world kingdom was divided by his four generals. One hundred fifty years later, Antiochus Epiphanes, leader of the Greek province of Syria, invaded Jerusalem and sacrificed a pig upon the brazen altar. Josephus called him the "little horn" of Daniel's prophecy — a prophetic type of the antichrist. [20] The designation has led many scholars to believe the future antichrist will be a Syrian. But, though Antiochus Epiphanes may have been a Syrian general, his lineage goes back to the Greek general who fell heir to part of Alexander's kingdom. Antiochus Epiphanes may have been from the tribe of Dan.

The father of Alexander was Philip II, who, in 359 B.C., became the king of Macedonia and quickly conquered the entire Greek peninsula. In later years, Philip called a meeting at Corinth of representatives from all the Greek city states (with the exception of Sparta). And the delegates to this league of Corinth sat on a council called the "Synhedrion." As incredible as it may seem, the parliament of ancient Greece was called by the same name as the parliament of ancient Israel. They were called the "Sanhedrin."

Is it any wonder that though the Old Testament was written in Hebrew, the New Testament was written in Greek? It may be more than a coincidence that the Hebrew alphabet, with its Aleph, Beth, Gimmel is remarkably similar to the Greek alphabet with its Alpha, Beta, Gamma. Though the Greeks were a mixture of ancient tribes (as was all of Europe for that matter), their political leaders may well have been Danites who migrated from the land of Israel over a thousand years before the birth of Christ. Perhaps from the ancient Spartans came the rulers of most of the thrones of Europe — who carried with them the symbol of the eagle.

The symbol of imperial Rome was a single headed eagle, but after Constantine divided the empire in the 4th century A.D., and moved his throne to Constantinople, a two headed eagle evolved as the symbol of the Byzantine Roman Empire.

In the ninth century, most of the thrones of Europe were established, including a huge Jewish kingdom, known as Khazaria — kingdom of the Khazars. It was located above the Black Sea and offered a refuge for all of the tribes of the Diaspora. Could the Khazars have been Danites? Strangely enough, there are four major rivers that ran through the kingdom of the Khazars emptying into the Black Sea. There is the Danube, the Dnister, the Dnieber, and the Don. It appears to have been a common thing for the people of Dan to name their rivers by their ancient forefather. Even the Jordan river that weaves like a snake along the eastern border of the land of Israel is named after the ancient tribe of Dan. Jordan means "the going down of the Dan."

The kingdom of the Khazars may have been a refuge for all of the tribes, but their political leaders ruled under the symbol of the two headed eagle. With all of that evidence, one is tempted to conclude that the lost tribe of Dan has thus been found. Some scholars believe that the prophet Ezekiel was referring to the prophet Daniel when he dampened the hopes of his people for deliverance, in Ezekiel 14:12-23, by saying that an individual will be saved only if he is righteous. To stress the point, Ezekiel wrote:

"Though these three men, Noah, Daniel, and Job were in the land, they should deliver but their own souls by their righteousness."

Scholars have no problems identifying Noah and Job in the Bible, but who is the Daniel mentioned by Ezekiel? Is he the great prophet contemporary with Ezekiel? Or is he the Danel of the Canaanite legend? In the book of Daniel, the prophet's name is spelled in the Hebrew, Dny'l. But in Ezekiel's passage, Daniel is spelled Dn'l — exactly as the name Danel is spelled in the ancient Canaanite legend. It is possible, then, that Ezekiel made reference not to his contemporary, but to the ancient tribe of Dan who was predicted to judge the children of Israel. Ezekiel, neverthless, declared that his people would not escape the judgment meted out by the Babylonians.

In Revelation 4:7, a description of four living creatures is given — each seeming to represent a quarter of the ancient zodiac:

"And the first beast was like a lion, and the second beast like a calf, and the third beast had a face as a man, and the fourth beast was like a flying eagle."

The lion, calf, and man seem to represent the constellations of Leo, Taurus, and Aquarius, but the eagle has replaced Scorpio. The symbolism is powerful. Aquarius, the water bearer, may be a picture of the first coming of Christ to pour out the Holy Spirit (symbolized by the water) upon his people. Leo appears to be a picture of the second coming of Christ to judge the offspring of Dan (symbolized by the snake, Hydra).

On the other hand, Taurus, the bull, and Scorpio, the transformed eagle, may represent the tribe of Dan and its quest for the throne. The name Taurus means "the coming Judge." That is the description given of Dan by his dying father, Jacob, in Genesis 49:16, *"Dan shall judge his people, as one of the tribes of Israel."*

The symbol of the eagle has replaced Scorpio in the book of Revelation, which may be another indication of the tribe of Dan who refused the symbol of the snake and adopted the symbol of the eagle in the days of Moses.

On the Gabbatha, or pavement at the fortress of Antonia, where our Savior stood before Pilate on the day of his crucifixion, there is an inscription carved in stone. It was discovered in the archaeological dig made at the site in the early 1930's, and is considered to mark the spot where our Savior was mocked by the Romans as "King of the Jews."

Among the pictures carved in the pavement, there is a symbol of Scorpio — used as an insignia of the brutal Roman army. The symbol may have been used interchangeably with the Roman eagle. Both may be a clue to the progenitors of the Romans, who came from the Trojans, who came from the Spartans, who admitted to being brothers to the Jewish people (and of the stock of Abraham) 150 years before the birth of Christ.

There is an ancient prophecy given in the apocryphal book of II Esdras which has baffled scholars for hundreds of years.

The book was written during the Babylonian captivity and was published between the Old and New Testaments for many years. However, it is not regarded as an inspired part of the Bible. We cannot consider the validity of its doctrine, but can get a glimpse at early Jewish theology from a reading of it.

In chapter 11, Esdras, a captive rabbi in Babylon, dreams a dream — which enlarges upon the eagle plucked from the back of the lion found in Daniel's vision:

"Then saw I a dream, and, behold, there came up from the sea an eagle, which had twelve wings, and three heads." [21]

In the vision, the prophet is told that the wings represent a dynasty of kings who would rule in succession and that the three heads represented the development (worldwide expansion) of the empire, with its various divisions. Verses 29 through 35:

"... behold, there awaked one of the heads that were at rest, namely, it that was in the midst; for that was greater than the two other heads.

"But this head put the whole earth in fear, and bare rule in it over all those that dwelt upon the earth with much oppression; and it had the governance of the world more than all the wings that had been.

"And after this I beheld, and, lo, the head that was in the midst suddenly appeared no more, like as the wings.

"But there remained the two heads, which also in like sort ruled upon the earth, and over those that dwelt upon the earth, and over those that dwelt therein.

"And I beheld, and, lo, the head upon the right side devoured it that was upon the left side." [22]

The passage is remarkable in view of the history of the Roman Empire. The head in the middle could be a prophecy of Imperial Rome, which ruled the world for 666 years. Please note: the head disappeared on its own. It was not killed. Such was the demise of Imperial Rome. The empire simply disintegrated in the fourth century.

The other two heads of the eagle could represent the succeeding Holy Roman Empire which was split under the leadership of Constantine. The division destroyed its imperial power and weakened Roman rule. Over the centuries, the Church at Rome devoured the Eastern Orthodox Church, which ruled from Constantinople. For nearly a thousand years, the power of the Holy Roman Empire was unchallenged.

The implications of the visionary eagle are incredible. It may well represent the historical development of the Roman Empire. May I point out that the Habsburg Dynasty provided most of the emperors of the Holy Roman Empire from 1273 to 1806. And before that, in A.D. 496, King Clovis, the grandson of Merovee, was crowned emperor of the Western Roman Empire following the death of Constantine, and the division of the government. As incredible as it may seem, the family crest of the Habsburg Dynasty is a two-headed eagle.

Could the vision of Esdras be accurate after all? His three headed eagle appears to be an uncanny portrayal of the history and development of Roman rule — or perhaps we should say, of Merovingian rule, for the Roman Empire was started by Aeneas, a Trojan prince, whose ancestors were Spartans, who claimed to be of the stock of Abraham!

In the vision of Esdras, he saw a lion come out of the woods and declare that the last head of the eagle represented the fourth dreadful beast of Daniel's vision. You may recall, Daniel's fourth beast had 10 horns, representing a ten nation European confederation which would attempt to establish the final world government, and whose leader would be the antichrist.

In chapter 12 of the ancient prophecy, the destruction of the eagle is described. A lion came out of the woods to proclaim an interpretation of the eagle. According to the prophecy, the lion represented the Messiah.

"And it came to pass, whiles the lion spake these words unto the eagle, I saw,

"And, behold, the head that remained and the four wings appeared no more, and the two went unto it, and set themselves up to reign, and their kingdom was small, and full of uproar.

"And I saw, and, behold, they appeared no more, and the whole body of the eagle was burnt, so that the earth was in great fear ..." [23]

In the final stages of the eagle, two leaders are predicted to reign over a small kingdom full of uproar. That may be a picture of the proposed world government during the short seven years of the Tribulation Period. Finally, the eagle will be burned, and all the world will be in great fear. Could that be a prediction of nuclear war? The description seems to fit with the other prophecies of the Bible.

The symbol of ancient Spartan Greece was an eagle. The symbol of ancient Trojan Rome was an eagle. The symbol of Germany, which also claimed descent from the Trojans, was an eagle, and the symbol of the Habsburg dynasty, which provided the emperors of the Holy Roman Empire for 500 years was an eagle. In fact, the name Habsburg means "hawk's castle." The hawk is a part of the same family as the eagle. There are 260 kinds of eagles. Furthermore, the type of eagle which lives in the Middle East is called the "hawk eagle." This may be one of the most important clues to tie their dynasty back to the ancient Israelite tribe of Dan.

Under Roman domination, the Jewish people suffered unmercifully. But the leaders of the cruel Roman oppression may have been from the tribe of Dan. The Jew has suffered in the various countries of Europe down through the centuries,

House of Habsburg

but those European kings may well have been from the tribe of Dan.

They also suffered under the pograms or massacres of the Russian Czars who came from an ancient tribe known as Varangians, whose symbol was the double headed eagle. The ninth century Varangians, who established the Czarist throne of Russia may well have been Merovingians of the ancient tribe of Dan. In fact, the symbol of the Russian bear may have come from the ancient Spartans who lived in the province of Arcadia in southern Greece. The Word Arcadia means "the people of the bear."

Perhaps, one day, a descendant of the tribe of Dan will surround Jerusalem with an army, enter the Jewish sanctuary on the Temple Mount, commit the prophetic abomination of desolation, establish a throne on the sacred site and declare himself to be god!

Yes, the prophecy of dying Jacob may be ultimately fulfilled — as he said, "Dan shall judge his people."

Chapter Notes

CHAPTER 6

1. Baigent, et al., HOLY BLOOD, op. cit., p. 235.
2. Gurney, KINGDOMS OF EUROPE, op. cit., p. 52.
3. Homer, THE ILIAD, Trans. W.H.D. Rouse (New York: Mentor Books, 1960), p. 62.
4. Ibid.
5. Baigent, et al., op. cit., pp. 238-239.
6. Flavius Josephus, THE WORKS OF JOSEPHUS, Trans. William Whiston, A.M. (Lynn, MA: Hendrickson Publishers, 1980), Antiquities of the Jews, Book XII, Chapter IV, par. 10, p. 256.
7. THE APOCRYPHA (London: Oxford University Press), I Maccabees 12:6-11.
8. THE HOLY BIBLE, King James Version, Ed. Rev. C.I. Scofield, D.D. (New York: Oxford University Press, 1945), Judges 14:8.
9. Ibid., Judges, Chapters 16-21.
10. Josephus, WORKS OF JOSEPHUS, op.cit., Antiquities, Book V, Chapter III, verse 1, p. 113.
11. "Ireland," THE WORLD BOOK ENCYCLOPEDIA, op. cit., p. 336.
12. "Mythology/Celtic Mythology," WORLD BOOK, op. cit., p. 822.
13. H.C. Kee, "Testaments Of The Twelve Patriarchs," in THE OLD TESTAMENT PSEUDEPIGRAPHA, Vol. 1, ed. James H. Charlesworth (Garden City, NY: Doubleday, 1983), p. 809.
14. Ibid.
15. Ibid., p. 810.
16. Merrill F. Unger, UNGER'S BIBLE DICTIONARY (Chicago: Moody Press, 1966), pp. 235-236.
17. Josephus, op. cit., Antiquities, Book XVII, Chapter VI, par. 2, p. 364.
18. Ibid., par. 3, p. 364.
19. "Ugarit," ZONDERVAN PICTORIAL ENCYCLOPEDIA OF THE BIBLE, Ed. Merrill C. Tenney (Grand Rapids, MI: Regency Reference Library, 1976), Vol. 5, p. 840.
20. Josephus, op. cit., Antiquities, Book X, Chapter XI, par. 7, p. 227.
21. THE APOCRYPHA, op. cit., II Esdras 11:1, p. 38.
22. Ibid., pp. 38-39.
23. Ibid., II Esdras 12:1-3, p. 39.

Ancient Mysteries and Legends

Chapter 7

The Secret Doctrine

Adolf Hitler believed in a unique race of people called Aryans. Such a concept is foreign to the vocabulary of most Christians in our Western culture. We normally classify the three branches of humanity as Caucasoid, Negroid, and Mongoloid. To put it more simply, they are considered to be the European (or white), the African (or black), and the Asian (or yellow). This concept agrees with the biblical teaching that the sons of Noah survived the flood and produced the three branches of humanity. We are the offspring of Shem, Ham, and Japheth.

Hitler, however, believed in something called the "Secret Doctrine," which promoted the idea that there were seven races of humanity — who all had their origins on the ancient continent of Atlantis. These seven races were known as the Rmoahals, Tlavatli, Toltecs, Turanians, Akkadians, Mongols, and Aryans.

The so-called Secret Doctrine first appeared among the Buddhists of ancient Tibet. It was not taught in an intellectual manner, nor was it passed down as a teaching from generation to generation. It remained a Secret Doctrine, revealed only to a special group of people who practiced astrology and Transcendental Meditation.

According to THE SPEAR OF DESTINY, by Trevor Ravenscroft, in a chapter entitled "The Secret Doctrine": "Only when the centers of the astral body of a novice had been brought to fruition and his etheric organism fully expanded could the Secret Doctrine be revealed to him."[1]

To prepare for such a moment of revelation, the novice learned step-by-step to read the cosmic script (also called astrology) through the art of Yoga or meditation. It was precisely the same process used by the ancient European Knights Templar in learning the ABC's of the Grail.

According to the so-called Secret Doctrine, "...when the third eye had been opened to a full vision of the Akashic Record, the initiate became a living witness of the whole evolution of the world and of humanity. Traveling back through tremendous vistas of time, the very spirit origin of the earth and of man was unveiled to him, and he was able to follow the unfolding destiny of mankind through ever-changing conditions of life and cycles of development."[2]

The concept for the Lost Continent of Atlantis originally came from this so-called Secret Doctrine, taught in ancient Tibet. It was expanded upon, however, by Plato, the Greek philosopher who lived some 400 years before the birth of Christ. According to Plato, Atlantis was a large, island continent in the Atlantic Ocean.

Plato wrote that a great empire existed on Atlantis. Its armies planned to subdue the Mediterranean countries and were supposedly successful in parts of Europe and Africa. But Athens, wrote Plato, resisted their attack and defeated them. Later, great earthquakes and floods shook Atlantis and submerged it. During a single day and night of rain, the island sank into the sea.[3] Such a fable does not at all agree with the historical teachings of the Bible, but appears to be a crude attempt to give an alternative opinion on the catastrophic flood of Noah.

This, of course, is a ridiculous perversion of history. It is, however, the basis for the so-called Secret Doctrine, which is at the heart of the mystery cults. It was believed and taught for truth by the Thule Society, which, as we previously mentioned, became known as the Nazi movement. It was their primary source of inspiration for the Nazi attempt to destroy all Jewish life on the planet. It is important that we understand Hitler's concept of the Aryan race, for it is the underlying reason why he killed six million Jews. Furthermore, it is one of the guiding forces of the New Age Movement today.

According to the so-called Secret Doctrine, the people of Atlantis were not crude and primitive creatures. Though they developed through a process of human evolution, they lived in a far different world than we know today. Water at that stage in the "evolution" of the earth was much thinner than water today, and air, correspondingly, was far more dense. Atlantis appeared to be veiled in a heavy mist. To put in plainly, they lived in a fog. They couldn't see beyond a few feet. Because of this, they supposedly developed the ability to see with their third eye — the eye of clairvoyant perception. Their mindpower was greatly enhanced.

Though modern man is most conscious when awake, the Atlantean experienced a lowering of consciousness during the day and at night experienced a heightening of consciousness and could communicate with celestial hierarchies. (I would call them your local friendly demons.) It was said that these ancient Atlanteans possessed magical powers and roamed the universe through astral projection, a phenomenon which occultists claim to experience today.

The Secret Doctrine taught that their speech was intimately connected to the forces of nature. Their words could not only advance the growth of plants and tame wild beasts, but also could bring about immediate and miraculous healing to the sick. On the other hand, their words contained terrible forces of destruction against their enemies.

The leaders of these seven sub-races of Atlantis were not in the ranks of ordinary "evolving" human beings. It was said that these leaders were, in reality, "lofty spirit beings" who were able to take on human form. Their physical bodies were softer and had greater plasticity. They had mental and spiritual qualities of a super-human kind and appeared to their contemporaries as super-men. One could call them divine, human, hybrid beings — sort of god-men. They were greatly venerated by all lesser mortals who accepted their guidance gratefully and obeyed their commandments without question.

Such super-men instructed the Atlantean people in the sciences, the arts, law, and religion and taught them the techniques of tool-making and the practice of crafts. These super-men selected certain of the Atlantean peoples to breed new races. Thus, over a period of time seven races emerged from ancient Atlantis. Some of these manipulated races produced by the super-men became monstrous and grotesque. That accounts for their so-called explanation for the giants who inhabited the earth thousands of years ago.

According to the so-called Secret Doctrine, the Atlanteans had a problem. They had developed great magical powers, but with the ability came an overwhelming greed to dominate everyone and everything around them. In their lust for power, they tried to kill off everybody else with various kinds of voodoo. The power of the mind was being used for all the wrong reasons. Everyone was trying to feed his own ego with perverse appetites, and it was destroying the continent.

In order to preserve humanity, a master race of Atlantis was founded. It was called the Aryan race. But, it was not formed by a mere refinement of the previous sub-races of Atlantis. It was a sort of quantum leap in the whole process of human evolution — achieved in order to fashion the Root Race which would live on after the great flood — the one which totally destroyed the continent of Atlantis.

This new man, the Aryan, did not have the same kind of body developed in the earlier races. Their bodies were not plastic and pliable. They did not contain soft cartilages. The body of the new Aryan man possessed a bony skeleton. Furthermore, this new man was designed to develop personal intelligence and direct vision in the sense world. But these faculties of thought and sense perception were gained at the price of a total loss of all magical powers.

The breeding of this new race took place in the bitter weather conditions of the mountainous regions in the far north of the continent. Gradually, with the passing of many generations, a body emerged which was firm enough to withstand the effects of adverse soul powers — those magical problems which had disfigured the earlier races of Atlantis.

The new Aryan race was designed and developed with a physical brain which became the essential instrument of thought. Over a period of several generations, the ego and the first human experience of self-consciousness was awakened. Those who were selected to be leaders of the new Aryan race were isolated in mountain training centers where they received the most rigorous schooling under the rule of uncompromising discipline.

They were taught that everything which confronted them physically on earth was directed by so-called "invisible powers" in the macrocosm of the universe, and that they should dedicate themselves without reservation to the service of these powers. Their education at the hands of these hybrid god-men or super-men brought them to the point where they would grasp (in thought) the principles upon which the Aryan race was to be further developed. Above all, they were taught to respect and protect the purity of their blood.

This new Aryan race lived on the north side of the continent of Atlantis. It was said that the degenerating races who lived on the south side of the continent saw the dangers of allowing the new race of Aryans to develop. As a result, the people of the south made war against the Aryans. Out of the foggy mists surrounding the foot of the mountains the Aryan warriors were confronted with terrifying hordes of marauding peoples — many of whom were huge in size and grotesque in shape — manifesting the most fearful magical powers and capable of feats of super-human strength.

Against them, the Aryans pitted their newborn intelligence. Their ability to improvise proved superior to all the magic thrown against them. According to the so-called Secret Doctrine, the details of these monstrous and magical creatures has come down to us in the form of legend and myth.

According to the Secret Doctrine, the masses of this new Aryan race were entirely cut off from any form of direct perception of the spirit. At night they entered the void of sleep, and during the day they were blind to the workings of the spirit in nature. The earlier magical power of memory dwindled, and each new generation became further isolated from all knowledge of man's so-called "spiritual origin."

In order to remedy the spiritual blindness of the Aryan people, a mystery religion was developed. The elite of the race were prepared for "initiation at the sun oracle." After a series of initiations and periods of meditation, the spiritual centers in the astral bodies of the chosen few were matured — and opened to the vision of the spiritual hierarchies.

Under the symbol of the sun wheel (also called the four-armed swastika) the new initiates took over the leadership of the race and became the mediators between the masses of the people and the unseen powers of the spirit world. They taught this new religion which sought to bring every facet of life into relationship with the so-called cosmic universal order in the world.

The Aryan peoples were led out of Atlantis by the great Manu — the last of the sons of god or super-men. Their migration took them across Europe and Asia into the area of the Gobi Desert — and from thence to the heights of the Himalayas in Tibet. There on the top of the world, at Shambala, the sun oracle was founded to mastermind and direct the seven civilizations of the post-Atlantean age.

The so-called Masters of Wisdom, trained at this oracle, were said to be reincarnated over the years as the leaders of the people who survived the flood and settled throughout Europe, Asia, and America. According to the World Book Encyclopedia the word "Aryan" refers to a language spoken by the people who migrated from ancient Persia. In fact, the Word "Iran" is really a modernized version of the word "Aryan." Some of the Aryans migrated into Tibet and India, while others migrated into Germany and Europe. [4]

It is not difficult to imagine why Adolf Hitler thought that the Aryan race should be called the Master Race. We can also understand why he thought the Aryans could produce a new brand of Nazi super-men who would preserve the purity of the bloodline by destroying everybody on the planet who was not of Aryan descent.

He estimated that there were some 11 million Jews in the world, and he planned to murder every one of them. But that was only to be the beginning in his purge of the planet. His plan was to destroy all but the Aryan race, whose mental powers could then be developed without hindrance as they gave themselves to the guidance of the super-men, the spirit beings or god-like spiritual hierarchies, who would come to live in their bodies and guide them in the redevelopment of their magical powers of the mind.

From the teachings of the Bible, we can only conclude that these so-called god-like creatures — these spirit beings called super-men — are, in reality, demonic spirits who would like for you to believe that you are a god and that you contain creative powers in your mind. This demonic theology was not confined to the Nazi movement. It can be found at the heart of every cult religion down through the centuries of human history to this very day. It is the very core of the philosophy of the New Age Movement.

The concept of the Secret Doctrine that man possesses a third eye is also as old as the Tower of Babel. This third eye is referred to by some as the "mind's eye." It is also called the "all-seeing eye."

There are many books available today which claim to teach you how to master the creative powers of your mind. It is my conclusion that they are demonic, even those masquerading as "Christian." Most promote the concept that man is a god.

These books teach the same spiritual garbage. They want you to think that you are a god and that you possess magical powers. All you have to do is nurture these powers through a series of initiations. You are encouraged to practice self-hypnosis, yoga, or Transcendental Meditation. You are directed to release control of your mind so that your local "spirit guide" can enter and possess you — and give you magical clairvoyant powers. It's the same old lie that was told to Adam and Eve in the Garden of Eden when satan said, "Ye shall be as gods, knowing good and evil."

Of course, you are not told that this magical force you are accepting as your guide is in reality one of satan's demons. It is referred to as your "spirit guide" or your "inner guide" or your "Master of Wisdom." Children are encouraged to practice this demonic initiation in some public school classrooms in America.

A book entitled, PONDER ON THIS, contains the psychic messages of an ancient Tibetan Master—Djwhal Khul, who transmitted his thoughts to Alice Bailey by way of Transcendental Meditation. The book was published by the Lucis Publishing Company. This company was originally established as the Lucifer Publishing Company, but changed its name in 1923-24, to the less startling, Lucis Publishing Company. Quoting from PONDER ON THIS:

"The third eye is the director of energy or force, and thus an instrument of the will of Spirit ... It is the eye of the inner vision, and he who has opened it can direct and control the energy of matter, see all things in the Eternal Now, and therefore be in touch with causes more than with effects, read the Akashic records, and see clairvoyantly ... It is through the medium of this 'all seeing eye' that the accomplished Adept can at any moment put Himself in touch with His disciples anywhere."[5]

"This is the path to be trodden by one and all, and the method is meditation — till he finally contacts the one initiator, is admitted into the secret place, and knows the mystery that underlies consciousness itself."[6]

"Man is in essence divine ... Man is in fact a fragment of the Universal Mind."[7]

The New Age Movement is also discussed: "The New Age

... will be brought into manifestation, through the collaboration of the well-intentioned many ... current affairs will undergo such a transformation, that we shall verily and indeed see the emergence of a new heaven and a new earth." [8]

"The New Age is upon us and we are witnessing the birth pangs of the new culture and the new civilization. That which is old and undesirable [religious doctrine] must go, and of these undesirable things, hatred and the spirit of separateness [especially the separation of Christians from the sinful world] must be first to disappear." [9]

The ideology of Adolf Hitler was not unique. The Nazi movement was only one of many secret societies which has been driving the world toward a so-called New Age wherein the Aryan race will bring the world from theism through atheism to Luciferic humanism.

There was a time not long ago when professors on college campuses across America no longer believed in the existence of a God. Man was only material, only matter in motion. However, atheism cannot long maintain itself. The pendulum continues to swing. Those who once believed in atheistic, materialistic evolution and who promoted it in the classrooms of America are now teaching that there is a spiritual dimension to life, and that students can nurture god-like qualities.

They use scientific terminology — extra sensory perception, psychic phenomenon, trance-channeling, and psychokinesis. This may be called New Age philosophy, but it reared its ugly head in the Garden of Eden and found fruition at the Tower of Babel. It is, quite simply, witchcraft, or shamanism. It is prohibited by the Bible in Deuteronomy 18.

New Age thought teaches that ancient wisdom is timeless, yet ever modern in its scientific applications and beneficial results. They believe at the core of their "Craft" is a faith in the spiritual and the mystical, meaning the so-called Secret

Doctrine — whose god is Lucifer. New Age philosophy is actually an occult ancient philosophy — and always involves "Secret Doctrines" in their "quests for truth."

The average member of most so-called New Age organizations is quite unaware of the ancient mystery-wisdom that led to the development of the so-called "Secret Doctrine." But one of these days, the mystery will be revealed! And Babylon the Great will fall, for there is a God in heaven, and His Son, Jesus Christ, will come — to destroy this foolishness and establish the kingdom of heaven on earth!

Chapter Notes

CHAPTER 7

1. Ravenscroft, THE SPEAR OF DESTINY, op. cit., p. 235.

2. Ibid., pp. 235-236.

3. Plato, TIMAEUS, THE DIALOGUES OF PLATO, trans. B. Jowett (Roslyn, NY: Walter J. Black, Inc., 1942).

4. "Aryan," THE WORLD BOOK ENCYCLOPEDIA, Vol. 1, 1973 Edition, p. 728.

5. Alice A.Bailey and Djwhal Khul, PONDER ON THIS (New York: Lucis Publishing Company, 1971), p. 409.

6. Ibid., p. 269.

7. Ibid., p. 275.

8. Ibid., p. 276.

9. Ibid., p. 279.

Great Seal of the United States — the All-Seeing Eye atop a pyramid.

Chapter 8

The
All-Seeing
Eye

On the reverse side of the one-dollar bill is a picture of a pyramid and its capstone. In the capstone is the picture of an "All-Seeing Eye" with a sunburst behind it. The average person may think little of these unusual exotic symbols. However, its meaning is far-reaching, and its history lies buried in antiquity.

The worship of the All-Seeing Eye has existed under many names and disguises for thousands of years. Through the ages its high priests have worshiped before unhallowed altars dedicated to the adoration of a nameless deity — an unknown god.

The identity of this deity has been concealed behind an elaborate system of veiled allegories and secret symbols. Followers of this pseudo-mystical, humanistic, occult system of belief affirm without proof that it is based on an unbroken, oral tradition handed down from an ancient priesthood in Egypt.

The cult projects a minimum belief in a god which totally excludes Christ as the divine Redeemer. The adherents of the cult reject Jesus Christ, the Son of God. The cult's leaders contend that the doctrine of the cult is based on a hidden master religion which they believe all men can embrace because it is founded on pre-Christian models.

The offspring of this ancient idolatrous mystery cult has existed in America for centuries, but its leaders have never dared to admit that they hope to replace Christianity with the cult. However, in recent years they have dared to establish small public temples in the United States — namely the Meditation Room in the United Nations and the prayer chapel in the United States Capitol.

This mystery religion can be partially identified today under the name The New Age Movement, and is sponsored by the Lucis Trust, a pseudonym for the Lucifer Publishing Company. As stated by Constance Cumbey in her books, THE HIDDEN DANGERS OF THE RAINBOW [1] and A PLANNED DECEPTION, [2] Lucis Publishing Company was originally incorporated in 1922 as the Lucifer Publishing Company, and then in 1923 changed its name to the less startling Lucis Publishing Co. According to the Lucis Trust president, Perry Coles, Lucis comes from the Latin word lux, translated "of light." He states that the word Lucifer, as used in his organization, means "bringer of light" or the morning star, but has no connection whatsoever with satan. [3]   Also, Mrs. Cumbey states that even while many New Age groups work to extol Lucifer's name, there has been a parallel movement within Christianity to clear his name and dissociate him from any satanic identity. The Amplified Bible, for example, denies Lucifer is satan! (See Amplified Bible notes on Isaiah 14 explaining why the name "Lucifer" was omitted from that chapter.) It is also interesting to note the address of Lucis Trust. It is 866 United Nations Plaza, New York, N.Y. 10017. It is the brains — from an occult planning basis — behind the New Age Movement.

These people are seeking to obliterate Christian ethics by attempting to destroy all honored standards and traditions set up during the past 19 centuries for the protection of the civilized world. The lure of famous names associated with the cult has drawn many naive supporters into its fold. These people would recoil in horror from its evil teachings if they only knew the truth about the system. The secret doctrine of the cult has been carefully guarded from public scrutiny and investigation. [4]

Every Christian needs to learn the meaning of that doctrine and the symbolism employed by the cult. It uncovers the trail of the serpent, and Christians need to be armed with knowledge if they are to detect and destroy this insidious menace which threatens the very foundation of Christian civilization.

Arthur M. Schlesinger, Jr., in his book, "THE COMING OF THE NEW DEAL," provided his readers with a remarkably candid report on Henry A. Wallace, one-time vice-president of the United States.

"The occult fascinated him. He saw special significance in the Great Seal of the United States, with its phrase 'E Pluribus Unum' and its conception of unity out of diversity." [5]

Henry Wallace saw even more significance in the reverse side of the seal with the incomplete pyramid and its 13 levels of stone, along with the apex suspended above it in the form of an All-Seeing Eye, surrounded by the inscription, "Annuit Coeptis" and "Novus Ordo Seclorum." [6]

Some have suggested that the pyramid may represent the Second Coming of Christ. Quite the contrary. It is, in fact, the opposite. It represents the All-Seeing Eye of big brother government headed up by none other than the god of this world, Lucifer.

Henry A. Wallace induced "the Secretary of the Treasury to put the Great Pyramid on the new dollar bill in 1935. He sold this idea to Secretary Morganthau on the prosaic ground that 'Novus Ordo' was Latin for New Deal."[7] At that time, of course, the term was popular under the presidency of Franklin D. Roosevelt.

Wallace had been drawn into the orbit of a White Russian mystic, Dr. Nicholas Roerich, an associate in the Moscow Art Theater. "Wallace occasionally called on him at the Roerich Museum on Riverside Drive in New York. The friendship continued after Wallace went to Washington."[8] On a number of occasions Wallace wrote letters to Dr. Roerich, addressing him as "Dear Guru."

Wallace was also associated with the Communist Party. This "culminated in his candidacy for the Progressive Party, which was nothing more nor less than the Communist Party under a false label."[9] This is the man who introduced the reverse side of the Great Seal of the United States on the dollar bill in 1935.

According to the original press release of the Treasury Department on August 15, 1935, announcing the appearance of the two sides of the seal on the dollar bill, the Latin mottos on the reverse side are translated in this manner:

"Annuit Coeptis" means "He (God) favored our undertaking" and "Novus Ordo Seclorum" means "a new secular order of the ages." The press release also stated that the eye and triangular glory symbolize an all-seeing deity. The pyramid is the symbol of strength, and its unfinished condition denotes the belief that there is yet more work to be done.[10]

The earliest known history of the All-Seeing Eye dates back

to ancient Babylon. It was worshiped as the Solar Eye — a picture of the sun god. It was also represented as the eye of Jove or Jupiter. It has been called the eye of Phoebus or Apollo. It was also referred to as the eye of Baal, and as the eye of providence.

The eye of Jove or Jupiter actually appeared on the front of a temple dedicated to Jupiter found in the excavated ruins of an ancient Spartan city in Peloponnesus, the southern peninsula of Greece. As the Solar Eye, it was said to be the symbol of the Arabian god of Jethro, the father-in-law of Moses. All ancient temples of Arabia were decorated with the eye. Furthermore, it was worshiped as the symbol of the gods, Osiris and Isis of Egypt.

The eye represented the mystical symbol of the so-called Egyptian trinity expressed in these words inscribed on the statue of Isis: "I am all that has been, that is, or shall be, and none among mortals has hitherto taken off my veil."

"She was the daughter of Saturn, and her name meant "ancient." She married her brother, Osiris, and was pregnant by him even before she had left her mother's womb.... She and her brother-husband comprehended all nature and all the gods of the heathens."[11]

She was the Venus of Cyprus, the Minerva of Athens, the Cybele of the Phrygians, the Ceres of Eleusis, the Proserpine of Sicily, the Diana of the Ephesians, and the Bellona of the Romans. The sun god, Osiris, was also worshiped under the names of Anubis, Bacchus, Dionysius, Jupiter, and Pan.

The Great Pyramid of Gizeh was once covered with a beautiful, polished limestone. Over the years most of the covering was removed and used in other buildings. Today only a few of the polished limestone building blocks remain along its base.

Somewhere in the ancient past when the Great Pyramid

stood with its polished limestone cover glistening in the sun, there was a capstone. It was made of purest crystal. It has been referred to in history as the "priceless gem of Egypt." It was also called "the terrible crystal." It was crystal clear and brought the pyramid to a perfect point at the top 485 feet above ground level. Where is this capstone today, this forerunner of the All-Seeing Eye? No one knows. Perhaps it was plundered by some ancient thief who thought he had found the world's largest diamond.

The Egyptian god Osiris was worshiped as early as the 27th century B.C. He was called the great deity of Amenti or Hades (the biblical word for hell). He was described as the judge of the dead, and he corresponds to the Christian's idea of the devil.

According to mythology, Osiris made a great expedition across and beyond the borders of Egypt during which he left his kingdom to the care of his wife, Isis, and her faithful minister, Mercury or Hermes. When Osiris returned, he found that his brother, Set (or Typhon), had aroused his subjects against him. Set murdered his brother and cut his body into 14 pieces. Isis recovered all the mangled pieces, or most of them, and Osiris was proclaimed to be a resurrected god.[12]

"The number 14 has a special occult meaning in the symbolism of modern-day secret societies as the 14 days of burial.... Plutarch, in his treatise, ON ISIS AND OSIRIS, explained the symbolism: 'The body of Osiris was cut into 14 pieces, that is, into as many parts as there are days between the full moon and the new.' "[13]

"Now, if the picture of the reverse side of the Great Seal is examined, it will be found that 14 rays of light issue from the triangle containing the eye of Osiris. This combination of symbols simply cannot be attributed to a chance arrangement."[14]

The phrase "Novus Ordo Seclorum" provides the clue as to the nature of that New Order of the Ages referred to in Latin. It is to be a golden age during which the Saturnian kingdom shall return. Saturn was the father of Osiris.

" 'Annuit Coeptis,' which are the Latin words for 'favored my daring undertaking' was not a supplication to God. In conjunction with the other motto, it can only refer to Saturn or Osiris." [15]

The Meditation Room in the United Nations is a monument to the All-Seeing Eye. The room is 30 feet long, 18 feet wide at the entrance, which faces north-northeast, and 9 feet wide at the other end.

It is, therefore, wedge-shaped or represents a pyramid turned over on its side. The room is very dimly lit. The only source of light comes from a special lens recessed in the ceiling which focuses a beam of light on the altar in the center of the room.

The altar is four feet high; it is a dark gray block of crystalline iron ore from a Swedish mine and weighs six and a half tons. The Swedish government presented this block of ore, the largest of its kind ever mined, to the United Nations in early 1957. The chunk of ore has been described as a lodestone or magnetite. It is strongly magnetic and possesses polarity. [16]

On April 24, 1957, the late Dag Hammarskjold, UN Secretary General, described this pagan stone as an altar to universal religion. He said, "The altar is the symbol of the god of all."

The picture or mural at the front of the room was designed in 1957 by Bo Beskow, an old friend of Dag Hammarskjold. The picture was painted to open up the wall, to give a feeling of space, of the void — in effect, to extend the room farther out to another dimension. The theme of the mural is infinity.

There are 22 triangles in the painting. They obviously represent a typology found in both the ancient pyramid of Gizeh and in the Tower of Babel.

The circle near the center of the painting represents the All-Seeing Eye. There is a vertical line down the center of the mural with waving lines around it. It is said to represent the tree of life. It may also represent the serpent in the tree.

"The mural was described as having been designed to give a feeling of space by the opening up of the wall. All right, let us ... open up the wall behind the mural. The Meditation Room is constructed in the shape of a wedge. If [you could imagine what the room would look like] from above, [looking down, you] will see at once that [the room is in the shape of a] pyramid with the apex [or capstone] cut off."[17]

Obviously, the Meditation Room in the United Nations is a chapel designed to worship the god of the All-Seeing Eye. It is another attempt at the Tower of Babel. Oddly enough, the United Nations has been called the modern Tower of Babel, and New York City has been referred to as Babylon-on-the-Hudson.

Another prayer room dedicated to the All-Seeing Eye can be found in the United States Capitol building in Washington, D.C. The movement for its construction was launched in 1952 and the prayer chapel was opened in 1955.

The room is located on the House side of the Capitol near the Rotunda. The lighting in this Meditation Room is subdued. The concealed ceiling light focuses on a white oak altar, similar to the light in the U.N. Meditation Room.[18]

There are ten chairs facing the altar, just as there are ten chairs in the United Nations Meditation Room. Ten? It reminds me of the beast of Revelation with its ten horns representing ten kings who will give their allegiance to the coming antichrist. Above the altar in the stained glass window the unfinished pyramid with its capstone containing the All-Seeing Eye is prominently displayed.

The New Age Movement, with its roots in the ancient Order of the Knights Templar, has been "working to set up a universal theocratic state. Already the high priests, the prayers, and the temples of this universal cult are with us. Curriculum is being drafted to indoctrinate our children in what John D. Rockefeller, Jr., called 'the church of all people.' "[19]

This New Age Movement even has an international prayer for use as an "Invocation of the United Nations," which they say our leaders may wish to substitute for the Christian prayers no longer permitted in our schools. That prayer reads in part:

"May the Peace and the Blessing of the Holy Ones pour forth over the world — rest upon the United Nations, on the work and the workers ...

"May the chalice the United Nations is building become a focal point for the descent of spiritual force ...

"May the consciousness of the United Nations become ever more at one, the many lights, one light in the light of the self."[20]

Recognizing this "goofy network to be a source of power and influence, United Nations officials have lectured at meetings of the Arcane School, the international 'group of New World Servers,' who form 'Triangles' to work for UNESCO."[21] The Arcane School, World Goodwill, Triangles, and The Group of New World Servers are all operated under the auspices of Lucis (Lucifer) Trust. The Arcane School, located in New York City, is one of the major divisions of Lucis Trust. It was personally founded by Alice Bailey, considered to be one of the primary writers and occultists who originated today's New Age Movement. Training received at the Arcane School prepares and enables people for active New Age discipleship and leadership.

A few years ago Dr. Hudson Smith, professor of philosophy at the Massachusetts Institute of Technology, visited Sydney, Australia. He lectured at the Blavatsky Lodge on the subject, "Is a New World Religion Coming?" The name Blavatsky refers to the late Madame Helena Petrovna Blavatsky, the Russian cult leader whose writings are used in the secret courses of instruction at the Arcane School in New York.

In a moment of frankness, Madame Blavatsky explained the influence of magic on history when she said, "What is one to do, when in order to rule men, it is necessary to deceive them? For almost invariably the more simple, the more silly, and the more gross the phenomenon, the more likely is it to succeed."[22]

The headquarters for the European Common Market today is located in Brussels, Belgium. It is rather interesting that Brussels, Belgium is also the headquarters for the world-wide Illuminati, the religious cult of the All-Seeing Eye. Is it a mere coincidence that the headquarters for the world-wide Illuminati just happens to be Brussels, Belgium — the headquarters for the European Common Market?

Plans are being made in our generation to establish a one-world government and a one-world religion. The political structure of our world today is preparing for the rise of the antichrist.

Chapter Notes

CHAPTER 8

1. Constance E. Cumbey, HIDDEN DANGERS OF THE RAINBOW (Shreveport: Huntington House, 1983).
2. Constance E. Cumbey, A PLANNED DECEPTION (East Detroit, MI: Pointe Publishers, 1985), pp. 246-247.
3. Ibid., p. 246.
4. Robert Keith Spenser, THE CULT OF THE ALL-SEEING EYE, op. cit., p. 5.
5. Ibid., p. 23, quoting Arthur M. Schlesinger, THE COMING OF THE NEW DEAL (New York: Houghton-Mifflin, 1958), p. 31.
6. Ibid.
7. Ibid., quoting Schlesinger, p. 32.
8. Ibid., quoting Schlesinger, p. 33.
9. Spenser, ALL-SEEING EYE, op. cit., p. 24.
10. Ibid., quoting Treasury Department Press Release No. 5-59.
11. Ibid., p. 32.
12. Ibid., p. 34.
13. Ibid., quoting Albert G. Mackey, AN ENCYCLOPEDIA OF FREEMASONRY (New York: 1900), p. 288.
14. Ibid.
15. Spenser, p. 35.
16. Ibid., p. 8.
17. Ibid., pp. 19-20.
18. Ibid., p. 41.
19. Ibid., p. 49, quoting Edith Kermit Roosevelt, "The Universal Theocratic State," Edith Kermit Roosevelt Syndicate, 1962.
20. Ibid.
21. Ibid.
22. Ibid.

This medieval painting of Christ having supper at Emmaus, shows the All-Seeing Eye above.

Chapter 9

The
Illuminati

The infamous Illuminati was organized on May 1, 1776, by Adam Weishaupt, a former Jesuit, lawyer, and professor at Ingolstadt University in Bavaria. The aim of his secret organization was to replace Christianity with a religion of "reason" (another word for humanism). Their ultimate goal was to replace all national governments with a single world government.

According to some accounts, the Illuminati helped foment the French revolution. The conspirators engineered the fall of the monarchy and the rise of Napoleon. The Illuminati also influenced the American revolution and had hoped to use the Colonies as a springboard for world conquest.

Is there really an Illuminati organization? Does it still exist today? If so, just how powerful is it? Who are the members? What are its goals? These are questions asked by concerned

Christians who see a decided development toward world government today.

This much we know — the organization existed at one time. Two reliable sources for documentation include Webster's Dictionary and the Encyclopedia Britannica. Webster's gives the following definition: "Illuminati: ... the members of an anticlerical, deistic, republican society founded in 1776 by Adam Weishaupt, professor of law at Ingolstadt in Bavaria." [1]

According to the Encyclopedia Britannica, "... a short-lived movement ... founded on May Day (May 1) 1776, by Adam Weishaupt ... a former Jesuit. The members of this secret society called themselves Perfectibilists. Their founder's aim was to replace Christianity by a religion of reason, as later did the revolutionaries of France ... The order was organized along Jesuit lines and kept internal discipline and a system of surveillance based on that model ... From 1778 onward, they began to make contact with various Masonic lodges, where, under the impulse of A. [Baron Von] Knigge, one of their chief converts, they often managed to gain a commanding position. " [2]

Though the organization, under the leadership of Adam Weishaupt, existed for only a short time, the parent organization had existed for centuries, and has continued until this very day. Historians have traced its existence to 1200 B.C. in Italy, France, and Greece. The Encyclopedia Americana says that the Illuminati has been in existence 2,000 years. [3] Other authors have stated that Weishaupt's knowledge of ancient secret societies influenced the structure of his organization.

In 1771, a merchant named Kolmer returned from Egypt to Europe. He was seeking converts to a so-called "Secret Doctrine," based on Manichaeanism — which he had learned in the East. On his way to France, he stopped at Malta, where he nearly brought about an insurrection among the people, and was driven from the island by the Knights of Malta. The following year, he met Adam Weishaupt on a tour in Germany. Over the next 5 years, he initiated Weishaupt into the mysteries of his so-called Secret Doctrine.

The concepts taught to Weishaupt represent the same Secret Doctrine held by Rosicrucianism, Hitler's Nazi movement, the Mormon Church, the Masonic Lodge, and the modern day New Age Movement. Weishaupt once wrote a friend to guard the origin of the Secret Doctrine in a most careful way. He said that the greatest mystery must be that the thing is new and that the fewer who know this the better. He wrote that the carefully guarded secret of the Secret Doctrine is that it is as old as Methuselah.

Weishaupt adopted an insignia to identify with the name, beginning, beliefs, and goals of the Illuminati. It was the emblem of the All Seeing Eye, which was drawn in ancient times as a circle with a dot in the middle. He said that although men would think it was new, it was "as old as Methuselah."

Satan's plan is not new. He has not changed his method since the Garden of Eden. He tempted Adam and Eve with the forbidden fruit, which promised to open their understanding and make them gods — knowing good and evil. In the book of Genesis, the serpent said to the woman,

"Ye shall not surely die: For God doth know that in the day ye eat thereof, then your eyes shall be opened, and ye shall be as gods, knowing good and evil (Genesis 3:4-5).

"And the eyes of them both were opened ..." (Genesis 3:7).

We know that neither Adam nor Eve were blind. So, this scripture is not referring to their physical eyes, but to their MIND'S EYE! Satan was able to introduce them to the opening up of their mind's eye — today sometimes called centering, deep relaxation, or meditation — which allows a "spirit" to enter and practice "mind control." The original temptation and deception that occurred in the Garden of Eden is no different than the tactics and subtleties that satan uses today. The serpent still beguiles men to partake of forbidden fruit.

The Bible does not say that the forbidden fruit was an apple. [*] In fact, the forbidden fruit has been regarded by some theologians as only symbolic — for such a fruit does not appear to exist on earth today. Ah, but perhaps it does! Perhaps the forbidden fruit eaten by Adam does exist today. It could have been a narcotic extraction such as those used in mind-expanding drugs — mescaline, heroin, marijuana, etc.

Mind altering drugs are used to open the mind's eye — the all seeing eye of clairvoyant perception. Mind-expanding drugs reportedly bring out the god quality — the ability to explore the universe and visit the palaces of the gods. In the Bible, it was called "sorcery," and it involved the use of drugs in religious ceremonies. In the temple of Apollo of ancient Greece, a priestess would chew a narcotic weed, breathe narcotic fumes, would fall into a trance, and speak in an ecstatic utterance the so-called language of the gods. The Indians of the Southwestern United States smoke peyote to open contact with the gods of their religion. The use of mind-expanding drugs was a common practice in the ancient mystery cults.

The emblem of the Illuminati (an all seeing eye) has been traced back to the mystery schools of secret wisdom in ancient Egypt during the 18th Dynasty — to the reign of Pharaoh Amenhotep IV (1350 B.C.). It was probably brought into Egypt by the children of Ham after the tower of Babel debacle. The Hamites were among those who designed the tower as a pyramid-like structure and migrated into Egypt after the confusion of tongues. They built the pyramid of Gizeh —

another "Tower of Babel."

Although its roots may go back even further, the teachings of the Illuminati were quite popular in the 9th century. Perhaps it is more than a coincidence that in the 9th century, all the thrones of Europe were established by the so-called sacred family of the Grail.

Many modern groups, though not related through organizational structure, nevertheless, claim to be offshoots of the original so-called Mystery Religion. They practice and believe the same so-called Secret Doctrine. Some organizations may even appear to be enemies, but their underlying philosophy is the same. They appear to be tributaries of the mainstream of Babylonian philosophy. They all carry the same symbols, such as the All-Seeing Eye, and believe in the same so-called Secret Doctrine.

Today, the largest religious organization adhering to the mystery religion of ancient Babylon is Hinduism. It also appears to be the fastest growing religion in the world. Gurus (holy men) set themselves up as gods and are worshiped by millions throughout India and the Far East. Even Americans, by the thousands, go to India in search of so-called "truth." They worship these gurus and believe in their occult powers. It is reported that some Americans traveling in India have disappeared — falling into the hands of fanatic bands of gurus who sacrifice them on unhallowed altars to Hindu gods. That idolatrous religion has darkened the minds and hearts of its people, and has kept them in poverty. In my opinion, the extreme poverty of India can be attributed to the satanic influence of the Hindu religion.

By the 2nd century A.D., this diabolical religion had begun to move westward into Persia, developing the ancient religion of Zoroastrianism. One of its followers developed the doctrine of Manichaeanism, teaching that the sun god became incarnated in Jesus Christ. This perversion of early Christianity led to the so-called "Secret Doctrine" of the Order of the Knighthood; the development of European Rosicrucianism; and eventually, the 18th century Illuminati.

The Illuminati may not exist today under its infamous name, but it does exist. Its structure, its secret doctrine, its symbols, and its goals are still alive — plotting and planning toward that day when a world government will be established — without God.

One of the tributaries of the ancient Mystery Cult is Rosicrucianism, which claims identification with the Illuminati. According to H. Spencer Lewis, author of the book CULTS AND THE OCCULT, "The order had its birth in one of the mystery schools of secret wisdom in ancient Egypt during the 18th dynasty, or the reign of Pharaoh Amenhotep IV, about 1350 years B.C."[5]

Rosicrucianism is also called the Ancient Mystical Order of the Rosy Cross. The rose was chosen for its color. In the 5th century, the Frankish king, Merovee, was said to have a birthmark on his chest above his heart in the shape of a red cross. When the order of the Knights Templar was established in 1118, their symbol became a bright red cross on a white shield.

Over the years, certain emblems were developed by European Rosicrucians. These identifying symbols appear on page 49 of the official ROSICRUCIAN MANUAL.[6] Among them is the Seal of the Founder (see page 169), composed of three items: on the bottom is a beetle, signifying all living things, including man; over the beetle is a crown, signifying a single monarch over all the world; and over the crown is a circle with a dot in the middle — the symbol of the All-Seeing Eye.

As in other Mystery Cults, the Rosicrucians also have orders. According to the ROSICRUCIAN MANUAL,

"Members who attain and complete the psychic instruction of the ninth degree or those above it may enter the Illuminati, which is a higher organization of the order wherein the worthy members continue to carry on specialized work and studies under the direction of the imperator of their jurisdiction and the personal cosmic masters. Members cannot ask for admission to the Illuminati, but must wait until they have been found ready and are invited in this additional work."[7]

Rosicrucianism traces its beginning to ancient Egyptian mysticism. The mentor of Adam Weishaupt was from Egypt. Rosicrucians, the Illuminati, and other fraternal organizations are linked together by their organizational structures, emblems, and practices. That is not to say that the average member of these organizations is a knowledgeable, willing part of some conspiracy. Good people have been involved without realizing the background and occult nature of the ancient mystery religion which shapes their underlying philosophies. Adam Weishaupt, founder of the Illuminati in 1776, manipulated several political groups, as indicated by the Encyclopedia Britannica.[8]

It is reported that Benjamin Franklin was a Rosicrucian. Thomas Jefferson, John Adams, and George Washington were Masons. It is interesting to note that though these men were a part of these orders, George Washington warned the Masonic Lodge in America of the dangers of the Illuminati, while Thomas Jefferson and John Adams later disagreed over the use of the Masonic Lodge by the Illuminati. John Adams, who is reported to have been the founder of the Masonic Lodges in New England, accused Jefferson of using the lodges that he himself had founded, for subversive Illuminati purposes. The three letters of Adams which deal with this problem are in the Wittenburg Square Library in Philadelphia. Many today are becoming convinced that Franklin, Adams, and Jefferson were manipulated by the Illuminati until John Adams became alerted.

This should not be interpreted as an indictment against the American founding fathers as being un-Christian or unpatriotic. Many good men are quite naive of the tremendous influence of ancient religious-political movements. Neither should we construe all members of modern esoteric organizations as part of an international conspiracy. Thomas Jefferson, for example, was an idealist — and some of Weishaupt's ideals corresponded with his own — but of course, we do not question Jefferson's patriotism. However, it is conceivable that in the past as well as today, that otherwise good men can be deceived — just as many of the liberal clergy of today are deceived by Communism — which, by the way, may also be a product of the Illuminati.

It is a well-known fact that Weishaupt wanted a theistic republic of global dimensions. It should be obvious to anyone who has read THE PROTOCOLS OF THE MEETINGS OF THE LEARNED ELDERS OF ZION,[9] that the book discussed Weishaupt's six points of subversive revolution plus 18 additional principles.

According to the Journals of Congress, 1776, Vol. I, pages 248 and 397, Thomas Jefferson, John Adams, and Benjamin Franklin (who were members of "secret societies") were appointed by the Continental Congress on July 4, 1776, to prepare a seal for the United States of America. This was 13 years before John Adams became concerned about a conspiracy. But those three men are credited with the design of the Great Seal of the United States.[10] It appears to be an Illuminati masterpiece. For a good view of the Great Seal, simply take a look at both sides of the U.S. one dollar bill.

The pyramid, with 13 levels, was said to represent the 13 colonies, but the association with ancient Egyptian and Babylonian mysticism is apparent. The eye above the pyramid has been construed to be the All-Seeing Eye of God. However, nothing could be further from the truth. It is the symbol of the Illuminati, as well as the symbol of the Rosicrucians, the Priory of Sion, the occultic symbol of Egyptian mysticism, and the Hindu symbol of the "mind's eye" with its magical powers of clairvoyant perception. We have previously made reference to the fact that the All-Seeing Eye is also symbolic of the Grail.

The symbol may represent a god, but it is not the God of the Bible. It is a human eye indicating that man is god. It represents so-called "mind power," the ability to manipulate one's world with thought. It is also considered to be linked to extra-sensory perception, the ability to read other people's thoughts; hypnotism, the ability to control other people's minds; psychic phenomena, the ability to conjure up the spirits of the dead; astral projection, out-of-body experiences; and psycho-kinesis, the ability to bend metal with one's mind or to make objects move and levitate. These so-called psychic powers are nothing but a deception created by demonic forces to make the adherent think that he is a god capable of these powers.

The words "Novus Ordo Seclorum" stem from Babylonian mysticism announcing the birth of a new secular order. It does not represent freedom OF religion, but freedom FROM religion. The goal of the Illuminati was to establish a new SECULAR order — apart from religion. Fortunately, our founding fathers were able to circumvent the intention of the Illuminati to destroy all religion. They established the First Amendment to our Constitution promising the freedom OF religion — not a "Novus Ordo Seclorum," a new secular order. Our founding fathers established a republic where God was honored and men were free. This was not the original intention of the Illuminati.

The words "E Pluribus Unum" means "out of many, one." "Pluribus" (or plural) stands for many, and "unum" (or unity) stands for one. It may sound idealistic, but the motto is still Babylonish in concept. According to Genesis 11, the Tower of Babel was built in order to resist God's division of mankind into races, languages, and nations. It was an attempt on the part of man to circumvent the plan of God and make of all races one nation, one empire — one world government.

Some years ago Dr. S. Franklin Logsdon, former pastor of the Moody Memorial Church of Chicago, wrote a book entitled, IS THE U.S.A. IN PROPHECY? He proposed the possibility that the United States may be the last Babylon mentioned in the Book of Revelation.[11] The reforming of all nations, races, and languages into a world order under a common leader is the goal of the Illuminati Society. It appeared that Weishaupt and other Illuminists of that day had designs to use America to bring their goals to fruition. It was only by the intervention of God and the awareness of some of our early founding fathers that this goal was not achieved — and has still not been achieved — yet.

The Illuminati emblem of the All-Seeing Eye continues to be associated with organizations and movements throughout the world which are working for a One-World, godless secular order. You can see it in the meditation room at the United Nations, in the prayer chapel at our nation's capitol, and in the meditation room of the Pentagon. How far are the Illuminati and other "secret society" groups willing to go to propel their revolutionary conspiracy?

A document, first published in 1903, entitled THE PROTOCOLS OF THE MEETINGS OF THE LEARNED ELDERS OF ZION, became one of the most infamous documents of the twentieth century. THE PROTOCOLS were alleged to be the secret minutes of the World Congress of Jewry held in

Switzerland in 1897. It was, instead, the purpose of that Congress to organize the various factions of Zionism to move toward the establishment of a legally recognized Jewish national homeland in Palestine. However, the PROTOCOLS claimed that its purpose was to make plans for world domination by the Jews.

The PROTOCOLS were convincing proof to a great many anti-Semites that there was an "international Jewish conspiracy." After being distributed to White Russian troops in 1919, some sixty thousand Jews were massacred, blamed for the 1917 Bolshevik Revolution.

Hitler also used the forged PROTOCOLS to inflame German hatred against the Jews. When the already anti-Semitic German public first read the book, they were convinced that their loss and humiliation in World War I was caused by the treason of Jews in the government and in banking. The PROTOCOLS are a vicious and insiduous forgery. Nevertheless, they are still being circulated to support the view that the Jewish people are behind the movement to establish a One-World government.

The PROTOCOLS promote a plan for nothing less than total world domination. They seem to be a program for a small group of people determined to impose a new world order, with themselves as absolute rulers. They advocate a "hydra-headed conspiracy dedicated to disorder and anarchy, infiltrating Freemasonry and other such organizations, and eventually seizing absolute control of the Western world's social, political, and economic institutions."[12]

According to HOLY BLOOD, HOLY GRAIL, a copy of the PROTOCOLS is known to have been in circulation as early as 1884 — a full thirteen years before the World Zionist Congress met. Therefore, they could not have been the minutes of the Zionist meeting.[13]

The PROTOCOLS ends with the statement, "Signed by the representatives of Sion of the 33rd Degree."[14] Joseph Carr, author of the book, THE TWISTED CROSS, says, "The PROTOCOLS are very explicit in their claim that the sponsors manage the world scene from the shadows.... [the] 'Representatives of the 33rd Degree,' ... is Masonic and not Jewish terminology."[15] They also indicate that the "Learned Elders of Zion" are "not to be confounded with the representatives of Zionism." Then perhaps the "Zion" they do represent alludes to The Priory of Sion.

The text repeatedly speaks of a coming "Masonic kingdom," and of a "King of the blood of Sion" who will preside over this "Masonic kingdom." It claims that the future king will be of "the dynastic roots of King David." It asserts that "the King of the Jews will be the real pope" and "the patriarch of an international church." And it concludes, "Certain members of the seed of David will prepare the Kings and their heirs ... Only the King and the three who stood sponsor for him will know what is coming."[16]

According to the authors of HOLY BLOOD, HOLY GRAIL the original text of the PROTOCOLS was not a forgery. "On the contrary, it was authentic. But it had nothing whatever to do with Judaism or an 'international Jewish conspiracy.' It issued, rather, from some Masonic organization or Masonically oriented secret society that incorporated the word 'Sion'.... The published version of the PROTOCOLS is not, therefore, a totally fabricated text. It is, rather, a radically altered text.... while such vestiges might have been irrelevant to Judaism, they might have been extremely relevant to a secret society.... they were — and still are — of paramount importance to the Priory of Sion."[17]

The PROTOCOLS may be the product of the Illuminati. It seems likely that neither Jewish elders nor Masons were entirely responsible for writing it. Neither group would have been so foolish to so obviously indict themselves in such a document — secret or otherwise. The title itself, which mentions the "learned elders of Zion," seems to refer to the mystery religion of the so-called Holy Grail and to the Priory of Sion organized by Godfroi de Bouillon in 1099 for the purpose of establishing a world government and providing a Merovingian king for its throne. The Illuminati, then, may be simply another name in the ongoing development of the Priory of Sion — the Guardians of the Grail.

Does the Illuminati still exist? Perhaps not in name, but in organizational structure it is bigger than ever. Most important of all, it is being promoted in this decade as a New Age Movement. This powerful organization is dedicated to the establishment of world government and vows to soon introduce a single dictator to sit upon the throne of this world. To this agree the words of the prophets — they call him antichrist.

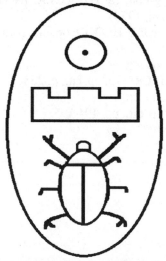

Rosicrucian "Seal of the Founder" is composed of three items: a beetle, signifying all living things; a crown, signifying a single world monarch; and a circle with a dot in the middle, signifying the All-Seeing Eye.

Chapter Notes

CHAPTER 9

1. WEBSTER'S NEW TWENTIETH CENTURY DICTIONARY, Unabridged, Second Edition (Springfield, MA: G. & C. Merriam, 1957), p. 906.

2. "Illuminati," ENCYCLOPEDIA BRITANNICA, 11th Edition (Later editions have eliminated all references to the organization).

3. "Illuminati," ENCYCLOPEDIA AMERICANA (Note as footnote No. 2 above).

4. THE HOLY BIBLE, Genesis 2:16-17, 3:1-6, 11-13.

5. Harve Spencer Lewis, CULTS AND THE OCCULT.

6. Harve Spencer Lewis, ROSICRUCIAN MANUAL, ed. Supreme Grand Lodge of AMORC (1955), p. 49.

7. Ibid., p. 74.

8. "Illuminati," ENCYCLOPEDIA BRITANNICA, op. cit.

9. PROTOCOLS, op. cit.

10. THE DAUGHTERS OF THE AMERICAN REVOLUTION MAGAZINE (Hall, July, 1982), p. 485.

11. S. Franklin Logsdon, IS THE U.S.A. IN PROPHECY? (Grand Rapids, MI: Zondervan, 1974).

12. Baigent, et al., HOLY BLOOD, op. cit., p.192.

13. Ibid.

14. PROTOCOLS, op. cit.

15. Carr, TWISTED CROSS, op. cit., p. 268.

16. PROTOCOLS, op. cit.

17. Baigent, et al., op. cit., pp. 194-195.

The
Money
Conspiracy

Chapter 10

Money Wars

Throughout our nation's history, the national economy has been subject to what economists call "the business cycle." Ours, as well as the world's economy has periodically suffered through "hard times" and "good times," with each complete cycle lasting approximately seven to twelve years.

This perceived "business cycle" has been credited (or blamed) with the ups and downs of our purchasing power, unemployment rate, budget deficits, national debt, recessions, and even severe depressions. But is an apathetic acceptance of hard times inescapable — a natural phenomenon, or, is it possible that the control of our economy is and has been manipulated by a few powerful men who reap huge profits from this economic roller-coaster?

At the onset of the 1980's, our nation plunged headlong toward depression. Interest rates were the highest in history at

21.5%. Unemployment was approaching 11%, as millions of workers were laid off. A 12% rate of inflation not only gobbled up all increases in productivity, but temporarily discouraged our national pride.

These unacceptable economic times eventually abated, but in the meantime the hardship of high interest rates worldwide created dangerous fissures in the financial system and hastened the arrival of the Third World debt crisis. It is said today that if this ugly accumulation of Third World debt is "not properly managed," it could crush the world financial system.

Today we face a distressingly weak dollar, which threatens to push the inflation rate out of control once again. Also, the sluggish level of U.S. and world economic growth could easily tail off into global recession, especially if American interest rates should rise appreciably. The national debt is approaching THREE TRILLION dollars and is rising on an exponential curve. One out of every seven dollars in the national budget now goes to pay interest on the public debt. If state and local government debt, along with all business and personal debts are included, we now owe over five times the value of all land and buildings in America!

Headlines indicate that the money problem is worldwide. "Banks begin to foreclose on Third World debt." "Over 200 bank failures so far ...!" It is a recognized conclusion that the banking systems of our world are on shaky ground and that a worldwide depression could occur at any time. Where will it all end — this mad manipulation of our money?

According to the World Book Encyclopedia, some economists and historians think there is a close connection between war and economic depression. They argue that in a worldwide depression, every country tries to protect itself at the expense of other countries. Each nation wants to cut down unemployment at home and tries to make sure that little is bought from abroad which could be made by its own workers at home. This can be accomplished by raising tariffs. It is sometimes called a way of exporting unemployment to other countries.

The chief concern of any government during a depression is to get people back to work. One way to do this is by building armaments. If anger can be stirred up against another country or if people can be made to feel that they are in danger of attack, funds for military preparation are readily voted. Besides, the armed forces themselves give employment to many.

When a nation makes war, its government always states the reason for the war. But, this is necessary if the people are to be united in the war effort. The reasons given for the war, however, may not be the same as its causes. The causes of war may be selfish, base, or even wicked, but the reasons stated are usually lofty and noble.' Is such the case today? Let us review U.S. history and examine the possible correlation between the problems of a sagging economy and war.

One hundred years before the Revolutionary War (in the mid-1600's), the British government would not allow the colonies to mint coins. But Massachusetts built a mint anyway, and from 1652 to 1683 several silver coins were minted.

Then came paper money, even though most of the early colonists used a barter system for trade. Colonial governments printed money to pay the cost of military attacks against Canada. In the 1700's colonial governments continued to issue notes to pay their debts. By 1750, the colonies had much more paper money than they had gold or silver for which to exchange it. As a result, many persons found that the notes were worth far less than the value printed on them.

In 1751, the British Parliament took steps to curb paper money (called colonial scrip), supposedly to keep it from becoming worthless. They prohibited Connecticut, Massachusetts, New Hampshire, and Rhode Island from printing any more paper money. In 1764, the British Parliament ordered the rest of the colonies to stop issuing paper money.

At the same time, the British government began to levy taxes against the colonies. On December 16, 1773, British ships lay in Boston harbor loaded with 340 chests of tea. When the tea arrived in Boston, a committee called "The Committee of Correspondence" protested its arrival and called on Thomas Hutchinson to order the loaded ships back to England. Hutchinson refused.

About 7,000 persons gathered at the Old South Church. They repeated the request to Hutchinson, who refused again. At a signal from Samuel Adams, about 50 men dressed as Indians boarded the unguarded ships, broke open the tea chests, and dumped the tea into the harbor. It has been notoriously referred to as "The Boston Tea Party." The incident lit the fuse to an explosive situation and helped to bring on the Revolutionary War.

During the years 1775-1781, the Continental Congress issued a great amount of notes called "continentals." The value of these notes was stated in terms of Spanish silver coins called "dollars." However, the continentals quickly lost value. It seems they greatly outnumbered the supply of Spanish dollars. Americans began to describe anything worthless as "not worth a continental."

In October, 1781, General George Washington's army of about 17,000 men surrounded Yorktown and began attacking British troops who were under the command of Major General Charles Cornwallis. The siege lasted for three weeks and ended with the surrender of Cornwallis and his 8,000 soldiers. This was the last major battle of the Revolutionary War.

One of the first acts of the Continental Congress at the close of the war was to redeem all of the colonial scrip (continentals) at 100 cents on the dollar. Question: Where did they get all that silver to redeem a currency that was "not worth a continental?"

At this point enters the story of a retired Harvard University professor who was teaching a high school history class in Durant, Oklahoma, just after the turn of the century. I was told that the date was somewhere around 1908. He closed the history book one day, sat down on the corner of his desk and said to his class, "Now let me tell you what really happened."

He told about the Revolutionary War of 1776, the War of 1812, and the Civil War. He declared that each was a money war, perpetrated by the international banking houses of Europe in an effort to gain control of the monetary system of the United States.

According to his story, George Washington and his colonial troops were becoming weary of the war when word came from certain European bankers through their agent, Alexander Hamilton, that a peace could be negotiated provided a central bank would be established allowing the European bankers, primarily the Bank of England, to control the currency. A private agreement was made, thus concluding the war.

When Thomas Jefferson heard of the negotiations, he was furious. He said that to allow the European bankers to establish a central bank, thus controlling our currency, was worse than putting a British soldier in every home.

I do not know how accurate these details may be. We have only the word of a history professor long-deceased. The story is not given in the history books. But if his story is not true, then why was Cornwallis allowed to leave the shores of the United States with his 8,000 troops and their armaments, artillery, and ammunition? We took no spoils of war.

Another question: Where did the silver come from with

which to redeem those worthless continentals? The money had been so worthless that people were papering their walls with it. Suddenly, several politicians, including Alexander Hamilton, became very wealthy men.

At the conclusion of the Revolutionary War, Alexander Hamilton established his central bank in New York City. It is said that Thomas Jefferson was so furious he resigned Washington's cabinet. History does affirm that Jefferson opposed Hamilton in the establishment of the bank, claiming it was unconstitutional.

Alexander Hamilton's national bank handled the payments of the public debt for the Treasury, received subscriptions for new issues of government securities, and even paid the salaries of public officials. [2]

Thomas Jefferson became president in 1801 and served until 1809. During those years he continued to oppose the bank and evidently persuaded several congressmen to agree that the bank was unconstitutional. When the 20 year charter for the central bank came up for renewal in 1811, it was denied.

Guess what happened in 1812! Another war! The British navy began to commandeer our ships and press U.S. citizens into the British military. England wanted to send us a message that the United States was not a "sovereign nation" after all — that we were still a vassal state! The conflict was called the "War of 1812," and again the British were defeated — or were they? The old Harvard professor called it another negotiated peace, for in 1816, a new 20 year charter was issued to the central bank.

One of the heroes of the War of 1812 was Andrew Jackson. He became president in 1829, voicing his hatred for the central bank. He called them "a bunch of snakes." In 1833 Jackson ordered the Secretary of the Treasury to remove government deposits from the Bank of the United States and place them in state banks. He paid off the national debt, thus making the United States free from the control of international bankers. Congress then refused to renew the charter for the national bank, driving it into bankruptcy.

In 1836, when the charter of the bank came up for renewal, Jackson managed to get it defeated. On January 8, 1835, Andrew Jackson paid off the final installment of the national debt. He was the only president in history ever to do so. The United States of America was at last out from under the control of European banking houses.

What happened next? Mexico invaded Texas!

On March 5, 1836, Mexican troops, led by Santa Anna, engineered the fall of the Alamo. It is believed that he intended to push northward to the Mason-Dixon Line and eastward to the Atlantic coast. Thus, the South would be ruled by Mexico. Other troops were stationed in Canada during those days in an effort to invade all of the territory north of the Mason-Dixon Line. When those two attempted invasions failed, certain politicians began to stir up strife between the North and the South.

The stated issue of the dissension was slavery, but was it the cause of the war? The retired Harvard professor said that though slavery is generally accepted as the reason for the war, the real cause lay in the control of America's economy. The Civil War was another "money war." We cannot say with certainty that the Civil War was fomented by the European banking houses, but immediately the question arises: Who backed the Confederate money used to fight the war? The answer: Europe's banking houses.

The matter was somewhat complicated in 1849, when gold was discovered in San Francisco, California, and in 1859, when the Comstock Lode was discovered in Colorado. Suddenly, the European banking houses were left out in the cold. Real money — gold and silver — provided a potential prosperity for the United States. This obviously would keep the United States from the control of the international bankers.

Two years later, in 1861, the Civil War began. Abraham Lincoln refused to borrow money from the European bankers with which to fight the war. Instead he printed the first United States notes — the greenback. The infamous "two-dollar bill" was used to finance the war.

In the years which followed there was a continual struggle in America's economy. The economy sagged in the mid-1870's; there was the depression in 1884 and a panic in 1893; and there was another panic in 1907. Each seemed to be an effort by the international bankers to cripple our economy in hopes of convincing Congress to allow a central bank. During those years, however, Congress refused, and though we suffered economic recession, that period witnessed America's greatest financial growth.

The industrial age flourished. Free enterprise had its heyday. In 1876 the telephone was invented and from it came our modern means of communication. From those days came the automobile and the airplane.

On March 4, 1912, Woodrow Wilson was inaugurated as the 28th president of the United States. Immediately, he set about to establish a central bank. He had campaigned on the platform that he would never allow a central bank. He said that he would lead the fight against those "wolves of Wall Street." But alas, he turned out to be one of those wolves in sheep's clothing.

The bill was introduced on June 23rd of that year. It was hotly debated for some six months, but finally was passed in December of 1913 (while most of the Senators and Representatives were out of town for the Christmas holidays), thus establishing the Federal Reserve System.

Guess what happened the next year! World War I — another "money war"!

Shortly before noon on June 28, 1914, crowds gathered in the capital of the Austrian province of Bosnia. They came to see the Archduke, Francis Ferdinand, of the House of Habsburg, and his wife, Sophie. Suddenly, a man jumped on the running board of the royal touring car and fired a pistol. Two shots struck Ferdinand, and one hit Sophie, who was trying to shield him. They both died almost immediately.

As a result, war was declared on July 28th. On July 30th, Russia ordered general mobilization. On August 1st, Germany declared war on Russia. On August 3rd, Germany declared war on France. On August 4th, Germany invaded Belgium, and on the story goes. It appears to have been another "money war."

Then came 1929 and the depression that rocked America. Our economy was devastated. Millionaires became paupers. Millions of others lost their life savings. Many committed suicide because they just couldn't take sudden poverty. The fateful day came on October 18th, 1929. President Hoover was blamed for the depression and as a result, lost the election in 1932. But who and what was really responsible?

A new president came to power at that time — Franklin D. Roosevelt. On March 6, 1933, following his inauguration, Roosevelt called for a bank holiday. Americans were told that all banks were closed in an effort to help stop the money panic that was spreading in the nation. Depositors had been withdrawing their funds at such speed that many banks ran out of money to pay over the counter. But was this the whole truth?

In the early 1930's, America did not lack industrial capacity, fertile farmland, skilled and willing workers, or industrious farm families. Communications between regions and localities were the best in the world, utilizing telephone, teletype, radio, and a well-operated government mail system. No war had ravaged the cities or the countryside; no pestilence weakened the population; nor had famine stalked the land. The United States of America lacked only one thing: an adequate supply of money to carry on trade and commerce.

The banking community, the only source of new money and credit, deliberately refused loans to industries, stores, and farms. Payments on existing loans were required, however, and money rapidly disappeared from circulation. Goods were available to be purchased, jobs waited to be done, but the lack of money brought the nation to a standstill. By this simple ploy America was thrust into a "depression" and greedy bankers took possession of hundreds of thousands of farms, homes, and business properties. The people were told, "times are hard," and "money is short." Not understanding the system, they were cruelly robbed of their earnings, their savings, and their property.

In 1934, Congress passed the Gold Reserve Act. The government stopped minting gold coins, and persons could no longer hold gold money. President Roosevelt called in all the gold held by citizens throughout the United States, redeeming it for $20.67 an ounce. Immediately after the gold was, shall we say, confiscated, the value of it was set at $35.00 an ounce. It seems obvious that someone profited overnight.

Guess what happened next! World War II — another "money war"!

On September 1, 1939, Germany attacked Poland, launching the most devastating war in the history of mankind. Casualties are estimated upwards to 50 million people. World War II cost more money, damaged more property, affected more people, and probably caused more far-reaching changes than any other war of history.

But the war ended the "depression." The same banking community, which in the early 30's had no loans for peacetime houses, food, and clothing, suddenly had unlimited billions to lend for Army barracks, K-rations and uniforms! A nation that in 1934, couldn't produce food for sale, suddenly could produce bombs to send to Germany and later, Japan. With the sudden increase in money, people were hired, farms sold their produce, factories added two shifts, and "The Great Depression" was over. The truth is, the lack of money (caused by the International Banking Community) brought on the depression, and an adequate money supply ended it.

Many were the reasons for the war, but what was the cause? Obviously, the world economy was affected when the United States went off the gold standard, and I am reminded of the prophecy in the New Testament epistle of James:

"Go to now, ye rich men, weep and howl for your miseries that shall come upon you.

"Your riches are corrupted, and your garments are moth-eaten.

"Your gold and silver is cankered; and the rust of them shall be a witness against you, and shall eat your flesh as it were fire. Ye have heaped treasure together for the last days.

"Behold, the hire of the labourers who have reaped down your fields, which is of you kept back by fraud, crieth: and the cries of them which have reaped are entered into the ears of the Lord of Sabbath.

"Ye have lived in pleasure on the earth, and been wanton; ye have nourished your hearts, as in a day of slaughter.

"Ye have condemned and killed the just; and he doth not resist you" (James 5:1-6).

Today, we face a rising trade deficit, a politically unmanageable budget deficit, and a dying dollar. The European Common Market nations have established a new European currency. What it will do to the dollar? How traumatic will be the effects?

In the early 1970's, Congress passed a bill allowing Americans to own gold. At that time the government began auctioning America's gold. Since then the price of gold has risen to new record highs, retreated to half its gains, leveled off, and currently is fluctuating. Some predict, however, that within a few years the price of gold could rise again to as high as $2,000 an ounce. But has the VALUE of gold really gone up? No, it simply means the VALUE of the dollar has declined.

Whether by accident or by manipulation, someday, a new one-world economy will be introduced. How do I know? Because the Bible predicts that a European confederation will arise to establish a loosely-knit world government through which they will introduce a new one-world currency.

Once this currency is established, no one will be allowed to buy or sell unless he has the proper identification — called in the Bible the "Mark of the Beast." Question: In the light of today's headlines, will the world soon wage another war?

"And ye shall hear of wars and rumours of wars: see that ye be not troubled: for all these things must come to pass ..." (Matthew 24:6).

All wars of history have been money wars — so says the World Book Encyclopedia. The Bible seems to concur and also predicts a series of future wars that will be fought over monetary control. At that time, a new world currency will be introduced. Even the infamous Armageddon will be fought as a result of this attempt at monetary control. According to prophecy, one day the antichrist will lead the way in a movement to establish this new world monetary policy — the "Mark of the Beast."

Chapter Notes

CHAPTER 10

1. "War," WORLD BOOK ENCYCLOPEDIA, Vol. 21, 1973, p. 22.
2. "Bank of the United States," THE WORLD BOOK ENCYCLOPEDIA, Vol. 2, 1973, p. 60.

In the legend of the Holy Grail, Percival enters the Grail Castle and sees a mystical ceremony taking place in the banquet hall. The king is ill, as shown above. (See chapter 3.)

Chapter 11

The
Conspiracy

Since the days of World War II, the bloodletting has continued. There was Korea, Vietnam, Laos, Cambodia, Thailand, and Pakistan. There was Iran, Iraq, Syria, Lebanon, Libya, and Nicaragua. The continent of Africa has been wracked with war and the countries around the Caribbean continually suffer the capers of Castro. What is this scourge we call war? Where does it come from? Why does it occur?

A few years ago on a nationwide telecast, Senator Clarence Long gave a somewhat profound assessment. He said, "It's a rich man's war and a poor man's fight." However lofty and noble appear its aims, the real reasons are rooted in the wealth of the rich. In fact, the first war ever recorded in the Bible was fought over taxes.

According to Genesis, chapter 14, the cities of Sodom and Gomorrah, which had served the kings of the Elamites for 12 years and who had paid tribute (or taxes) from the fruits of their labors, in the 13th year rebelled. It was a tax rebellion. In the 14th year, the kings of the East invaded Sodom and Gomorrah along with the other cities that lay around the southern edge of the Dead Sea.

In those days, the region was filled with vegetation. Described as being like the Garden of Eden, Sodom and Gomorrah lay in fertile ground — lakefront property. But alas, they had no national security and the first war ever recorded in the history of the human race was fought over that region. Chedorlaomer and the Elamite kings overwhelmed the Sodomites and took them captive.

When Abraham heard of it, he gathered 318 of his finest soldiers and pursued the army almost all the way to Damascus. He was able to rout the enemy and rescue his nephew, along with the other citizens of Sodom. It is amazing that the fracas turned out to be a rich man's war and a poor man's fight! This could be said, I suppose, of every battle throughout history. The wars of this century are no different. They too, were fought over finances. It also seems inevitable, with the demise of the dollar and the corruption of currencies around the world, that men are not going to take it lying down.

It seems that if we are made weary of war, we will be more willing to accept slavery as the alternative. It is my opinion that there is a conspiracy afoot throughout the world, and I am not referring to a communist conspiracy. The communists appear to be only pawns in a gigantic game of chess. We too, appear to be pawns in this game, and the conspirators are not necessarily communists. Perhaps we should call them super-capitalists, for today's attempt at the enslavement of man is guided by one goal — world government and its implementation through a new one-world economy. The Bible calls it the "Mark of the Beast."

Rich man's war, poor man's fight. Is war caused by conspiracy, or is it just an accident of history? Is man so depraved that he cannot live in peace, or is the love of money the root of that evil we call war?

There are those who deny any connection between the bloodletting of one war and the bloodletting of another. They contend that there is no truth to the conspiratorial theory of history, that the theory is nothing more than that — just a theory. They feel that those who consider such a theory are deluded. Just what is the case? Has there ever been a war without a conspiracy? There are good men — godly men — who have disagreed on the conspiratorial theory of history. Perhaps some would prefer, like the ostrich, to bury their heads in the sand and refuse to admit that particular potential evil of man.

Conspiracy is one of the darkest words in the history of humankind. There is hardly a single page of the past which does not partially reveal the deadly eye of conspiracy at work. It was a conspiracy that directed Brutus against Caesar in the Roman Senate on the Ides of March. It was a conspiracy that plotted the betrayal of West Point by Benedict Arnold during the American Revolution. It was a conspiracy that led John Wilkes Booth to the assassination of President Lincoln on Good Friday, 1865. The past record of man is burdened with accounts of assassinations, secret combines, palace plots, and betrayals in war.

The tenet of conspiracy has been a dominant force in all of history. But in spite of this clear record, an amazing number of people scoff at the possibility of conspiracy at work today. They dismiss such an idea merely as a conspiratorial "theory" of history. Unfortunately, it is a conspiratorial FACT. There is a secret and powerful combine at work today. They constitute an unseen government — men behind the scenes pulling the strings, and it might be best described as a capitalist conspiracy.

In 1963, the nation was held spellbound by the testimony of a gangster, Joe Valachi, as he exposed the inside workings of the international crime syndicate known as the Cosa Nostra, or the Mafia. No matter how carefully criminal conspiracies are organized, eventually they are exposed because someone on the inside goes to the authorities and talks. The same is true with political conspiracies. For example, over the years there has been a steady stream of defectors from communist countries. Through their testimony we now have a clear idea of how that conspiracy is organized and operated.

But one large piece of the puzzle has always been missing. It is a matter of record that some of the greatest help to world communism has often come from prominent and respectable leaders within Europe and the United States. Obviously, these men are not communists. As a matter of fact, most of them are extremely wealthy and are thought of as capitalists, who supposedly would have the most to lose under socialism and communism. And yet, the record is disturbingly consistent.

Americans have repeatedly asked why some of the richest people in the United States, both inside and outside the government, aligned themselves with leftist policies that would appear to be the path of their own destruction? And if there is a conspiracy at work among these men, why hasn't someone exposed it?

The answer is, someone has. Dr. Carroll Quigley, a professor of history at Georgetown University, who also taught at Princeton and Harvard Universities, is the author of the widely used textbook, EVOLUTION OF CIVILIZATION.[1] In addition, he is a member of the editorial board of the monthly periodical, "Current History." He has been a frequent lecturer and consultant for such groups as the Industrial College of the

Armed Forces, the Brookings Institute, the U.S. Naval Weapons Laboratory, the Naval College, the Smithsonian Institution, and the State Department. Dr. Quigley has also been closely associated with many of the family dynasties of the super-rich. He is, by his own boast, an insider with a front row view of the world's money power structure.

When Dr. Quigley wrote his 1300-page book of dry history entitled TRAGEDY AND HOPE, [2] it was obvious that it would never be read by the masses. It was intended for the intellectual elite. And to such a select readership, Dr. Quigley cautiously exposed one of the best kept secrets of all time. But he also made it quite clear that he was an extremely friendly apologist for this group and that he fully supports their goals and purposes.

In his book he said that the international bankers remain different from ordinary bankers in distinctive ways:

First, they were cosmopolitan and international.

Second, they were close to governments and were particularly concerned with the question of government debts.

Third, he said their interests were almost exclusively in bonds.

Fourth, they were accordingly fanatical devotees of the necessity of creating inflation.

And fifth, he said they were equally devoted to secrecy and the secret use of financial influence in political life. [3]

It may seem strange that Dr. Quigley would make such statements when it is clear that he warmly supports the goals and purposes of the international banking network. But if that is the case, why would he want to expose this world-wide conspiracy and disclose most of its secret operations? Obviously, disclosing the existence of a mammoth power network which is trying to take over the world could not help but arouse the resistance of millions of people who are its intended victims. So why did Quigley write his book? Dr. Quigley feels that it is now too late for the little people to turn back the tide. In a spirit of kindness he is urging us not to fight a power that is already established.

Throughout his book, Dr. Quigley assures us that we can trust these benevolent, well-meaning men who are secretly operating behind the scenes. They are, he claims, the hope of the world, and all who resist them represent "tragedy" — thus, the title of his book, TRAGEDY AND HOPE.

Dr. Quigley wrote, "I know of the operations of this network because I have studied it for 20 years and was permitted for two years, in the early 1960's, to examine its papers and secret records. I have no aversion to it or to most of its aims and have, for much of my life, been close to it and to many of its instruments ... In general, my chief difference of opinion is that it wishes to remain unknown...." [4]

Dr. Quigley points out that during the past 200 years, while the masses of our world were gradually winning their political freedom from monarchies, the major banking families of the world were nullifying the trend toward representative government by setting up new dynasties of political control (behind the scenes) in the form of international financial combines.

These banking dynasties had learned that all governments — whether they be totalitarian or democratic — must borrow money in times of emergency, and that by providing such funds from their own private resources (with strings attached) they could bring both kings and democratic leaders under their control.

It should be noted that while some Jewish bankers cooperated together in these ventures, this was by no means a Jewish monopoly as some have alleged. Men of finance of many nationalities and many religious and non-religious backgrounds collaborated together to create this super-structure of hidden power. Its essence was not race, religion, nor nationality. It was simply a passion for control over other human beings. Dr. Quigley identified this group simply as the "International Bankers."

These are not the same as the local commercial bankers with whom we deal in everyday life. International bankers deal not with the general public, but with the industrial giants of the world, with other financial institutions, and especially with governments. The key to their success has been to control and manipulate the money system of a nation, while letting it appear to be controlled by the government. The net effect is to create money out of nothing, lend it to the government, and then collect interest on it — a rather profitable transaction to say the least.

For example, in 1694 international banker William Paterson obtained the charter of the Bank of England, and the power over England's money system fell into private hands. In a boastful mood, Paterson said, "The bank hath benefit of interest on all monies which it creates out of nothing."[5] Two hundred thirty years later, Reginald McKenna, British Chancellor of the Exchequer said, "The banks can and do create money... And they who control the credit of the nation direct the policy of governments and hold in the hollow of their hands the destiny of the people."[6]

Yes, there is a conspiracy. The international bankers have set about to establish a one-world government and a new one-world monetary system. Surely, in these days we are seeing the fulfillment of that ancient prophecy — the "Mark of the Beast."

In 1946 England's labor government revoked the charter and nationalized the Bank of England. Officially, it became a part of the government. It is important to note, however, that as late as 1961 Lord Cromer, of the banking family of Baring, was named governor of the bank, and the board of directors included representatives of Lazard, Hambros, and Grenfell—the same banking families who had previously controlled the board! Nothing had changed except for outward appearances for the benefit of the uninformed.

Turning to the United States, Dr. Quigley tells us, "The structure of financial controls created by the tycoons of 'Big Banking' and 'Big Business' in the period 1880-1933 was of extraordinary complexity, one business fief being built upon another, both being allied and semi-independent associates, the whole rearing upward into two pinnacles of economic and financial power....

"One, centered in New York, was headed by J. P. Morgan and Company and the other, in Ohio, was headed by the Rockefeller family. When these two cooperated, as they generally did, they could influence the economic life of the country to a large degree and could almost control its political life, at least on the Federal level."[7]

In the United States, it was inevitable that international banking interests would attempt to establish the same kind of private monopoly over the money system that had been achieved in England, France, Germany, Italy, and Switzerland. The same formula would be used: Make it look like a government operation, but keep the control in private hands.

John D. Rockefeller had purchased the Chase Bank, and his brother William had bought the National City Bank of New York. The Rockefeller Chase Bank was later merged with the Warburg's Manhattan Bank to form the Chase-Manhattan Bank, one of the most powerful financial combines in the world today.

Acting in concert with the Morgan banking dynasty, they spent untold millions of dollars to promote legislation that would grant to them a private franchise over this nation's money system. To sell this scheme to the voters, the monopolists created the propaganda line that the proposed banking law somehow would work against the monopolies. Politicians took up the cry, "Banking reform!" and "Down with Wall Street." And then, to make it look convincing, the financial tycoons publically pretended to oppose the measure — all the while, they were financing it behind the scenes.

When the Federal Reserve Act was passed into law, total control of the nation's money fell into private hands. The Federal Reserve System is totally responsible for creating money in the United States. The Treasury prints only what the Federal Reserve tells it to print. The far greater amount of checkbook money is also determined by this group. Yet it is not a government agency and is entirely beyond the reach of the American voter.

Dr. Quigley revealed the goal of this operation as nothing less than creating a world system of financial control in private hands able to dominate the political system of each country and the economy of the world as a whole. This system was to be controlled in a feudalist fashion by the central banks of the world acting in concert by secret agreements arrived at in frequent private meetings and conferences. The apex of the system was to be the Bank for International Settlements in Basel, Switzerland — a private bank owned and controlled by the world's central banks which are themselves private corporations.

Each central bank sought to dominate its government by an ability to control treasury loans, manipulate foreign exchanges, influence the level of economic activity in the country, and influence cooperative politicians with economic rewards in the business world. Dr. Carroll Quigley's book, TRAGEDY AND HOPE, lays out the whole sordid story of how the super-rich, who own and control the international banking houses, have hoarded gold and silver and have set about to establish a fiat money system — of course, for the good of mankind. The term "fiat money" means, "a paper currency made legal tender by law, although not backed by gold or silver and not necessarily redeemable in coin."[8] World government and world economy go hand in hand. It is impossible to control one without the other. Upset the financial interests of the super-rich in a country and they control the political power to bring about a war.

There is a conspiracy in this world determined to set up a one-world political and economic system through which every citizen on planet Earth will eventually become a slave. It is a very real conspiracy, and who is behind it? His name is Lucifer.

Chapter Notes

CHAPTER 11

1. Dr. Carroll Quigley, EVOLUTION OF CIVILIZATION, An Introduction to Historical Analysis (Brooklyn, NY: Revisionist Press, 1984).

2. Quigley, TRAGEDY AND HOPE; A History of the World in Our Time (New York, NY: The Macmillan Co., 1966).

3. Ibid., p. 52.

4. Ibid., p. 950.

5. Ibid., p. 49.

6. Ibid., p. 325.

7. Ibid., p. 72.

8. WEBSTER'S NEW WORLD DICTIONARY OF THE AMERICAN LANGUAGE, College Edition (Cleveland and New York: The World Publishing Company, 1956), p. 538.

This castle in southern France near the Rennes-le-Chateau reminds us of the one that once sat atop the hill belonging to the Merovingian kings. A castle similar to this one was the setting described in Wolfram von Eschenbach's epic poem, "Parzival." (See chapter 2.)

Chapter 12

The Coming Financial Crisis

The United States dollar has been the leading currency in the world — the basis for our world's economy. As a student of prophecy, I am carefully watching the decline of our dollar and know that according to prophetic Scripture, a new world currency will soon emerge. America's dollar and economic status must decline in order to give way for the emergence of western Europe. On the back of our one dollar bill is the Great Seal of the United States — a pyramid with an eye above it. Below are the words "Novus Ordo Seclorum," meaning "a new order of the ages." According to Daniel 7 and Revelation 13, a new order of the ages will indeed come. It will spring from the old Roman Empire.

Over the years, we have observed an apparent movement to capture the economic systems of this world and establish a single worldwide system. If all goes according to schedule, someday all paper currency will be revalued and along with Electronic Funds Transfer, a one-world monetary system will be forced upon the population. That seems to be the direction our dollar has been driven for several years now. In 1978, United States Senator Jacob Javits told the Senate, "The world monetary system eventually will be restructured in a way that would gradually replace reliance on the dollar. This new arrangement will make the monetary system more responsive to international financial reality."

In the early 1980's, representatives of the International Banking Community met in Toronto, Canada, to air their fears of an impending financial collapse of international banking. A general monetary breakdown was expected to cause possible world chaos. Some 500 billion dollars in loans to underdeveloped nations was coming due. According to the International Monetary Fund, these loans could default — causing a possible collapse of the International Banking System.

I believe the international banking community used the impending panic to further their goal for the creation of a new world currency. The so-called panic was part of a conspiracy planned to create a one-world money system designed to eventually replace currency and coin with computers. A similar case can be made regarding the more recent failures of many of our banks and the subsequent plan for the American taxpayer to bail out our bankrupt savings and loan industry.

Our Federal Reserve System is a part of the International Monetary Fund and the World Bank. It is said that plans have been made by these organizations to establish a new monetary system to replace the old. Before a new currency will be accepted, however, the value of all present currencies must be restructured. The phasing out of the one-dollar bill and the issuance of the "new currency" may coincide with the new world order of Daniel 7 and Revelation 13.

The prophet John, in Revelation 13, predicted that a great depression will come. Money will collapse and the economy of the world will crumble. Men will not be able to buy or sell without a personal identification number.¹ A new world currency will be instituted and eventually will require an engraving upon the flesh — a mark in the right hand or in the forehead. Many Bible scholars agree that those who control the money of this world will play a major role in the fulfillment of this and other Bible prophecies. Just how close are we to this new universal currency?

In the "International Money Line" newsletter, published by Julian Snyder, it was reported, "The United States is trying to solve its problem through currency depreciation. It will not work. If the crash does not occur this year, it could be postponed" — but not for long.

The dollar could become obsolete within a few years, and all paper currencies within the decade. Bill Newkirk, reporting for the Associated Press, said recently, "A new world exchange system which will dominate the economies of nations for the next 25 years is but months away." The development of a new one-world money system is one of the most significant fulfillments of Bible prophecy. The Bible is clear. It will become the "Mark of the Beast." One of the four horsemen of the Apocalypse carried a balance in his hand. A cry went forth:

"... A measure of wheat for a penny, and three measures of barley for a penny ..." (Revelation 6:6).

What a vivid description of the world's economy during the last days!

Some years ago, George Humphrey, then Secretary of the Treasury, declared, "We are on the verge of something that will curl a man's hair to think about it." He said, "It will make the 1930's look like rip-roaring prosperity."

In the mid-1970's a publication entitled "World Bank"

(paper number 447, article 3) predicted that the economics of the world would remain fairly stable until the 1980's, beyond which time it predicted their falling in domino fashion. Is there any wonder Ludwig Earhardt, finance minister of Germany following World War II, declared, "Give us problems or give us depression, but do not give us inflation, for it is the sure eventual death to every economy."

Mr. James Dines wrote in the "Invisible Crash" publication: "Today's crisis has been building since 1933. There has been no precedent for such monetary instability in the financial history of the world. The man on the street has no concept of the financial panic which could lie just before us."[2]

Banking is not new. It is almost as old as the human race. The concept first began in the ancient past when gold was left in the care of a trusted friend who gave a receipt on parchment or leather. Loans were made for which usury or interest was paid, even before the days of Moses.

In early America, banks issued their own paper money. Confusion set in as people moved from one state to another carrying various forms of paper money. In 1863, Abraham Lincoln influenced the passing of the National Bank Act, providing for a uniform standard of values and regulations. In 1870, America's banks went on the gold standard, allowing any American to exchange his paper money for gold.

On December 23, 1913, Woodrow Wilson influenced legislation which established the Federal Reserve System. With the passing of the Federal Reserve Act, Congress forfeited the right to create its own money. Paul Warburg was the man behind the Federal Reserve Act of 1913. The honorable Louis McFadden, chairman of the Banking and Currency Committee in 1933, said in a speech to Congress, "Paul Warburg came here from Germany for one purpose: to take over the Treasury of the United States as the international bankers have done with the treasuries of Europe."

Warburg's son, James, stood before the United States Senate on February 17, 1950. He announced in his speech, "We shall have world government whether we like it or not. The only question is, whether the world government will be achieved by conquest or consent."

Karl Marx, in his COMMUNIST MANIFESTO declared, "Money plays the largest part in determining the course of history."

In 1852, Lord Gladstone, who also served as chancellor of Britain's exchequer, or treasury, said, "The government in the matters of finance must leave the money power supreme and unquestioned."

In 1881, President James Garfield said, "He who controls the money of a nation controls the nation."

In 1920, nine years before the stock market crash, Congressman Charles Lindbergh of Minnesota said, "From now on depressions will be scientifically created."[3]

In 1924, Reginald McKenna, who served as chancellor of England's exchequer, said, "I am afraid that the ordinary citizen will not like to be told that the banks can and do create money, and they who control the credit of a nation direct the policy of the governments and hold in the hollow of their hands the destiny of the people."[4]

Sir Drummond Frazier, once vice-president of England's Institute of Bankers, said, "The governor of the Bank of England must be the autocrat who dictates the terms upon which alone the government can obtain money."

In 1933, Vice-president John Garner referred to the international bankers when he said, "You see, gentlemen, who owns the United States."

Mayer Amschel Rothschild once said, "Permit me to issue and control the money of a nation, and I care not who makes its laws."[5]

The original international banker was Mayer Amschel Rothschild, born in Frankfurt, Germany in 1743, and father of 5 sons. With one son he set up a banking house in Frankfurt. He sent another son to Vienna, another to London, another to Paris, and another to Naples. They established international banking houses through which they loaned European governments money. The scheme was to force those governments to repay their national debts to the Rothschild banking houses by levying taxes against their people.

By 1850, the House of Rothschild represented more wealth than all the royal families of Europe and Britain combined. The House of Warburg and the House of Rothschild, along with a few other powerful banking houses, became known as International Bankers. They now control the currencies of all the countries of the world.

From 1870 to 1933, the American dollar was fixed to the gold standard. When a currency is backed by gold, there is a built-in discipline and the government cannot manipulate the currency. In 1933, however, President Roosevelt accepted the advice of Englishman John Maynard Keynes, who insisted that deficit spending would be like a shot of adrenalin in the heart of the economy. This required removing the dollar from the gold standard and allowing the government to begin the slow, but sure, process of debasing the currency.

In 1933, President Roosevelt asked Congress to pass legislation demanding that the American people give up their gold. In 1934, when it was ordered to be turned in to the government, all gold was confiscated by the government for $20.67 an ounce. Immediately its value was increased to $35.00 an ounce, which produced a huge profit for the government — a $3 billion profit.

In August, 1979, the decision was made in Washington to

remove the $35.00 price of gold and allow the price to be set by demand and find its own "value" at market levels. Some feared that the price of gold would escalate, and indeed it did. Over the next few years, the price of gold soared to $850 per ounce. The price has since decreased and stabilized but will eventually rise, some say, to new record heights. It could go to $2,000 an ounce — even $3,000. But why? Why should the price of gold be manipulated on the money markets throughout the world? Obviously, the dollar is destined to die.

What happens when the price of gold is increased? The value of the dollar comes down. In 1934, our government began to print more dollars without any increase in substance — and spend them. Year after year our Congress approved deficit federal budgets which required the printing of additional dollars to finance those deficits. Our national debt now is around three trillion dollars. It has more than doubled since the early 1980's! Someday, perhaps soon, the cost of servicing the national debt will eat up all the government tax money available.

Meanwhile, however, huge trade and budget deficits continue unabated, the value of the American dollar continues to be weakened in relationship to other currencies, and the potential for impending WORLDWIDE financial disaster is nearer than at any time since the Great Depression of 1929! Although the accuracy of predictions by economists is often not reliable — in this instance, they surely are not far wrong. It is only a matter of time until our government and our nation will have to face the stark reality of national bankruptcy.

If and when our dollar fails, the other currencies of the world will also crumble. The resulting depression will be felt around the world. Isn't it strange that the problems we have faced here in America have also been felt by every other country in the world? Is every other economy so closely tied to the United

States dollar that when we fall, they shall fall? It was not so in 1929. Why should it be so today? Is it by mere coincidence that every other nation has been as derelict with their budgets as our nation seems to have been? Can we really blame ourselves for the death of the dollar?

The world-wide recession of 1982-83 was either the biggest coincidence in the history of humanity — affecting every nation at the same time — or else there is a conspiracy afoot to debauch the dollar and destroy the economies of the world. In 1910, Vladimir I. (Nicholai) Lenin, leader of the Russian Communist revolution, said, "The surest way to overthrow an established social order is to debauch its currency."

In more recent times, former Soviet Premier Nikita Krushchev said, "By a continuing process of inflation, governments can confiscate, secretly and unobserved, an important part of the wealth of their citizens." [6]

I realize we do not like to think in terms of a conspiracy. We all are thankful for some relief during the Reagan years. Our financial problems are not over, however. As individuals, we are still suffering. If there is a conspiracy, what would be the goal, the aim, the motive for destroying the American dollar and, along with it, all of the other currencies of the world?

The answer to that question can only be found in the prophecies of the Bible.

"And he causeth all, both small and great, rich and poor, free and bond, to receive a mark in their right hand, or in their foreheads:

"And that no man might buy or sell, save he that had the mark, or the name of the beast, or the number of his name" (Revelation 13:16,17).

A worldwide economic system is being developed. According to the prophecy, there will come a day when the economies of the world will require a mark in the flesh of the hand or forehead in order to participate in the market place. No exchange of money will be possible without that mark. Believe it or not, such a system is under development today.

Electronic Funds Transfer appears to provide all of the answers to our monetary problems. It will take the place of paperwork in the writing and processing of checks. It will remove the need for most currencies, which some argue is the inspiration for all crime, burglaries, and robberies. When all of the world is on the computer, all economic systems can be stabilized, thus solving both problems of theft and inflation.

Sounds like a utopian dream, doesn't it? The plastic debit card which is presently replacing credit cards across the nation seems to be the ultimate answer to make everybody honest — no more money under the table. Organized crime will just fade away. Sounds good — but wait a minute! There are some built-in problems: plastic cards can be stolen; computer theft is a growing menace; and the big question is, who is going to control the computer?

Whoever controls the bank account controls the individual. No matter which way one looks at it, people will no longer be free! Once the computer card replaces currency, it will only be a matter of time until the mark in the flesh of the hand or forehead will be required in order to activate one's bank account.

With the development of computerized banking has come the debit card, a system for transacting business without the need for currency or coin. As the plastic money system was developed, however, certain problems arose. How do we keep someone from stealing a card and using it?

Indentification is a very difficult procedure. Eventually, with the world's growing population, only one way can be effectively used to identify the holder of one's bank debit card.

Today, those who possess a bank debit card are asked to memorize a secret code. But that does not guarantee against some dishonest person counterfeiting the plastic card and obtaining the secret number. The only way to identify the holder of a card as being its owner is to let the computer read the identifying marks from the flesh of the one in possession of that card. It is inevitable. There is no other way to guard against a gross misuse and abuse of a computerized cashless medium of exchange.

The development of Electronic Funds Transfer fits the prophecy perfectly. Computerized money offers a perfect explanation of that description given in the book of the Revelation, chapter 13. Now, I realize the chapter is written in somewhat cryptic language, but remember, please, it was written 2,000 years ago in the primitive language of that day. There was no vocabulary with which to adequately describe the development of the computer. It is referred to in verse 14 as "an image." According to the Scripture, life was given to the image so that it could speak.

Though science has never been able to create life, the computer is admittedly the nearest thing to it. Computers can simulate the thinking process and speak today. The computer is a sort of mechanical brain. It is the nearest thing to the creation of life ever developed by the ingenuity of man. Is it not, obviously, the fulfillment of this ancient prophecy? The events of our generation leave little doubt as to the importance of the computer in our society and of its inevitable use by a world-wide government for the enslavement of man.

In March, 1980, a new banking act was passed by the Congress of the United States. It required 40,000 banks to join the Federal Reserve System. Until then, only about 4,600 banks were members. The CHRISTIAN SCIENCE MONITOR alluded to the Monetary Control Act of 1980, as "Big

Brother comes to the banking system."[7]

The Federal Reserve has an underground facility built into the side of a mountain in the lush, green foothills of Virginia overlooking the Shenandoah Valley. The facility, located near the small town of Culpeper, Virginia, controls a nation-wide network for the Federal Reserve Banks. It acts as a switching system for all banking transactions across America.

Every bank transaction goes through the computer at Culpeper. Over 70 trillion dollars each year are fed through the system. It is called a "store and forward communications system." Every bank transaction is required to be entered into the computer so that if there was a computer failure somewhere in the nation, the Federal Reserve would not lose the message.

According to Al Tinkelenberg, director of the facility, there are a number of concerns connected with computerized banking. He said that as the use of "Fedwire" increases, he and his crew "have nightmares about computer failure." If the wire is interrupted for 25 minutes, it is major news in the WALL STREET JOURNAL. An interruption of a few hours would send costly ripples into every corner of the economy.

Another concern is security. With billions of dollars in the electronic pipeline and no paperwork to authenticate these transactions, officials acknowledge the potential for sophisticated thievery. Not surprisingly, Tinkelenberg is tight-lipped about the codes and checks that protect the switching system. He said, "We recognize there is a growing potential for computer crime, so we are increasing our efforts to keep the risk at a proper level."

The system is designed particularly for use in case of a national emergency. Tinkelenberg said, "The reason we are underground, the reason for the dormitories and such, is so personnel from the Board of Governors in Washington could come here prior to an emergency and stay until all danger of radiation was over." [8]

The switching system at Culpeper is prepared to house, feed, and put to work more than 400 key workers who would be evacuated from the Federal Reserve in Washington, D.C. and Richmond, Virginia. The system is designed primarily for emergencies in the case of nuclear war. The giant computer is the main switching system for Electronic Funds Transfer in the United States.

Through an organization called "Society of Worldwide Interbank Financial Telecommunications," also called SWIFT for short, there is a satellite communications connection with another switching system in Brussels, Belgium. The computer in Brussels has the ability to record the bank accounts of some two billion people.

Five years ago newspapers across our country were reporting that a cashless society would be possible within a decade. All transactions then, would be electronic. To accomplish this herculean task, another giant computer has been built in Luxembourg, at the European Common Market facilities. It is the computer that has been widely acclaimed as "The Beast." The computer has the ability to assign every person on the face of the earth a bank account number. As I understand it, all banking systems throughout Europe and America are presently connected to the giant computer system. Electronic Funds Transfer has also now been introduced, offering an alternative to the use of currency and coins.

The development of this system has progressed so rapidly over the past few years it is mind-boggling. Within the next few years it is conceivable to believe that most currencies could be replaced by the computer. Plastic credit or debit cards could be replaced by one Electronics Funds Transfer card.

What a coincidence that this gigantic computerized system of cashless banking was developed and implemented at the same time the dollar is suffering. What a coincidence that while the dollar is faltering, the currencies of the other countries in the world are likewise faltering. It seems to me that one person's loss should be another person's gain. And yet, around the world there are uniform losses and nobody seems to be gaining. If everybody's currency is losing value, who is picking up the profit? Soon, world government will be the winner and the individual will be the loser.

In December, 1979, Dr. Franz Pick, renowned world currency authority, was quoted in the "Silver and Gold Report" as saying, "The most serious problem we face today is the debasement of our currency by the government. The government will continue to debase the dollar until ... it will be forced to create a new hard currency. When that day comes, it will take at least $100 to buy a new dollar. A currency reform is nothing but a fancy name for a state bankruptcy. The currency reform completes the expropriation of all kinds of savings. It will wipe out all public and private bonds, most pensions, all annuities, and all endowments."

Many investment analysts are charging that there is a "hidden agenda" behind the plans for a currency recall. We are only told that "something" must be done to stop the decline of the dollar against the world's currencies. That "something" must be a plan to issue new money!

Many foreign countries have ALREADY redesigned and reissued their currencies. A curiosity noted when examining these reissued foreign currencies is that all have very noticeable blank spaces on their faces. Why? Analysts say that in the event of a serious economic emergency, currencies could be hand stamped in the blank space by individual banks — at the time of issuance. At the same time, presumably, old currency would be decreed worthless. The conceivable emergency? It might be a currency trading breakdown, such as occurred in the 1970's, when currency trading around the world came to a complete halt because of the weakness in the U.S. dollar. We may be nearing such a currency crisis again as we enter the decade of the '90s.

It is believed that if such a crisis develops again it may be necessary to revalue all currencies in the world, require a call in of old currency, and reissuance of "over-printed currency" using the blank spaces. If all currencies were recalled at once, it would lead to a new form of world currency. This could be arranged under the auspices of the World Bank or the International Monetary Fund, which supervises international monetary matters.

It should also be noted that there could be a limit on the amount of cash that would be permitted to be exchanged at the time of a currency recall. Also, limits could be put on the amount of any bank transfers (checks) that could be written against the new deposits.

Implicit in the plan for an instantaneous recall and exchange is the possibility of a massive devaluation of the dollar — perhaps a four-to-one or a ten-to-one or even a one hundred-to-one exchange ratio. In this situation, an American's standard of living could fall overnight to a fraction of its former level due to our sudden inability to purchase imported goods of any kind!

Perhaps we will wake up one morning and find that our money has been destroyed through inflation and the banks have foreclosed on all property. The dollar, as we know it, could then be canceled and new money issued. But this new money would be an international money, controlled by computers.

Willard Cantelon, in his book, THE DAY THE DOLLAR

DIES, wrote concerning this group: "The world system will be praised and promoted by brilliant men. With elegance and apparent logic they will persuade men that this is the path to peace and security. The world leader will rise to power with flattery and gain complete control of the military and monetary powers of all nations." [9]

Quoting from NEWSWEEK, May 18, 1987, "A truly global economy has emerged. Major countries are tied together by financial, trade, and communications connections whose magnitude was barely imagined a few decades ago ... We don't fully understand all the interactions among nations, but most countries have clearly lost some control over their own affairs." [10]

On the cover of the respected journal, THE ECONOMIST, is a phoenix, rising from the ashes of burning world currencies. About its neck is a gold coin on a chain, imprinted with the words, "Ten Phoenix." The coin is dated in the year 2018. Significantly, the picture is entitled, "Get Ready for a World Currency." In the article accompanying the picture, the editors state their view that only a world currency can possibly heal the economic instability of today's world economy. The article ends with the statement, "Pencil in the phoenix for around 2018, and welcome it when it comes." [11]

Yes, a new world money system is inevitable. It was predicted in the prophecies of the Bible. Today, it is being planned and promoted by the money masters of the world.

Chapter Notes

CHAPTER 12

1. THE HOLY BIBLE, Revelation 13:16,17.
2. James Dines, INVISIBLE CRASH (New York: Ballantine), p. 5.
3. Gary Allen, NONE DARE CALL IT CONSPIRACY (Seal Beach, CA: Concord Press, 1972), p. 53.
4. Lindsey Williams, TO SEDUCE A NATION (Kasilof, Alaska: Worth Publishing Co., 1984), p. 217.
5. Ibid., p. 214.
6. Robert L. Preston, WAKE UP AMERICA (Hawkes Publishing Inc., 1972).
7. CHRISTIAN SCIENCE MONITOR, July 29, 1980.
8. "The Culpeper Connection," AMERICAN WAY, February, 1981, pp. 25-28.
9. Willard Cantelon, THE DAY THE DOLLAR DIES (Plainfield, NJ: Logos International, 1973), p. 145.
10. NEWSWEEK, May 18, 1987.
11. "Get Ready for the Phoenix," THE ECONOMIST, January 9, 1988, pp. 9-10.

Chapter 13

The United States of Europe

Prospects for the United States of Europe have now become a reality. On January 1, 1986, Spain and Portugal became the eleventh and twelfth members of the European Common Market. Either Austria or Turkey will be considered next. The establishment of the political arm of the unified confederation, the European Parliament, is now in place.

Joseph Lonz, former Secretary General of NATO said, "The slowly but steadily advancing unity of Europe is the most promising guarantee of our ideals of one world government." This is the ultimate goal of the European Common Market. Let's take a look at the history of the European Common Market — its formation, its framework, and its fruition as a fulfillment of Bible prophecy.

The European ideal for world government was first formed back in 1949, when the Council of Europe was established —

within a year after the organization of the state of Israel in 1948. A few years later, in 1951, the European Coal and Steel Community was organized in order to unify the coal, iron, and steel industries of the various countries of Belgium, France, Italy, Luxembourg, the Netherlands, and West Germany. These six nations set out to establish the European Economic Community and were successful in creating this new organization in 1957 — within a year of the Arab-Israeli conflict over the Gaza Strip.

The European Economic Community was created to begin removing barriers to the movement of goods, workers, capital, and services among its members. Also in 1957, the same six nations agreed to establish the European Atomic Energy Community to work together to develop atomic energy for peaceful uses. These six member nations became known as the European Community. Both the European Community and the European Economic Community adopted the name European Common Market in 1967, the year of the Six Day War in Israel.

Was it coincidence that the European Coal and Steel Community was organized after the Middle East war of 1948? Was it a coincidence that the European Community was established after the Middle East war of 1956-57, at the same time as the European Economic Community, which was also formed in 1957? And was it a coincidence that they just happened to merge their executive agencies to form a unified administrative system called the European Common Market during the year of another Middle East war — the Six-Day War of 1967?

The six original nations forming the European Common Market were Belgium, France, Italy, Luxembourg, the Netherlands, and West Germany. However, on January 1, 1973, the countries of Denmark, Ireland, and Great Britain became members of the European Common Market, bringing the total number to nine. Was this also a coincidence that it happened in 1973, the year of the Yom Kippur War in Israel? It seems that the formation of the European Economic Community has been woven around each war of Israel's recent history.

Early significant developments in the European Common Market have been made during the years which witnessed war in the Middle East — 1948, 1956, 1967, and 1973. The inclusion of Greece in 1981, along with Spain and Portugal in 1986, were coincidental to Israel's war in Lebanon in 1982-83. The next great development in the rise of this world government may be no different. The arrival of the antichrist could also be attended by war. Following World War I, politicians cried for a "League of Nations." After World War II, politicians cried for a "United Nations." It stands to reason, then, that with the next big war will come a cry for "World Government!"

1979 was the year the ECU (European Currency Unit), was established. The European Parliament was elected in June, 1979, and convened in January, 1980. Greece took its place as a member of the European Common Market on January 1, 1981, and Spain and Portugal joined in 1986. Turkey, or possibly Austria is now slated to become the thirteenth member in the near future. We believe the coming establishment of the "United States of Europe," slated for 1992, represents a revival of the Roman Empire predicted in the prophecies of the Bible. It is likely more than a coincidence that the treaty which was signed in 1957 organizing the European Common Market was called — the Treaty of Rome.

When Greece became the tenth member of the Common Market, it culminated 22 years of effort by Premier Constantine Caramanlis to join his country economically with Europe. A host of officials representing the nine European

Common Market nations, including French President Valery Giscard D'Estaing, were on hand for the glittering signing ceremonies in Athens. In addition to the signature of the French president, who was also then president of the European Common Market, four other premiers were present — Giulio Andreotti of Italy; Wilfried Martens of Belgium; Gaston Thorn of Luxembourg; and Jack Lynch of Ireland.

Eight foreign ministers of the European Common Market were also present to initial the treaty and the last one to sign was the 72-year-old premier of Greece, Constantine Caramanlis. In a voice quivering with emotion Caramanlis said, "I believe that the unification of Europe will be the most important political event in the history of our continent, an event which will effect not only the destiny of Europe, but the course of humanity as well, for it will even up the balance of power in the world. It will strengthen the independence of Europe and will contribute to the consolidation of world order and peace."

At no other time in history has such an alliance been formed which includes the countries once a part of the original Roman Empire. One of the most significant things about this confederation is that it now is comprised of twelve nations. According to Bible prophecy, this current alignment cannot continue. There are not twelve nations prophesied in the Bible, only ten. It is likely that two or more nations will withdraw from membership for some presently unknown reason.

The country of Turkey has also sought membership in the European Common Market. This too, cannot be, for Turkey is prophesied as confederated with Russia when she makes her invasion against Israel. That is found in Ezekiel 38:5. Turkey is referred to as the "house of Togarmah." Ezekiel 38:13 makes reference to the ten-nation confederation during the Battle of Gog and Magog. This European alliance is referred to as the "merchants of Tarshish." Notice, the use of the term "merchants" corresponds with the European ECONOMIC Community. It all revolves around money and commercial trade.

To contemplate the following possibility is truly exciting! At the time of this writing, Austria is considering its application for membership in the EEC. Austria may be considered to be "Europe's lucky 13th." If the EEC should accept Austria into the club, it would be a snub to Turkey, but the acceptance of Turkey, at this time, is not unanimous.

Austria is a natural for being the next (and probably last) member of the elite group. It is politically neutral and, in its own description, a "bridge between East and West." A fascinating scenario is currently developing! Could it be that Austria will be the 13th nation to join the eventual "ten-nation confederacy" spoken of by Daniel when he interpreted the dream of King Nebuchadnezzar in Daniel 2? Is it a coincidence that Austria would be the only nation in the European Economic Community (besides Spain) which had been ruled by a king of the Habsburg dynasty? Otto von Habsburg, although now an old man, is heir to the throne in Austria if a monarchy should ever be re-established. His son, Karl, is next in line. Could it be possible that the next nation to be admitted to the EEC would provide the "little horn" or eleventh king of Daniel 7:8 and 7:24?

"And the ten horns out of this kingdom are ten kings that shall arise: and another shall rise after them; and he shall be diverse from the first, and he shall subdue three kings" (Daniel 7:24).

We are living in the most exciting generation in the history of man. We are privileged to see the fulfillment of Bible prophecy as no other generation. We are witnessing the revival of the Roman Empire. Great theologians of past generations wrote about it and warned that it would come, but our generation has seen its formation. Long before there was a Roman Empire, the prophet Ezekiel wrote of its rise upon the world scene. He called them the merchants of Tarshish.

"Sheba and Dedan, and the merchants of Tarshish, with all the young lions thereof, shall say unto thee, Art thou come to take a spoil?..." (Ezekiel 38:13).

Sheba and Dedan are ancient names for the people who settled in present-day Saudi Arabia. The merchants of Tarshish referred to the European block and the term "young lions" is Ezekiel's way of describing the established colonies of Europe — among them must surely be the United States.

Tarshish was a great-grandson of Noah (Genesis 10:4). His descendants migrated to western Europe, which included the coasts of Spain and Great Britain. Later, Tarshish became the name of a biblical city on the southern coast of Spain. Yes, long before there was a Roman Empire, Europe's coastlands were populated by the merchants of Tarshish. Ezekiel mentions all the "young lions," or offspring, of the merchants of Tarshish. The fact that he calls them "young lions" tells me that the mother lion was eventually to become Great Britain, whose insignia is a lion. The young lions, then, could include the United States, Canada, Australia, New Zealand, and all the former colonies of Great Britain.

An inscription discovered in 1780, on a cliff above Mt. Hope Bay in Bristol, Rhode Island, contained an engraving written in Tartessian Punic. It read: "Voyagers from Tarshish this stone proclaims." The story of the discovery was published in "Reader's Digest," February, 1977. The inscription was believed to have been inscribed around 533 B.C. Harvard University's Department of Archaeology has found five locations within the continental United States where the merchants of Tarshish had colonies. Yet, Ezekiel wrote 2,500 years ago about this future empire. The merchants of Tarshish prophesied by Ezekiel hold the key to the fulfillment of end time Bible prophecy.

Now, let us examine these countries a little more closely. Sheba and Dedan refer to Saudi Arabia and indicate that it is a country to be allied with the West. Today, Saudi Arabia remains our friend, though Iran has become a radical Islamic Fundamentalist state under the regime of the fanatical Ayatollah Khomeini. Saudi Arabia continues to sell us oil. And though publicly, Saudi Arabia deplores the peace treaty between Israel and Egypt; privately, she continues her economic aid to Egypt. There are some fears today in political circles that Saudi Arabia will be next to fall into the Communist camp. But according to Bible prophecy, Saudi Arabia will remain friendly to the West. I believe they will continue to supply oil to Egypt, Europe, and the United States.

According to the Old Testament book of Daniel, chapter 2, a ten-nation confederation will arise out of the Roman Empire. The prophecy is given in a dream by Nebuchadnezzar, king of Babylon and then ruler of the world. In this dream there appeared the image of a giant man. The head was made of fine gold; his breast and arms were made of silver; his belly and thighs were made of brass; his legs were made of iron, and his feet were part of iron and part of clay. On the feet were ten toes, also made of iron and clay.

In the interpretation of the dream, Daniel referred to the head of gold as representing the Babylonian empire under Nebuchadnezzar. The breast and arms of silver represented the second world empire of Medo-Persia. The mid-section of brass represented the world empire of Greece under Alexander the Great. And the legs of iron were to represent the fourth world empire, Rome. The feet, mixed of iron and clay, were to represent the disintegration of the iron rule of Rome. And the ten toes of iron and clay represented the revival of the old Roman Empire by ten nations, which will keep their separate identities as nations, but will merge or confederate parts of their political structures to form a one-world economic union.

Nebuchadnezzar envisioned a stone cut out without hands which will smite the image upon its feet. That great smiting stone will be none other than the Lord Jesus Christ, who will judge the nations pictured in the ten toes of the vision and set up a world empire — a millennium ruled not by men, but by God. Quite a dream, isn't it?

This was Daniel's prophecy:

"And in the days of these kings shall the God of heaven set up a kingdom, which shall never be destroyed..." (Daniel 2:44).

Daniel was shown the vision of a great empire which would arise within the borders of the Roman Empire just seven years prior to Christ's final return. In verse 41 there is an interesting Scripture. It reads:

"And whereas thou sawest the feet and toes, part of potters' clay, and part of iron, the kingdom shall be divided ..." (Daniel 2:41).

For centuries the Roman Empire has been broken down. All attempts to revive it have failed. By the way, the riddle of "Humpty Dumpty" was written about the collapse of the great Roman Empire. Not until our generation has any fruitful effort been made to restore the empire. In the year of Israel's independence, 1948, the "Benelux Agreement" was signed, thus establishing the European Economic Community. All the king's horses and men, began putting Humpty Dumpty's Roman Empire together again.

Daniel had much more to say about this ten-nation confederation. In Daniel's prophecy (chapter 7), there is a further description of this last great world power. It is described in

Daniel 7:7 as a beast, dreadful and terrible, and strong exceedingly, and with great iron teeth. It will devour and break in pieces and will stamp the residue with its feet. The beast is described as having ten horns, which represent ten nations that will comprise this revived Roman Empire.

Daniel saw the rise of a great world ruler from among the ten nations. This "little horn" who rises up above the others is believed to be the predicted antichrist. With the arrival of this world ruler there will be a war — possibly the war of Gog and Magog. In the course of the battle, three of the ten nations will be destroyed. The scenario is portrayed in Revelation 13 and describes the creature as a beast with seven heads and ten horns. The passage indicates the possibility that Russia will invade Europe as well as the Middle East. The scriptures in Ezekiel 38 include the merchants of Tarshish, though the ancient prophet Ezekiel sees the battle from an Israeli point of view. The great seven-year period of tribulation may begin with seven nations that survive the Battle of Gog and Magog, with three European nations left in ashes.

The predicted monster is now here and has taken the form of the European Common Market. How do we know? One only needs to research the structure and goals of the European Common Market to find that the EEC plans to establish a one-world government with a one-world monetary system.

On March 13, 1979, Western Europe implemented the new European monetary system. The new European currency, commonly called the ECU, is now prepared for use in most of Europe, in accordance with biblical prophecy. The new European currency is designed to replace the dollar. According to an article in U.S. NEWS AND WORLD REPORT, our government is not interested in saving the value of our United States dollar. They are interested rather in converting to a new system — perhaps to the European currency.

"And he causeth all, both small and great, rich and poor, free and bond, to receive a mark in their right hand, or in their foreheads:

"And that no man might buy or sell, save he that had the mark, or the name of the beast, or the number of his name.

"Here is wisdom. Let him that hath understanding count the number of the beast: for it is the number of a man; and his number is Six hundred threescore and six" (Revelation 13:16-18).

According to this prophecy, members of the human race will one day have to submit to an engraving upon the flesh before they will be permitted to buy or sell. The currency unit at that time will require a number. How close are we to such a requirement?

According to reports, the European Economic Community's computer in Luxembourg, which they affectionately call "The Beast," has the capability of containing a brief history of every individual on earth. It can contain one's history, economic status, earning capability, all business transactions, and credit. According to reports, every person in the world will receive an identification number containing 18 digits — three sets of six numbers each. A sister computer has been built in St. Louis, Missouri, and is designed to be compatible with any brand computer on the market. Banks will be connecting their computers to the main computer sometime within the foreseeable future. Perhaps we are close to that day when the United States currency will be converted to the one-world monetary system of a computerized, cashless society.

The Burroughs Corporation announced that the Society for Worldwide Interbank has chosen them to extend the nation's system of computerization to an international system with the main switching station to be in Brussels and Luxembourg, the headquarters for the Common Market of Europe. The fact that computerized money is coming is unavoidable. The question is, when?

At a meeting of the European Common Market some years ago, the question was posed: What if some one person refuses to accept this new computerized, cashless currency? The answer from the rostrum was that the individual would not be able to buy or sell. The problem would soon be eliminated, of course, for that individual would simply starve to death.

The European Parliament (the community's legislative body), the Council of Ministers (the decision making body), and European Court of Justice (the judicial branch), were formed as the political arms of this powerful confederation. It is probable that we have witnessed the birth of the Revived Roman Empire described in the book of the Revelation, chapter 13.

By the end of 1992, according to the plans of European Commission President Jacques Delors, Europe will have arrived at complete unity. It will share common economic goals and a common currency, as well as a common defense and social policies. The goal of the European Community is the creation of a Europe without national rivalries — a Europe that will become a top competitor on the world market.

Will all this come to pass on schedule? In spite of the momentum and the many dialogues among top European leaders, no one really knows. There is, in fact, much cultural resistance to such a merger, in addition to the natural language barriers and social prejudices. Jacques Medecin, the Mayor of Nice, France, was recently quoted as saying, "In December of 1492, Europe discovered America, and 500 years later Europe must still discover itself."

French Finance Minister, Edouard Balladur, proposed the concept of forming a European central bank, in the hope of putting the matter on Western Europe's economic and political agenda. "The moment has come," said Mr. Balladur, "to examine the possibility of creating a European central bank that would manage a common currency."

Among certain groups in Western Europe, pressure is steadily increasing for the organization of a central bank. The current morass of money changing bureaucracies, border delays, and reduced ability to compete in the world market has convinced most economists that Europe's only answer is to adopt a common currency. Europe has long been known in the world market as a loose collection of wildly fluctuating, separate economic policies. In recent years, however, the nations of Europe have converged their monetary policies, generally following the lead of Germany's conservative Bundesbank. As a result, they have created an arena of monetary stability in Europe.

Commenting on the movement toward a central bank of Europe, the editors of the June 25, 1988, ECONOMIST wrote, "The limit of such convergence in monetary policy is to adopt a common currency. If governments do that, they surrender national monetary control altogether and replace it with a uniform, region-wide policy ... And a common European currency allied with free internal trade would merge EEC member countries into a unit economically indivisible as America's united states."

The ECONOMIST speculates that 1992 is the most likely year to look for such a union, based on an agreement now in force among the nations of Europe. That agreement centers around 1990, when all but four members of the European Economic Community have promised to do away with their current capital controls. Money will then be free to flow anywhere within the Community's borders, ultimately allowing Europe to receive the full benefits of free trade.

By 1992, the European Monetary System should be in full force, with its own currency. A Central Bank of Europe will be in full control of monetary policy. The European Currency Unit features a portrait of Charles V, (Habsburg) Emperor of the Holy Roman Empire (1519-56). The Holy Roman Empire is considered a forerunner of the United Europe, now known as the European Economic Community.

On the cover of the January 9, 1988, ECONOMIST, an eagle — the symbol of the Roman Empire, is pictured standing on a bonfire, fueled by the various currencies of the world. The headline reads, "Get Ready for a World Currency." The eagle is wearing the crown of a European monarch, and around its neck is the coin of a new One-world currency. It is called a phoenix. It may look like an eagle, but is referred to as a phoenix — the legendary bird who dies, only to re-emerge

from its flames with new life.

The eagle was the symbol of most of the monarchies of Europe as well as the Roman Empire. But the Roman Empire fell apart. The Holy Roman Empire also disintegrated. Over the last two centuries, the monarchies of Europe have also lost their political power. Now comes the announcement that a new world power will emerge out of the ashes — just like the legendary phoenix.

But, in the book of the Revelation, the final form of world government predicted to emerge from the ashes of the Roman Empire is given the symbol of a dragon — a winged dragon with 7 heads and 10 horns.

Could the eagle and the dragon somehow be related? The symbol of the Holy Roman Empire was a two-headed eagle, while the symbol of Revelation is a seven-headed dragon. Are they the same creature? A partial answer to the riddle can be seen in Revelation, chapter 4, where John saw four living creatures around the throne of God. Theologians have written that they depict the four major constellations of the heavens.

"The first beast was like a lion, and the second beast like a calf, and the third beast had a face as a man, and the fourth beast was like a flying eagle" (Revelation 4:6).

These creatures represent the major constellations in the four quadrants of the zodiac. The lion is typical of the constellation Leo. The calf is typical of the constellation Taurus. The man is typical of the constellation Aquarius. And the eagle replaces the constellation Scorpio. Scorpio, in the ancient Egyptian zodiac, was a many-headed serpent. Why did the eagle replace the serpent or dragon? And why is the eagle called a phoenix?

While visiting in Korea, I went to the palaces of the Lee Dynasty. A young Korean lady guided our group through the grounds which covered over 100 acres. I saw the royal

audience hall and throne with its ornate designs. In the ceiling above the throne was a picture of two winged dragons trying to eat a disk — from which emitted streams of fire. The Korean guide explained that these creatures were called phoenix. She said that in the West, the phoenix was depicted by an eagle, but in the East, the phoenix was pictured as a dragon. I heard her say, "They are the same creature." These two symbols of the ancient tribe of Dan are really the same creature!

The revival of the Roman Empire is more than a dream. It is a reality, whose time seems to have arrived. It has already begun as an economic union. It will end as a spiritual abomination. But in its rudimentary form, it may be observed today as it swiftly rises to world prominence.

There is a great deal of movement among European political figures to bring back the powerful days of that great empire. Today, Europe's royal families are quietly putting in place the foundation stones of a new united Europe.

In February, 1987, young Archduke Karl von Habsburg was on a speaking tour in the United States. This young man is a future leader of Europe with a plan. His goal is, "... the creation of a European federation that would be occupied with the things that the individual nations are not able to solve — problems of economy, agriculture, security, and foreign affairs." [1]

The young Habsburg was quoted as saying that the International Pan-European Movement, of which he is the youngest board member, has been around since 1921, when a small number of European aristocrats saw a unification as the only way to avoid another war like the one that had just devastated the continent.

"The idea was well received by the elite," he said, "but support never went beyond that."

World War II temporarily halted the movement, which remained dormant until 1973, when Karl's father, Archduke Otto von Habsburg became its leader.

Karl stated, "My father decided the only way the movement was going to be able to succeed was to make it a mass movement rather than an elite movement. That strategy has turned out very well. We now have branches in all European countries and 180,000 members."

Habsburg reportedly sees the foundation of the European Economic Community in the 1950's as the first step toward European unification.

"The creation of the European Parliament in 1979 was even more significant," he said. "True, its power is only budgetary at this point, but history shows that power flows toward that which controls the purse strings."

The young Habsburg was described as "exuding confidence" that his dream would one day be a reality. "Of that, I'm absolutely sure," he said. (See last paragraph, page 96.)

The European Parliament is a loose confederation of trading partners, which currently operates only in an advisory capacity. However, it seems to be the foreshadowing of the United States of Europe, which would join into an economic and legislative structure of enormous power. The initial stage of this unification is currently set for 1992. According to Scripture, the antichrist will emerge from such a confederation.

Daniel 9:26 and 27 tell of this time: *"... and the people of the prince that shall come shall destroy the city and the sanctuary; and the end thereof shall be with a flood, and unto the end of the war desolations are determined. And he shall confirm the covenant with many for one week: and in the midst of the week he shall cause the sacrifice and the oblation to cease ..."*

The *"prince that shall come"* (the antichrist) is shown as a descendant of those who destroyed Jerusalem in A.D. 70. If the current effort to unify Europe constitutes a revival of the empire, it is likely that he will come from there.

Chapter Notes

CHAPTER 13

1. "Archduke says unified Europe is a certainty," COLUMBUS DIS-
PATCH, February 8, 1987, p. 1D.

The
Magdalene
Connection

Chapter 14

Are We MYSTERY BABYLON?

How does the United States fit into the prophetic picture? If this should be the last generation and if the Second Coming of Christ is near, then why should the prophets fail to include the greatest industrial, military, economic, and political power ever to emerge among the family of nations?

If America is included in Bible prophecy, then where? By what names were we called? There was no United States of America in existence when Jeremiah and Ezekiel penned their prophecies. Our nation did not exist when John wrote the Revelation. If those two great prophets were allowed to look into the far future, to the days of the return of Israel, to the days of a Russian military development, and to the days of Armageddon, could they have failed to see the role the United States would play? If their visions included the United States, how can we tell?

Some suggest that the United States is made up of the ten lost tribes of Israel — that the northern tribes migrated into Europe and from there to the United States. I find that theory impossible to accept. I believe when God speaks of Israel in the end time, He is referring directly to the land of Israel and to the returned Jewish people. So, we are left with the probing question, "Where is the United States in prophecy?"

The term, "United States" was not used by the prophets, probably because our nation did not exist at the time. This may have been one reason why symbolism was used in the Bible — not to confuse, but to identify. Symbols are much more readily understood in the Middle East than in our Western culture. Daniel recorded a vision which may shed some light on the use of symbols. Furthermore, his vision may contain a prophetic reference to the United States. Daniel wrote:

"The first was like a lion, and had eagle's wings: I beheld till the wings thereof were plucked, and it was lifted up from the earth, and made stand upon the feet as a man, and a man's heart was given to it" (Daniel 7:4).

This vision culminates in the Second Coming of Christ. The symbols of animals could represent the leading nations of that last generation. The lion could represent Great Britain. Notice, in this passage the lion had eagle's wings. Daniel wrote, *"I beheld till the wings thereof were plucked ..."*

If the lion represents Great Britain, then the eagle's wings plucked from the back of the lion may represent the United States, whose symbol is that of an eagle with outstretched wings. In the vision, the eagle's wings were plucked from the back of the lion, and in like manner the United States was freed from British rule through the Revolutionary War of 1776. Here then, is one possible indication of the United States in prophecy.

There is another possibility in Ezekiel 38:13. The chapter

gives a prophetic picture of the Russian invasion of Israel. In verse 13 we have a list of nations who will rebuke the mighty Magog:

"Sheba, and Dedan, and the merchants of Tarshish, with all the young lions thereof, shall say unto thee, Art thou come to take a spoil? Hast thou gathered thy company to take a prey?"

Sheba and Dedan are ancient names for the people who populate modern Saudi Arabia. The merchants of Tarshish (as we mentioned before) seem to refer to the nations of Europe. Even more distinctly, they are called *"merchants,"* indicative of the European Common Market. They could represent a ten-nation confederation of the revived Roman Empire.

There is another group listed in verse 13, namely *"the young lions"* of the merchants of Tarshish. The symbol of the young lions refers to the offspring, or colonies, established by the merchants of Tarshish.

Harvard University's Department of Archaeology has found five locations within our continental United States where the merchants of Tarshish had established colonies during the days of Ezekiel — 2,500 years ago.

The United States may be found in the prophecies of Ezekiel and become involved when Russia makes her military move into the Middle East. Though the United States is not mentioned by name, the nation may be included through the use of symbols.

Two small references, however, do not seem to be enough for the nation which has been involved in our planet's two greatest world wars and whose industrial base has provided the military hardware which may fuel the flames of Armageddon.

Being a patriotic citizen, I would much rather write about the good of our country than the bad. My heart still leaps when I see the flag and hear the national anthem. God has blessed

America during these past two centuries because the nation was founded upon the principles of the Word of God. "In God We Trust" is found on our nation's currency and coin, and is indicative of our historic faith in God.

But, let us consider the possibility that the U.S. could represent a major factor within the pages of prophecy. Among all of the nations mentioned in the Bible as existing in the last days, there is one which seems to stand out above the others. It is not given a name as other nations; rather, it is simply called "MYSTERY, BABYLON THE GREAT" — not Babylon as was known in the days of Daniel, Jeremiah, and Ezekiel, but a MYSTERY, a nation prominent among the nations of the world in the last days, and a nation which shall be destroyed during the Tribulation Period.

According to the Revelation account, a detailed portrait is given of that future BABYLON which will be destroyed:

"And there came one of the seven angels which had the seven vials, and talked with me, saying unto me, Come hither; I will shew unto thee the judgment of the great whore that sitteth upon many waters:

"With whom the kings of the earth have committed fornication, and the inhabitants of the earth have been made drunk with the wine of her fornication.

"So he carried me away in the spirit into the wilderness: and I saw a woman sit upon a scarlet coloured beast, full of names of blasphemy, having seven heads and ten horns.

"And the woman was arrayed in purple and scarlet colour, and decked with gold and precious stones and pearls, having a golden cup in her hand full of abominations and filthiness of her fornication:

"And upon her forehead was a name written, MYSTERY, BABYLON THE GREAT, THE MOTHER OF HARLOTS AND ABOMINATIONS OF THE EARTH" (Rev. 17:1-5).

MYSTERY, BABYLON THE GREAT! She has remained a mystery to Bible scholars down through the centuries, though many have tried to discover her identity. The beast upon which she sits may be identified as the ten-nation confederation of the revived Roman Empire. But MYSTERY BABYLON uses those ten nations as a vehicle upon which to rise to power. She appears to control the direction and provide the motivation for those ten nations.

BABYLON THE GREAT, then, may not be a part of the European group of nations. It may represent a nation who is in control of those nations. The United States today certainly fills that role. European nations are indebted to the United States for their very existence. Their economic and industrial growth has been funded by the United States. During World War II, those European nations were under the heel of Hitler. Had it not been for the United States of America, Europe might still be trying to dig out from under that cataclysmic war.

Also in the Revelation account, a description is given of the destruction of BABYLON THE GREAT and of the nations who bewail her burning:

"And the kings of the earth, who have committed fornication and lived deliciously with her, shall bewail her, and lament for her, when they shall see the smoke of her burning.

"Standing afar off for the fear of her torment, saying, Alas, alas, that great city BABYLON, that mighty city! for in one hour is thy judgment come.

"And the merchants of the earth shall weep and mourn over her; for no man buyeth their merchandise any more" (Revelation 18:9-11).

The economic progress of the entire world will be due to BABYLON THE GREAT. The nations have enjoyed the prosperity afforded by her natural resources, her industrial achievements, and the strength of her currency.

How fitting is the picture! It could be a description of the United States, which has made the nations rich with her goods! The strength of the dollar is the strength of the industrialized nations. When confidence in the dollar is shaken, confidence in every currency in the world is shaken.

Primarily, BABYLON is a city, but in the Bible, cities often represent nations. Today, the most renowned city in the world is New York City. Wall Street rules the economic world. At the United Nations, representatives from around the world come to resolve their differences.

There are some who say that the United Nations Building is a modern "Tower of Babel." It may also be interesting to note that the term "New York" has a numerical value of 666. How is that, you may ask? Let me explain. Take the English alphabet and add the number six (the biblical number of man) to each succeeding letter of the alphabet. Then calculate the numerical value of "New York" and arrive at that conclusion.

According to that method, the letter "A" would equal 6; "B" would equal 12; "C" = 18; "D" = 24; "E" = 30; etc.

A=6	H=48	O=90	V=132
B=12	I=54	P=96	W=138
C=18	J=60	Q=102	X=144
D=24	K=66	R=108	Y=150
E=30	L=72	S=114	Z=156
F=36	M=78	T=120	
G=42	N=84	U=126	

Adding up the letters in the words "New York": the letter "N" equals 84; the letter "E" = 30; the letter "W" = 138; the letter "Y" = 150; the letter "O" = 90; the letter "R" = 108; and the letter "K" = 66 — for a combined total of 666.

N	=	84
E	=	30
W	=	138
Y	=	150
O	=	90
R	=	108
K	=	66
		——
		666

Using ancient pagan, or occult numerology, a similar result is obtained. From our study in Chapter 4, by assigning a number value for each letter and then combining the digits to arrive at a single digit value, "New" equals 555 and "York" equals 7692.

NEW   YORK,   NEW   YORK
———— ————   ———— ————
5 5 5 7 6 9 2 5 5 5 7 6 9 2
 15   24   15   24
  6   6   6   6
            24
             6

Such evidence is not conclusive, but at least seems to point to the possibility. Furthermore, you might take a look at a map of New York City. Located right on the eastern edge of the city along the southern shore of Long Island, there is a suburb called Babylon, New York.

BABYLON THE GREAT — is it possible that the prophets made reference to the United States? Dr. S. Franklin Logsdon in his book, IS THE U.S.A. IN PROPHECY? goes into further detail. He has compared the prophecies of BABYLON recorded by Jeremiah with certain characteristics of modern America:

"It is not our purpose ... to render a verdict or to finalize a conclusion, but simply to adduce evidence."

I agree with Dr. Logsdon that we cannot be dogmatic on this subject, but like him, I would have you consider Jeremiah's prophetic scenario:

1. Jeremiah 50:12:

"Your mother shall be sore confounded ..."

In this prophecy against BABYLON, Jeremiah referred to a *"mother"* nation. Dr. Logsdon suggested that historic Babylon did not have a mother. The city was built by Nimrod.

Babylon, the capital of Babylonia, situated on the Euphrates, was one of the largest and most splendid cities of the ancient world some 1,600 years before the Christian era and was almost entirely destroyed in 683 B.C.

A new city was then built by Nebuchadnezzar nearly 100 years later. This city was taken by Cyrus in 538 B.C., and Babylonia became a Persian province. Then came Alexander the Great and the famous city fast declined. It is possible that Jeremiah's prophecy did not concern ancient Babylon, which did not have a mother nation.

On the other hand, should the United States be the end time nation in view in this prophecy, then Britain, by the simplest deduction, would be the mother, and, to be sure, today Britain is *"sore confounded."* The word confounded in this verse means "to pale, to become dry, or to lose strength."

On January 16, 1968, United Press International released an article entitled "The Nightfall of an Empire." It read, "Britain yesterday abandoned her role as a world power. British Prime Minister Wilson's announcement before the House of Commons came after more than 31 hours of agonizing soul searching by the British Cabinet."

This political *"mother"* nation paled as Jeremiah indicated: *"Your mother shall be sore confounded ..."*

2. Jeremiah 51:7:

"BABYLON hath been a golden cup in the Lord's hand, that made all the earth drunken: the nations have drunken of her wine; therefore the nations are mad."

These words seem to indicate that this prophesied nation (spiritual BABYLON) is a country which has been exceptionally blessed of God. However, the *"golden cup"* in the Lord's hand is in the past tense. The nation mightily used of God had become so debauched that the nations (according to Logsdon) have been made drunken with her wine.

3. Jeremiah 50:37:

"A sword is upon their horses, and upon their chariots, and upon all the mingled people that are in the midst of her ..."

The nation in view consists of a *"mingled people."* The country is cosmopolitan in character. How very indicative of our country which has been called the "Melting Pot of the World."

4. Jeremiah 51:13:

"O thou that dwellest upon many waters, abundant in treasures, thine end is come, and the measure of thy covetousness."

Dr. Logsdon suggested that the description could hardly fit the empire of ancient Babylon. The city was situated on the banks of the Euphrates River with its southern-most point touching the Persian Gulf. The description in Jeremiah 51:13 seems to be indicative of the United States with the Atlantic Ocean along our eastern coast, the Pacific Ocean along our western coast, and the Gulf of Mexico to our south. *"O thou that dwellest upon many waters ..."*

5. Another description is given in Jeremiah 50:23:

"How is the hammer of the whole earth cut asunder and broken!"

Consider the word *"hammer."* The verb form means "to for-

mulate, to shape, or to create as if by hammer strokes; to force
or drive as if by repeated blows; to overpower, to overwhelm,
or to rule by persistent force or influence."

The word *"hammer,"* while referring to force or power,
does not indicate destructiveness. A hammer is not catego-
rized as a weapon, but rather as a tool. The hammer of
diplomacy, for instance, can register telling blows when
wielded by a great political power. Could that be a description
of the United States?

Dr. Logsdon suggested that the omniscient God looked
down through the corridors of time and saw the nation, which
He is here describing as wielding the greatest influence of any
country, the hammer of the whole earth. The United States has
unquestionably held that distinction.

6. Another description is given in Jeremiah 51:55:

*"Because the Lord hath spoiled BABYLON, and destroyed
out of her the great voice; when her waves do roar like great
waters, a noise of their voice is uttered."*

Jeremiah described MYSTERY BABYLON as speaking
with a *"great voice."* He indicates that her pronouncements
gained wide attention, that her suggestions could tip the
balance in the direction of her wishes, that her voice was
prestigiously regarded.

If the Bible quotation concerning the great voice should
point to the United States, then let it be said with patriotic
pride, her *"voice"* has been one, for the most part, of honor.
Our leaders have sat at the conference table with warring
nations in an effort to bring peace to our planet. We can be
thankful for that.

7. Yet another description was given in Jeremiah 51:53:

*"Though BABYLON should mount up to heaven, and though
she should fortify the height of her strength..."*

Ancient Babylon was never able to mount up to heaven,

though she may have tried to do so in the construction of the Tower of Babel. But the United States has *"mounted up to heaven."* We have sent our rocket ships to other planets and have put our men on the moon.

Again and again, the descriptions of Jeremiah's BABYLON lend themselves to the hour in which we live. Is the United States the MYSTERY BABYLON of the Bible? I don't know, but if it is, then we must remember that God has promised to judge her, for she is a wayward nation. That great woman called MYSTERY BABYLON is destined to be destroyed.

8. John, the Revelator, wrote:

"And the ten horns which thou sawest upon the beast, these shall hate the whore, and shall make her desolate and naked, and shall eat her flesh, and burn her with fire.

"For God hath put in their hearts to fulfill his will, and to agree, and give their kingdom unto the beast, until the words of God shall be fulfilled.

"And the woman which thou sawest is that great city, which reigneth over the kings of the earth" (Revelation 17:16-18).

If those ten nations represented by the beast are indeed the ten-nation confederation of the European Common Market, and if that great city which reigns over the kings of the earth be New York City, then we have a bizarre picture of Europe turning against the United States. Can you imagine New York City being destroyed by fire at the hands of Europe?

9. John adds an admonition to the Jewish people living in BABYLON THE GREAT:

"And I heard another voice from heaven, saying, Come out of her, my people, that ye be not partakers of her sins, and that ye receive not of her plagues" (Revelation 18:4).

"Come out of her my people ..." What people? In the middle of the Tribulation Period the only people who could possibly be described as God's people would be the Jews. Today, more

Jews live in New York City than live in the entire nation of Israel. As many Jews live in New York City as live in the entire country of Russia. More Jews live in New York City than in any other one area in the world.

In the midst of the Tribulation Period, when BABYLON is about to be destroyed, the cry goes forth, *"Come out of her, my people."*

The resulting war may offer the oportunity for the antichrist to move his throne to Jerusalem. He will enter the Jewish sanctuary established on Mount Moriah, will set up his throne in the Holy of Holies, and proclaim himself to be God. This is called in the Bible the "abomination of desolation." Then will begin the Great Tribulation, the last three and one-half years of God's judgment on unbelieving mankind.

MYSTERY BABYLON! Is it the United States? Down through the centuries, the MYSTERY BABYLON of Revelation 17 has been thought to refer to Rome and may, indeed. However, Dr. Logsdon has suggested the possible alternative that she could be the United States. Well, it may not be long until the mystery is solved.

Chapter 15

Death by Suicide

"The citizens chafe impatiently at the least touch of authority and at length they cease to care even for the laws, written or unwritten. And this is the fair and glorious beginning out of which springs tyranny. The excessive increase of anything causes a reaction in the opposite direction. Dictatorship naturally arises out of democracy and the most aggravated form of tyranny and slavery out of the most extreme form of liberty" (Socrates).

That sounds like our society today. Human nature has not changed in 2,000 years. Socrates wrote that society naturally "progresses" to a point where it does not respect authority or the laws of that society. He defined this condition as the beginning of tyranny. He also explained that if people receive an excessive amount of anything — including liberty — it will cause a reaction in the opposite direction. The United States of

America is not immune to world diseases and the disease of sin is just as prevalent here as anywhere in the world — perhaps more so!

Dictators rise into power through national emergencies. In the past, the wrong kind of leader has often risen to power through the misguided hopes of a desperate people. It does not take a large political organization to catapult the man with the answers into power. Adolf Hitler started with only a handful of men. He skillfully and deceitfully set the stage for his own rise to power. It was Adolf Hitler who said, "The streets of our country are in turmoil. The universities are filled with students rioting and rebelling. Communists are seeking to destroy our country, and the republic is in danger. Yes, danger from within and without. We need law and order. Without law and order our nation cannot survive."

Each one of history's dictators has been a champion of some particular cause popular with the people. Like Hitler, Lenin, Mao, and other dictators before them, every dictator seems to be obsessed with ridding his country of political corruption, lawlessness, the hoarding of wealth by a minority, and other immoral forces which work against social order. That's not such a bad idea when you first think about it. Any man who is able to rid his country of corruption certainly deserves to be heard. But that's how a dictator rises to power — on the crest of a wave of popularity. After the dictator takes over the reins of government, the people learn — too late — that his policies are bad for the people and the country.

A dictatorship in its extreme form is total government. All freedoms are removed from the people and every aspect of life comes under the scrutiny of some bureaucracy. Some dictators have been elected to office only to usurp additional power and authority. Then they remain in power through their own decree, and elections become a thing of the past.

Now the question: Could it happen in the United States of America? Is it possible that a nation built on the electoral process could fall into the hands of a dictator? We know that one day, perhaps soon, a world leader will rise to power whom the Bible calls the antichrist. He will attempt to establish a world government and although his prestige and political power will be worldwide, he will not be elected to his office:

"And in his estate shall stand up a vile person to whom they shall not give the honor of the kingdom, but he shall come in peaceably and obtain the kingdom by flatteries" (Daniel 11:21).

Is it possible to imagine that the office of President of the United States could be filled by one who is not elected? One who will usurp the authority of the office? Well, it is possible to have both a President and a Vice-President who are not elected by the American people. If it happened once, as in the mid-1970's, it can happen again. When Spiro Agnew resigned as Vice-President back in the early 1970's, Gerald Ford was appointed to the post. Then when Richard Nixon resigned as President, Mr. Ford automatically moved up to the Presidency. Nelson Rockefeller was then appointed Vice-President to fill the vacancy left by Ford. Suddenly, without the consent of the American people, we had a President and a Vice-President who were not elected.

Today, the President of the United States has emergency powers that can enable him to seize personal property such as businesses, homes, cars, and other assets, all in the interest of national security. President Franklin Roosevelt proclaimed a state of emergency when dealing with the Great Depression. President Harry Truman proclaimed a state of emergency at the outbreak of the Korean War. President Nixon declared two states of national emergency: one — to bring an end to the Postal Service employees' strike in 1970 and two — to end several trade agreements a year later. These are only a few examples.

There are, in fact, 470 provisions of federal law which serve, among other things, to give the President literal dictatorial powers. But could such a thing be done today? Are our politicians so determined and our nation so gullible as to allow such things? Let us consider just such a possibility.

As the 1940's ended, the United States hit its peak and possessed a much greater percentage of the world's riches than at any other time in its history. During this period America had three times as much in gold reserves as the entire rest of the world. We produced 60% of the world's steel and drove 73% of the world's cars and trucks. We produced 51% of all the gasoline used around the world and owned 67% of all the telephones on earth. Americans owned a much higher ratio of radios, refrigerators, freezers, washers, air conditioners, and other luxury items than any other people on earth.

In productive capacity we far out-stripped all others. In technical know-how we were in a league by ourselves. America was the greatest, a giant among pygmies, and the rest of the world looked on in awe and held the United States in high esteem.

In the years since then, something has gone terribly wrong. Now, instead of the nations of the world being at America's feet, most of them appear to be at America's throat. When one looks objectively and analytically at the America of the 1940's and compares it with the America we see today, the contrast is staggering and rather frightening. One is prompted to ask, "What is America trying to do, commit suicide?" For truly, America is being weighed in the balance and found wanting.

In the United States today people have more money, more freedom, more opportunities, more privileges, and more luxuries than any nation in history, and yet, paradoxically, they are among the most mixed up and unhappy people on earth.

I read an editorial some years ago that appeared in newspapers across America. I have long since misplaced its source, but here is what it said:

"We are overpopulated, undercivilized, divided, corrupted, and bewildered; destitute of faith and terrified of skepticism. War, crime, pollution, racial tension, political cynicism, and pessimism are our companions.

"The spectacle of this great nation which does not know its own mind is as humiliating as it is dangerous. America's allies around the world are deeply concerned about what is happening to this country and curiously question the ability of the United States to deal effectively with any of its major problems. Thirty years ago, the image which America projected to the world was one of a colossally powerful, vibrantly alive, fantastically rich and benevolent giant who could confidently be trusted to lead the world through the challenges of the future. However, in the process of time, that image has become tarnished, dented, chipped, smashed, and broken.

"Our new image around the world is one of a lumbering, stumbling, bumbling, grumbling dolt, who staggers from one crisis to another through a blinding haze of fear and indecision. It is one of a dissipated giant who throws crumbs (bought with borrowed money) to his neighbors in order to keep them out of his hair while he engages in a mammoth orgy of crime and violence. It is the image of a terribly sick giant, who, having exchanged his God-given Christian heritage for a bowl of atheistic, socialistic pottage, has lost his sense of destiny and has purged his mind of any trace of morality."

The late J. Edgar Hoover, who headed up our Federal Bureau of Investigation for some 50 years, made this statement shortly before his death: "Whether we like it or not, the morals to which we subscribe as a people are vital for our survival as a free nation. Concerned citizens are beginning to wonder if we may not be in grave danger of rejecting those things which are the source of our nation's strength. Are we entering an age that must end in anarchy? Are we rearing a generation almost wholly lacking in self-discipline? In short, do we deserve our magnificent inheritance? Are we good enough to preserve the great republic to which we have pledged our allegiance? Will we retain the capacity to do our duty as Americans?"

A former police chief of Los Angeles, Chief Parker, also expressed pessimism about the future of our society. He said that he was very much concerned about the way in which things are going: "It is very hard for me to believe that our society can continue to violate all the fundamental rules of human conduct and expect to survive. I think that I have to conclude that this civilization will destroy itself as others have done before it. This leaves only one question — when?"

President Abraham Lincoln gave a speech in Springfield, Illinois, in January, 1837. He took note of the future with great clarity of vision and insight. He recognized that no foreign power or combination of foreign powers "... could by force take a drink from the Ohio or make a track on the Blue Ridge ... At what point, then, is the approach of danger to be expected?" Lincoln said, "If it ever reach us, it must spring from among us, it cannot come from abroad. If destruction be our lot, we must ourselves be its author and finisher. As a nation of freedom, we must live through all time or die of suicide."

President Lincoln clearly understood that the only real danger facing the American nation as it marched into the future was the corrupting of its people, or what has been called "the subverting of the American spirit."

When the United States entered the 20th century, it was basically sound. It throbbed with life and vitality. Most people were deeply patriotic, loved their country, and lived by a definite standard of morality. They respected their country, their neighbor, and themselves. The home and family were held in high esteem. Men were masculine, women were feminine, and both sexes were content with their natural role and God-given responsibilities. In the years since then, all of these pillars of sound society have been eroding away, and we have now reached the point where the average person is left without a set of clearly defined principles by which to run his life. They are left floundering on the quicksand of doubt, fear, and indecision.

As one person put it, "A nation which stands for nothing will fall for anything." The result? The fruit is all around us for everyone to see. Look at any phase or facet of society. You will see chronic diseases gnawing away relentlessly at the nation's vitals. The true state of a nation is reflected in its leading institutions. It is reflected in education and in the churches, in literature and music, in government and in the home. And it is mirrored in the financial mess in which the government and most individuals find themselves.

What went wrong? Who has turned the American dream into the American nightmare? What has come over us? What are the causes for the effects which we see all around us in the world? Our homes and families are falling apart with blind, shattering rapidity. Our schools and colleges spawn alienated, frustrated, venereal diseased pill-poppers whose lives are wrapped up in doing their own thing.

Our courts force law abiding citizens to lock themselves up in their homes and apartments at night while criminals are allowed to roam the streets almost at will to terrorize the populace. Governments grow and grow and grow while they tax and tax and tax and spend and spend and spend while the nation groans under an awesome, mind-boggling national debt nearing $3,000,000,000,000. Throughout all strata of society — lying, deceit, graft, corruption, and hypocrisy are the order of the day.

Over the past 20 years there have been some men of insight who tried to warn us of our approaching dilemma, but it seemed that nobody was willing to listen. The politicians certainly would not listen, and the American public wanted to stick its head in the sand, like the proverbial ostrich, in hopes that the problem would go away. Many preachers during the early 1960's cried from their pulpits for national revival. When the Supreme Court, on June 25, 1962, eliminated prayer and Bible reading from the American classroom, preachers everywhere became alarmed. We tried to warn our nation of the result, but no one would listen. We were accused of being right-wing extremists crying "wolf" when not many could see the wolf.

Across our nation, ministers began to establish Christian schools while at the same time others were becoming involved with conservative political organizations. Bus ministries began to pick up millions of children all across America and bring them to Sunday School in an effort to salvage the young minds of our youth from the humanistic and socialistic values they were being taught five days a week in the public schools. But alas, the nation would not listen, for most people were too busy going to the lake on Sunday instead of recognizing that there is a God in heaven who is concerned in the affairs of men.

It has been said by some that it is not the responsibility of, nor is it proper for, Christians to be involved in upholding America's traditional values or speaking out on moral issues. Today's churches are lowering their standards in a foolish attempt to accommodate the world and its philosophy. The sin of complacency, apathy, and lukewarmness of which we Christians are so guilty today has allowed the godless atheists and humanists to have a free reign in society, even in many churches.

Presumably, very little thought has been given to admonitions offered us throughout the Bible, such as Matthew 5:13: *"Ye are the salt of the earth."* Salt preserves and seasons. Matthew 5:14: *"Ye are the light of the world."* Light overcomes darkness. Proverbs 29:2: *"When the righteous are in authority, the people rejoice, but when the wicked beareth rule, the people mourn."* It was Edmund Burke who once said, "The only thing necessary for the triumph of evil is for good men to do nothing."

For over 20 years conservative organizations have begged our politicians not to overspend our nation's budget. But alas, no one would listen. This is one reason why our dollar is in danger of dying. Back in 1973, the Arab nations began to raise the price of oil. Suddenly, we found long lines waiting at the gas pump in every major city in America. President Gerald Ford assessed the energy crisis at that time. He said, "It is difficult to discuss the energy problem without lapsing into doomsday language. The danger is clear. It is severe. No one can foresee the extent of the damage or the end of the disastrous consequences if nations refuse to share their natural resources for the benefit of all mankind."

At that time our politicians promised that in the years ahead our nation would set upon a course to become energy-independent of foreign oil. The Alaskan pipeline was finished and oil began to flow into the United States from the far regions of the north. Did our leaders follow through with their promise? That oil reaching our West Coast from the Alaskan pipeline has been and is being loaded onto ships and exported to other countries. Meanwhile, our nation has been allowed to become even more dependent upon Arab oil.

In December, 1974, Edward Teller, the father of the American hydrogen bomb, gave an address before the United Nations. At that time he expressed his fears that the energy crisis brought on by the Middle East war of 1973-74 could lead to dictatorship. He said, "The financial disorder triggered by the energy crisis has not yet run its course. Its ultimate consequences might be as disastrous or more disastrous than that of the Great Depression. Let us remember that it was this depression that brought Hitler to the helm in Germany and as such is the cause of the Second World War."

Did you comprehend that? Edward Teller said that World War II was brought on by the Stock Market Crash of 1929. The monetary crisis of Wall Street, U.S.A. created reverberations in every country of the world. Watch out, America! It could happen again! And this time, it could lead to Armageddon.

Chapter 16

The New Age Movement

A popular song some years ago declared, "This is the dawning of the Age of Aquarius." What did the authors of the song have in mind when they wrote and sang of the so-called New Age Movement? It seems to be some kind of a new revolution which is quietly taking over planet Earth. Its goal is to establish a new, one-world government, along with an economic system designed to make all human beings one big happy brotherhood. But what is the New Age Movement? Where does it come from and what do its leaders believe?

On May 14, 1982, one of the leading spokesmen for the New Age Movement held a press conference at the Ambassador Hotel in Los Angeles, California. Mr. Benjamin Creme, British artist and lecturer, declared the coming of the New Age with his introduction of Lord Maitreya. Claiming an esoteric theology, Benjamin Creme declared that all reli-

gions expect a superhuman savior to soon appear upon the
world scene, and he called his christ, "Maitreya Buddha."

Creme stated, "It is important to remember that all of the
great religions await the coming of a teacher or an Avatar.
The Christians await the return of a Christ at the same time
the Buddhists await the coming of another Buddha, the fifth
Buddha, foretold by Gautama Buddha. And they call him
Maitreya Buddha. And they expect him now, at the dawn of
the New Age.

"At the same time, the Moslems await the Imam Mahdi.
Some of them believe he is already in the world. The Hindus
await the return of Krishna Bodhisattva, and the Jews, as
always, await the coming of the Messiah.

"I speak out of the esoteric tradition, and esotericists know
all of these under one name — The World Teacher — and
await his return now, at the dawn of the New Age."

That is clue number one. Mr. Creme has called his christ
Maitreya Buddha, indicating the underlying theme of the
entire movement. It is, in fact, Buddhism and Hinduism
exported to America. The religion, however, has been
clothed in scientific garb with new terminology which makes
it seem quite innocent. H. G. Wells called it a "consciousness revolution," a good and open conspiracy that would save
the world from destruction. In fact, he suggested that this
"open conspiracy" is the "natural inheritor of socialist and
communist enthusiasms; it may be in control of Moscow," he
said, "before it is in control of New York!"

If one probes deeply enough, he may find out that it was
the underlying philosophy behind the communist revolution.
Though the movement appears to be political in nature, it is
actually a religion — quite different, however, from Christianity. We believe in one God — the Creator of the universe;
Buddhism believes in many gods. We believe God is the

Creator of man, but the Buddhist believes that man is God.

Quoting Creme again: "Maitreya says that when you share, you recognize the god in your brother. He says, 'The problems of mankind are real but solvable. The solution lies within your grasp. Take your brother's need as a measure for your actions and solve the problems of the world. There is no other course. We share or we die.' That is the simple message. His aim, his goal, his mission is to take us into the sense of our oneness, that we are one — one family, brothers and sisters of that one humanity."

The central theme of the New Age Movement is said to be "the emergence of a new planetary consciousness." It sees each of us as "cells in the body of humanity," as planetary citizens. Marilyn Ferguson has called this movement the "AQUARIAN CONSPIRACY.' According to her, "New Age thinking involves a new openness to one another, to ourselves, to nature, to a universal force pervading the whole cosmos which produces an awakening of unimagined powers of the mind." Like Hinduism and Buddhism, upon which it is based, the Aquarian Conspiracy claims to embrace all beliefs, all religions, on the premise that all is one.

Creme: "It is nothing less than the transformation of all our structures — political, economic, and social — gradually, logically, relatively painlessly, with the minimum of cleavage, the minimum of trauma, but still change — change so far reaching that we can become the one humanity, which essentially we are — with the divisions broken down. The caste system must go in the interest of that one humanity. And that is what the christ has been saying."

This belief lies at the heart of Buddhism and Hinduism. The mystical religions of the Far East are diametrically opposed to the teachings of the Bible. In Genesis chapter 11, the identical concept could be seen at the Tower of Babel:

*"And the whole earth was of one language and of one
speech.*

*"And they said, Go to, let us build us a city and a tower,
whose top may reach unto heaven; and let us make us a name,
lest we be scattered abroad upon the face of the whole earth"*
(Genesis 11:1,4).

"Let us not scatter throughout the earth," was the cry. "Let's
stick together, build us a city, and make us a name." Like the
builders of the Tower of Babel, the New Age Movement is
promoting the idea that man is god and can be guided into his
higher state of consciousness through a system of meditation,
yielding himself to the control of a so-called "spiritual guide."
Such "guides," if real, can only be demons.

Creme also stated, "My information from my master (I stand
in relation to one of the masters), — my information comes
from my master, who is one of the disciples of the christ.
And I have been in rapport — telepathic rapport — with that
master for 23 years and have been trained and prepared by
him over the last nine years for the work which I am now
doing."

Who is this master teacher about which Mr. Creme speaks,
and why does he have to reach him only through meditation
and telepathic means? This type of contact with the spirit
world can only be demonic and is a prime example of the kind
of philosophy — or perhaps we should say theology — of the
New Age Movement.

On the inside cover of NEW AGE magazine is an advertise-
ment inviting readers to meditate with Rama, a Hindu deity.
He lives, of course, in the body of Dr. Frederick Lenz. The ad
reads that in the year 1531, he was the Zen master in Kyoto,
Japan. In 1602, he was the head of the Zen order. In 1725, he
was the master of a monastery in Tibet. And in 1834, he
became a yoga master in India. In 1912, he was a Tibetan

lama, the head of a monastic order in Tibet. And finally, in 1950, a little over 400 years later, he became the self-realized spiritual teacher and director of spiritual communities in Los Angeles and San Francisco.[2] That's what the New Age Movement is all about.

On the front cover of the NEW AGE magazine is the title of an article in favor of a nuclear freeze. The New Age Movement is, in fact, one of the major organizations behind the nuclear freeze movement. Who are these people? Consider these advertisements on page 79: "Wicca Seminary offers complete training program in witchcraft, sorcery, and herbology."

Another ad: "Tarot Counseling. Clarify your choices. $10.00. Send handwritten question, birthdate, picture if possible."

Another ad: "Oasis presents Emma, established psychic card-reader, who will answer your handwritten questions. Focus on illumination of inner blocks to personal success. Emphatic, helpful, practical. Amazingly accurate forecasts."

Consider this ad: "Nude beaches, resorts, events, directory of U.S.A., Europe, and Caribbean."

These ads are common in the NEW AGE magazine! Who are these people who produce such a magazine? They are professors in our leading universities. They are scientists working in America's prestigious laboratories. They are government personnel in the Pentagon, the State Department, and other government agencies. And they practice witchcraft!

The goals of the New Age Movement are as much political as they are religious. The New Age Movement is determined to usher in what they call the Age of Aquarius. Benjamin Creme's news conference on May 14, 1982, was for the purpose of declaring the whereabouts of his Maitreya Buddha, the one he called, "the christ."

Creme: "He is in England and has been in England for all

these years since July, 1977. The large town is London. He has been living in London — the community. He has been living as an ordinary man, accepted by them as a marvelous man, an extraordinary, wonderful man; a man to whom they can bring all their problems. He is their counselor and teacher — but still unknown to them in his true light, his true status. The community is the Pakistani-Indian community of South London, the immigrant community of Pakistan and Indian people living in South London. He said, 'Look for me in the dark places where hunger and strife abound.' "

That was in May, 1982. In the following weeks, Maitreya was supposed to be introduced to the world. Benjamin Creme said that Lord Maitreya would appear on television and speak telepathically to every person on the face of the earth.

Creme: "My estimate is that within the next 24 hours the media is to go to London into that community and speak to the christ, the Lord Maitreya, and know for themselves that the Avatar for the Age, the Representative of God, the Messiah of the Jews, the Imam Mahdi of the Muslims, Krishna returned, is living among us.

"The christ comes not really to save — he comes to teach. We are grown up. We are big boys and big girls now. Humanity has come of age. We must save ourselves — is our response to the teacher."

It has been years now, and Lord Maitreya has failed to make his appearance. Nevertheless, the movement continues full-steam ahead promoting its doctrine of Eastern mysticism.

There are literally hundreds of front organizations promoting the philosophy of the New Age Movement. For example, there is the Association for Humanistic Psychology, the Holistic Health Organizing Committee, and the Association for World Education. There is the Political Science Committee of the Institute for the New Age — and the Institute for the

Study of Conscious Evolution. There is the Naropa Institute, the Hunger Project, Planetary Citizens, Planetary Initiative for the World We Choose, Movement for a New Society, and a host of others. The list is almost endless. It is believed by those in the New Age Movement that world utopia will be brought about through acceptance of basic Hindu philosophy. And it is political, for the common goal is a New World Order, a world government.

The Association for Global Education, Cooperation, and Accreditation declared, "Only by the birth of global consciousness within each individual can we truly achieve transnationalization." Their goal is the emergence of a new universal person and civilization. National patriotism is to be overturned in favor of planetary citizenship. This goal explains why our children are being taught what is termed "globalism" in their classrooms today.

The doctrine of the organization is based to a large extent upon a denial of the Judeo-Christian God of the Bible in exchange for the belief that we are all God. This is ancient Hinduism — yet it is being accepted today as a non-religious, modern science. By a handful of naive fanatics? No, by millions of well-educated sophisticates.

In her book, THE AQUARIAN CONSPIRACY, Marilyn Ferguson wrote, "The Aquarian Conspirators range across all levels of income and education ... schoolteachers and office workers, famous scientists, government officials and lawmakers, artists and millionaires, taxi drivers and celebrities, leaders in medicine, education, law, psychology ...

"There are legions of conspirators ... in corporations, universities and hospitals, on the faculties of public schools, in factories and doctors' offices, in state and federal agencies, on city councils and the White House staff, in state legislatures ... in virtually all arenas of policymaking in the country." [3]

A member of the New Age Movement worships the mind, convinced by scientific experiment and his own experience that the universe itself is a great mind, which his own mind is a part of and can tap into through "altered states of consciousness." He believes he not only can move and bend and otherwise affect physical objects at a distance, but also that ultimately he can create his own reality with his mind.

Members of the New Age Movement have been too easily convinced that the so-called mind powers they seek are desirable. In fact, these are not mind powers at all — at least not powers which are within the capabilities of human minds. Please understand that the New Age Movement is based upon beliefs that have always been regarded instinctively by the human race as witchcraft and demonic. Whatever the explanation, through altered states of consciousness, paranormal mind powers both real and imagined, have been experienced by millions of people in the West under the stimulation of drugs, yoga, hypnosis, Eastern meditation, etc. As a result, the Hindu view of reality has become the predominant world view in the West today. This is true in science, medicine, psychology, sociology, education, politics, and business.

It is certainly the case with feminism, which is in the forefront of the New Age Movement. The women's movement is one of the most important parts of the New Age Movement. It is at the heart of the consciousness revolution that is sweeping the Western world. In universities across America, a new group of courses called "women's studies" have come into existence within the past two decades. There are also centers for feminist therapy; and national attention was given to the Equal Rights Amendment, which so far, has failed to reach its goal of becoming an amendment to the United States Constitution.

Many of those involved in the feminist movement may

sincerely believe it is a political crusade to gain equality with men. In fact, it is more than that. It is also a spiritual movement based partly upon a reawakening of the "goddess consciousness," and its real goal is "matriarchy," not equality.

One major spiritual force behind some aspects of the feminist movement is witchcraft, which is based upon the power of female sexuality derived from a mystical relationship with "Mother Nature" and "Mother Earth."

Take, for example, the Women's Conference held in southern California. Its title was "Women: the Leading Edge of the New Age." The organizers declared, "The New Age will allow us to experience a sense of wholeness, a sense of being connected with nature." Any witch would immediately recognize the significance of that statement. However, for those who don't know, "nature" religion is witchcraft.

Also, in 1982, leaders in the women's movement held a planning meeting at the West Los Angeles Center for Feminist Therapy. One of the brochures available that day stated, "1982 is the year for revolution in religion, higher education, and New Age learning, in which the holistic, interconnected nature of reality is widely recognized and in which women are encouraged to express their new spirituality which is the oldest on earth."

Any witch will proudly inform you that the oldest spirituality on earth is Wicca, or witchcraft.

A conference on "Women's Spirituality and Healing" was held in Los Angeles, California. One of the seminars was entitled "Introduction to Goddess Consciousness and the Craft." One would have to be very naive not to know that the "Craft" is witchcraft. The brochure described the seminar in this manner: "In this workshop, women will discover their own lost heritage by exploring ancient concepts of deity as goddess. Various aspects of the universal goddess will be shown. Their psychological and spiritual ramifications for our lives and for our time will be discussed, and the positive benefits of incorporating into our value structure a feminine image of the divine — will be explored."

Goddess worship, Wicca, and witchcraft are all names for a form of natural religion that is centered around the mystery, sexuality, and psychic abilities of the female.

Words like witchcraft, spiritism, satanism, devil-worship and voodoo are becoming prevalent, though not well-accepted words in our society. Therefore, new names have been given to these practices in order to make them palatable. For instance, there is the word "traditional." It sounds so much better.

The World Health Organization, under the auspices of the United Nations, has given official approval to "traditional healers." In Zimbabwe, Africa, there are 8,000 of these traditional healers who still practice their witchcraft— straightening their animal-skin headdresses, removing their shoes, and going into a hypnotic trance in order to prognosticate diseases.

Dr. Halfdan Mahler, former Director General of the World Health Organization, declared, "Nothing should be sacrosanct simply because we have been led to believe that it is witchcraft."

Another popular word used by the New Age Movement is "alternative." There is alternative medicine, which is a return to the old methods of pagan occultism, and there are alternate lifestyles, nice $40 words for homosexuality or lesbianism. Whatever way of life one chooses to adopt is simply a "style" that can be changed like hair or dress styles without any moral implications — or so one is led to believe. God still calls it sin.

Then there is the term "values clarification," which really means a desire to get rid of Christian morals by denying an absolute standard available for measuring moral values. "Values clarification" destroys the very meaning of the word "value."

The uses of such courses in public schools encourages the student to look within himself for inner guidance. The only thing that matters is how the student feels about a situation. Above all, he must be true to himself! The study of "values clarification" conditions the unsuspecting student to accept New Age philosophy. Over the years, while we have slept, Hinduism and Buddhism have been seductively presented to our children as a part of the New Age education. Yes, believe it or not, the New Age Movement has a stranglehold on our society.

What do those involved in the New Age Movement say is the meaning of New Age? In their own words, from THE 1988 GUIDE TO NEW AGE LIVING, the editor of the NEW AGE JOURNAL states, "In its broadest sense, new age thinking can be characterized as a form of utopianism, the desire to create a better society, a 'new age' in which humanity lives in harmony with itself, nature, and the cosmos. This desire ... the idea of a 'new heaven and a new earth' can be traced back as far as the Book of Revelation.

"But unlike the biblical 'Second Coming' or most other millenarian visions, the new age being discussed today by a number of philosophers, scientists, and social critics will not result from a future upheaval brought about solely by God. Rather, they say, society is now in the midst of the transformation, a change potentially as sweeping as the Renaissance or the Protestant Reformation." Some see it as "a transition that will change all the institutions of society, just as happened with the scientific revolution." [4]

David Spangler, a New Age Movement pioneer and founder of Findhorn, a "spiritual" community in Scotland, said, "The

New Age has little to do with prophecy or the imagination of a new world, but everything to do with the imagination to see our world in new ways that can empower us toward compassion, transformative actions and attitudes."

However, some New Agers "DO predict that a literal apocalypse is imminent and that it will be brought about by mystical, extraterrestrial, or cosmic forces." Of course, informed and aware Christians know that satan himself, as well as his demons, are responsible for the manipulation and control of these forces.

What are some of the recent developments from the realm of New Age thinking? "Once considered taboo, the study of consciousness is increasingly being viewed as a promising new frontier of human understanding ... A number of researchers ... are popularizing concepts and techniques previously accepted and practiced only by mystics." [5]

And, "Holistic medicine, still questioned by much of the medical establishment, is now gaining credibility, particularly in the area of stress reduction." It is called "behavioral medicine, which includes holistic techniques such as biofeedback, relaxation training, and hypnosis."

The New Age Movement is usually described as focusing primarily on metaphysical phenomena, such as channeling, which is said to occur when ancient entities allegedly speak through ordinary people, and the spiritual use and even worship of crystals, which supposedly help the body balance and realign its "energy" field.

Some of the underlying "values" that tie together this movement's philosophies are "human potential, holistic health, recycling, organic foods, grass-roots activism, practical spirituality, meditation, ecology, appropriate technology, feminism, [and] progressive politics." These are their own descriptive terms, but I will add a few observations of my own.

They say that their movement is not a religion but admit that it has an underlying spiritual dimension. Spiritual awareness is exemplified by their exploration of meditation, lucid dreaming, therapeutic prayer, positive visualization, and other spiritual and consciousness-altering pursuits. In fact, David Spangler maintains, "the essence of New Age thinking is the process of seeing the heaven that is right here on earth every day, a process he calls 'renaming the sacred.' "

Spangler says, "the sacred is only what we encounter on whichever Sabbath day we celebrate, or a being we turn to hopefully in prayer ... To rename the sacred is to have a different view of the universe ... It is to re-expand those boundaries we have placed around God, even to redefine the nature of divinity ... It is to look at the objects, people, and events in our lives and to say, 'You are sacred.' "

New Age leaders consistently confuse the terms, Christianity and religion. They seem always ready to defend the criticisms of Christians who contend that the New Age Movement "is a satanic, Nazi-like cult bent on world domination, and a threat to Judeo-Christian values." They explain simply that New Age thinking embraces "the spiritual and moral truths that are the genesis of all religions, both Eastern and Western (though it has no religious doctrine or teachings of its own)." Why is it they cannot see that the foregoing explanation is THE reason why Christians are critical of their thinking processes? The mixing of pagan and false religions with Christianity is not only strictly forbidden throughout the Bible, it is precisely this unequal yoking, this watering down of the beliefs of God-fearing, Bible-believing Christians which will bring about the apostasy of the last days and will usher in the worship of the one-world leader — otherwise known as the antichrist.

Despite its name, most New Age ideology comes from a

collection of "alternative thinkers" such as "Lao-tse, Gandhi, and Rudolf Steiner, to Albert Einstein, Aldous Huxley, Carl Jung, and Marshall McLuhan. Perhaps the most influential ideas to shape contemporary New Age thinking were those that grew out of humanistic psychology and the human potential movement of the '60s and '70s."

They obviously seriously believe that "If the divine is present in an individual soul it must be sought and found in man's institutions as well. For people will not readily achieve individual salvation without a saving society ... Sooner or later, if human society is to evolve — indeed, if it is to survive — we must match our lives to our new knowledge." [6]

In order to fully comprehend the thinking and direction which the New Age Movement is taking its adherents, it is important for Christians to understand that at the root of all New Age philosophy is the New Age belief that each person has his own "inner adviser." Christians know these "friendly guides" to be nothing more AND nothing less than demons from hell! The following is from an article written by a medical doctor in NEW AGE JOURNAL, March/April 1988.

> "Begin by selecting a quiet and private location where you won't be interrupted for about twenty to thirty minutes ... Loosen any clothing or jewelry that is tight or restrictive. Get into a comfortable position, either lying down or sitting ... Begin by taking a couple of deep, full breaths ... As you breathe comfortably and easily, invite your body to relax and let go of any unnecessary tension ... Take the time to bring your attention to each part of your body, and invite it to release and relax ... relaxing more deeply ... more pleasantly ... more comfortably ... imagine yourself at the top of an imaginary staircase that leads to an even deeper and more comfortable state of mind and body ... descend one step at a time ... going deeper, more comfortably relaxed with each descending stair ... Let it be an enjoyable experience ... Head for that special inner place of peacefulness and healing.
>
> "Ten ... nine ... deeper, more comfortably relaxed as you go

down the stairs ... eight ... seven ... not being concerned at all with how deeply you go or how you go more deeply ... six ... easy ... comfortable ... five ... just allowing it to happen ... and four ... comfortable and pleasant ... three ... two ... body relaxed yet mind still aware ... one ... And go in your mind to a special inner place of deep relaxation and healing ... an inner place of great beauty, peacefulness, and security for you ... a place you have visited before, or one which simply occurs to you now ...

"When you are ready, focus your attention on the symptom or problem that has been bothering you ... Simply put your attention on it while staying completely relaxed ... Allow an image to emerge for this symptom or problem ... Accept the image that comes, whether it makes sense or not ... whether it is strange or familiar ... whether you like it or not ... Just notice and accept the image that comes for now ... Let it become clearer and more vivid, and take some time to observe it carefully ... let another image appear that represents the healing or resolution of this symptom or problem ... Recall the first image and consider two images together ... Which is larger? ... Which is more powerful? ... If the image of the problem seems more powerful, notice whether you can change that ... Imagine the image of healing becoming stronger, more powerful, more vivid ... Imagine it to be much bigger and much more powerful than the other ... Imagine the image of the problem or symptom turning into the image of healing ... Watch the transformation ..."

If some are not yet convinced of the evil of this procedure, please continue:

"After you've gotten comfortable with your imagery, you may want to explore it further, searching for new ways to support your self-healing. You may want to meet your inner adviser ..."

Please note that New Agers call this "inner healing" or "exploring your healing imagery." But, realistically, all they have accomplished in this exercise in hypnosis is the relaxation and the opening up of their minds and inviting the onslaught of satan's demons to do whatever the old serpent wills to do. This technique teaches one not to go to God for resolution of a problem, but to ask one's "inner adviser" for help. Parents should also be informed that this very same operation is performed almost daily at many elementary schools in this country!

The New Age medical doctor continues:

> "Spooky? Not really. Having a talk with an imaginary wise figure — an inner adviser — may sound strange, yet this is one of the most powerful techniques I know for helping you understand the relationships between your thoughts, your feelings, your actions, and your health ... Your inner adviser should be thought of as a friendly guide to these valuable unconscious stores ...
>
> "Have you ever struggled with a problem and ultimately come to terms with it by listening to that 'still, small voice within'?[7] ... you may be guided by something deep inside — a part of you usually hidden from conscious awareness. Imagining this guidance as a figure you can communicate with helps to make it more accessible ...
>
> "Talking with an inner adviser is not a new idea. Most of the major philosophical, religious, and psychological traditions of mankind speak of inner guidance in one form or another. Many primitive cultures used rituals that included music, chanting, fasting, dancing, sacrifice, and psychoactive plants in order to invoke a vision that could inform and guide them at important times.
>
> "Some Native American tribes sent braves into the wilderness unarmed, without food and water, to build a sweat lodge and pray for contact with a guiding spirit. From such a visionary experience they would draw their names, their power, and their direction in life ...
>
> "Catholic children are taught in catechism that they have a holy guardian angel who protects them and who can be called on in time of need. Many other religions teach a similar idea ...
>
> "All these experiences point to a common human notion — there is guidance available to us when we appeal to it and when we are receptive to it ...
>
> "It's not necessary to have any particular belief about the inner adviser in order to use it, but it's helpful for the technique to make

sense to you one way or another. Whatever you believe — that the adviser is a spirit, a guardian angel, a messenger from God, a hallucination, a communication from your right brain to your left, or a symbolic representation of inner wisdom — is all right. The fact is, no one knows what it is with any certainty. We can each decide for ourselves.

"... an inner adviser acts as a source of support and comfort; there is often a sense of peacefulness, of inner calm and compassion that stems from meetings with an adviser ... If you make a bargain with your adviser, make sure you keep it. Remember, you are dealing with a part of yourself here; you can't disrespect it without cost. Consider this a real relationship, and treat it with respect ...

"Inner advisers often come as the classic 'wise old man' or 'wise old woman,' but they come in many other forms as well. Sometimes they come in the form of a person you know, a friend or relative who has fulfilled this function for you in real life. These people may be living or dead ...

"Advisers may also be animals or birds, plants, trees, or even natural forces like the wind or the ocean. Sometimes people will encounter religious figures like Jesus, Moses, or Buddha, while others will find an angel, fairy, or leprechaun. People sometimes encounter the adviser as a light or a translucent spirit ...

"The best way to work with this and any other imagery experience is just to let the figures be whatever they are. Welcome the adviser that comes and get to know it as it is ...

"Meeting your inner adviser is simple ... let yourself relax and go to your special inner place. When you're comfortable, quiet, and relaxed there, allow an image to appear. Accept whatever image comes — whether or not it is familiar. [8] Take some time to observe it carefully, and invite it to become comfortable with you, just as if it were real. After all, it is a real imaginary figure! Ask your adviser its name, and let it have a voice to answer you ... It's important not to edit or second-guess the imagery at this stage.

"Take some time to become comfortable in the presence of your inner adviser, and as you grow more familiar with it, notice if it seems to be wise and kind. Notice how you feel in its presence. If it feels comfortable to you, ask your adviser if it would be willing to help you, and let it respond. If it is willing, tell

it about your problem or illness and ask if it can tell you what you
need to know or do to get better. Let it answer you and stay open
and receptive to the answers that come."[9]

The Bible, in II Timothy 3:1, declares that in the last days,
perilous times shall come. It is also clear that Paul warned us
that many would depart from the faith which he preached in
the latter days. *"Now the Spirit speaketh expressly, that in the
latter times some shall depart from the faith, giving heed to
seducing spirits, and doctrines of devils"* (I Timothy 4:1).

The New Age Movement professes to be a broadminded
organization incorporating all religions, but its basic, underlying philosophy represents a carefully calculated undermin-
ing of Judeo-Christian beliefs. The true primary goal of its
"Plan" is to establish a New Age "messiah" to lead a One-
World Religion and a global government. It has begun to wage
a total spiritual war against Christian believers. The New Age
Movement's ultimate goal is to eliminate every vestige of
Christianity. It is a sinister system designed to destroy faith in
Christ in hopes of introducing upon the world scene the
coming antichrist.

Chapter Notes

CHAPTER 16

1. Marilyn Ferguson, THE AQUARIAN CONSPIRACY (Los Angeles: Tarcher, 1980), pp. 19-21.

2. NEW AGE, January, 1983, (inside cover).

3. Ferguson, AQUARIAN CONSPIRACY, op. cit., pp. 23-25.

4. "What is New Age?" GUIDE TO NEW AGE LIVING, 1988, p. 5.

5. Ibid., p. 6.

6. Ibid., p. 12.

7. See THE HOLY BIBLE, I Kings 19:12. New Age terminology duplicates and counterfeits words and phrases from the Bible as often as possible in order to sound "spiritual."

8. Ibid., See Leviticus 20:6, 27; Deuteronomy 18:11; II Kings 21:6; I Chronicles 10:13; and II Chronicles 33:6.

9. "The Healing Power of Imagery," NEW AGE JOURNAL, March/ April, 1988, p. 52-56.

Charles V ruled Spain during the years Spanish galleons were hauling gold and silver from the "new world." His father was a Habsburg. His mother was the daughter of Ferdinand and Isabella.

Chapter 17

The Last Temptation

The movie version of "The Last Temptation of Christ," released by Universal Studios in 1988, is the most vile and wicked bit of blasphemy ever to be shown on the silver screen. In 1984, Paramount Pictures attempted to film it, but because of public pressure, the movie was shelved. Now, probably due to a greater potential for public acceptance, Universal Studios released it. It tells a sordid story about Jesus Christ and a so-called "love affair" with Mary Magdalene. Christians across America are furious — and have every right to be.

The movie, produced by Martin Scorcese, is taken from a book by the same title written by Nikos Kazantsakis, published in 1960. The movie had mixed reviews across America. Some ministers have praised the film while others have taken a firm stand against it. Some ministers, and most of the news media have suggested that the demonstrations against the film actually helped sell more tickets. Therefore, they were saying that we could hurt the film most by turning our heads and pretending it never existed. The truth is quite the contrary. Tickets will not be sold if movie houses refuse to show it — and Christian groups have been successful in convincing many theater owners across America not to allow it to be shown. In fact, the movie lost over $12 million!

Christians cannot afford to sit silently by and allow such theological garbage to go unchallenged. The movie is more than mere theatrics. It is a deliberate attempt to pervert the historical concept of Jesus Christ. If the book and film remain unchallenged, the next generation could grow up with a twisted view of Christ. Satan could accomplish his goal of brainwashing the world into thinking that the virtues of Christianity are nothing more than mere human hypocrisy.

One only has to review the life of Nikos Kazantzakis in order to understand the man's motivation for filling his novel with historical inaccuracies and theological heresy. He was born in 1883 on the island of Crete where his father kept a small farm. It was there that he first came to know the shepherds, the farmers, the fishermen, the innkeepers, and the peasants who peopled his novels. His childhood was "spent in an atmosphere where dare-devil hard-drinking heroism was the highest virtue, a virtue best exemplified for Kazantzakis by his own father."[1]

He earned his degree at the University of Athens, then went to Paris to study philosophy with Henry Bergson. He also traveled to Mt. Athos in Macedonia, a land of incredible beauty, with its famous ancient monasteries built high among the clouds on the craggy peaks of blue-green mountains overlooking the Aegean Sea. The monasteries are well-known for their total exclusion of all females — cows and hens, as well as women. Kazantzakis tried to gain some sort of spiritual peace through spiritual and bodily exercises while isolating himself for six months, alone in a tiny cell.

His life was filled with frustration. He married for the first time in 1911, but the infuence of his stay on Mt. Athos, which no female had penetrated since the 10th century, had evidently wrought its toll on his personality. He and his wife lived apart for much of their marriage. It ended in divorce.

He was a student of Friedrich Nietzsche. It was Nietzsche's existential philosophy which gave rise to the liberal concept that "God is dead," long considered by conservative theologians as heresy. During the early 1920's Kazantzakis was so enamored by Nietzsche's idea of man making himself by his own will and perseverance into a superman that he went on a pilgrimage to all the towns in Germany where Nietzsche had lived.

Trevor Ravenscroft, in his book, THE SPEAR OF DESTINY, summarized the philosophy of Friedrich Nietzsche when he wrote that the tragic philosopher sought to make a "re-evaluation of all values" by proving that so-called evil was good, and what was habitually believed to be good was, in fact, evil! He also explained that Adolf Hitler was incapable of distinguishing between good and evil for the sad reason that he had absorbed (as early as age 15) the works of Friedrich Nietzsche. If the diabolical teachings of Nietzsche had such a profound effect on Adolf Hitler, who threw a world into chaos, then we can rightfully conclude that Kazantzakis' reliance on the philosophy of Friedrich Nietzsche also made his writings potentially dangerous.

Trevor Ravenscroft had serious misgivings about Nietzsche. While evaluating the influence of Nietzsche upon Hitler, he wrote:

"When Adolf Hitler came to consider the significance of Christ in Christianity, the Spirit of the Anti-Christ, which speaks so powerfully through all of Nietzsche's later writings, now seized his own fertile imagination. There was no need as far as he was concerned to assess the value of Christianity because Nietzsche had already done it to perfection in a masterful analysis of this religion 'for slaves, weaklings, and the desiccated residue of racial scum!' " [2]

The following excerpt from "The Anti-Christ" by Friedrich Nietzsche reflects not only his philosophy, but also the probable viewpoint of lives he affected:

"The Jews are the strangest people in the history of the world because, confronted with the question to be or not to be, they chose, with uncanny deliberateness, to be at any price; this price was the radical falsification of all nature, all naturalness, all reality, of the whole inner world as well as the outer.

"Out of themselves the Jews created a counter-movement to natural conditions: they turned religion, cult, morality, history, psychology, one after the other, into an incurable contradiction of their own natural values.

"We encounter the same phenomena once again in immeasurably large proportions, yet merely as a copy: the Christian Church cannot make the slightest claim to originality when compared to the 'holy people.' This is why the Jews are precisely the most catastrophic people of world history: by their effect they have made mankind so thoroughly false that even today the Christian can feel anti-Jewish without realizing that he himself is the *ultimate Jewish consequence.*

"What is formerly just sick is today indecent — it is indecent to be a Christian today. And here begins my nausea ... I pronounce my judgment. I condemn Christianity. I raise against the Christian Church the most terrible of all accusations that any accuser uttered. It is to me the highest conceivable corruption. With its ideal of anaemia, of 'holiness,' draining all blood, all love, all hope for life; the cross is the mark of recognition for the most subterranean conspiracy that ever existed - against health, beauty, whatever has turned out well, courage, spirit, graciousness of soul, against life itself.

"This eternal indictment of Christianity I will write on all walls, wherever there are walls ... I call it the one immortal blemish on mankind."

Signed, "The Anti-Christ: Friedrich Nietzsche."[3]

Nietzsche hated the Jews. He hated Christianity. So did Adolf Hitler, and so did Nikos Kazantzakis.

Kazantzakis wrote that Nietzsche had taught him the only way a man could be free was to struggle — to lose himself in a cause, to fight without fear and without hope of reward. This apparently helped to prepare him for his next allegiance — the Eastern mysticism of Buddha.

In 1922, while staying in Vienna, he embraced the doctrine of complete renunciation, of complete mutation of flesh into spirit. Buddha was, for Kazantzakis, a superman who had conquered matter. In case you haven't yet made the connection, the existential philosophy of Friedrich Nietzsche and the Eastern mystical teachings of Buddhism are at the root and core of the New Age Movement.

In 1924, Kazantzakis became friendly with a group of communists. The Marxists seemed to be fashioning a new world and even a new god for the world. Now, here seemed to be a cause to which he could give himself! This was precisely what he had been seeking — if he would but seize the occasion. Lenin became Kazantzakis' new god. By 1928 he had made four trips to Russia. The Soviet government had given him a railroad pass and he traveled from one end of the vast country to another, writing about his new savior.

Eventually, however, he also tired of Communism. In the early 1930's he realized that Lenin could not satisfy the spiritual needs of men. He continued to dream, however, of an ideal system which he called "metacommunism" — a combination of Communism and metaphysics. Metaphysics is another term for the philosophy popularized by the New Age Movement.

According to P. A. Bien, translator of his book from Greek into English, at the age of 50, Kazantzakis had become a "priest of the imagination." His writings were a perverted combination of "Christianity, Buddhism, Bergson's vitalism, and Nietzsche's superman; an intellectuality balanced by distrust of pure ideas." [4]

During those years Kazantzakis lived in near solitude, working feverishly from dawn to dark, eating but one scanty meal a day. In 1948, at the age of 65, he decided to try his hand at writing his first novel.

In two months he had completed his first perverted work, THE GREEK PASSION. It raised such a furor in Greece, he was almost excommunicated from the Church. This unbelievable spurt of corrupted creativity continued — and enabled him to produce, over the next nine years, a total of eight books, including THE LAST TEMPTATION OF CHRIST.

Bien wrote, "By the time he was 70, he found himself known all over Europe: his novels were translated into 30 languages and he was nominated repeatedly for the Nobel Prize, losing in 1952 by just one vote. But with all this success came increasing bitterness." [5]

When he published his book, FREEDOM OR DEATH, the newspapers branded him a traitor to Crete. The publication of THE LAST TEMPTATION OF CHRIST worsened his reputation. He was branded a heretic by the Greek Orthodox Church, and rightly so. Perhaps a no more brazen piece of heresy has ever been written. It is said that Kazantzakis wanted to lift Christ out of the church altogether. Since (he believed that) the 20th century brought about the death of the old era, he wished to make Jesus a figure for a "new age." [6]

Kazantzakis desired to make evil into good while transforming good into evil. He is promoted today by those who push for a New Age Movement. So much was Kazantzakis a proponent of the New Age Movement that he is quoted extensively in Marilyn Ferguson's THE AQUARIAN CONSPIRACY. In the opening of her book she quotes Nikos Kazantzakis, along with two other believers in metaphysics, on the subject of the conspiracy espoused by the New Age Movement:

> "And I strive to discover how to signal my companions ... to say in time a simple word, the password, like conspirators: let us unite, let us hold each other tightly, let us merge our hearts, let us create for earth a brain and a heart, let us give a human meaning to the superhuman struggle."[7]

Kazantzakis is quoted no less than six times in THE AQUARIAN CONSPIRACY, the New Age treatise calling for personal and social transformation in the 1980's.[8]

THE LAST TEMPTATION OF CHRIST, by Nikos Kazantzakis, appears to be a combination of his life experiences with Nietzsche, Buddhism, and Communism. He was a bitter man and when he died in 1957, the Archbishop of Greece "firmly refused to allow his body to lie in state in a church in the normal manner."[9] He had enraged his own countrymen with his blatant heresy.

It is obvious that those who would take Kazantzakis' piece of literary trash and make it into a movie must also possess a like-minded bitterness against Christendom. According to reports, Martin Scorsese, producer of the movie, was himself expelled from seminary and was not allowed to prepare for the Roman Catholic priesthood. Scorsese, who has been recognized for outstanding movie production, has at last lowered himself to retaliate against a system that denied him the priesthood. Both the author and the movie producer of THE LAST TEMPTATION OF CHRIST were filled with one frustration and disappointment after another. Perhaps that is the reason why he portrays Jesus as a man who was likewise frustrated with his destiny.

Chapter Notes

CHAPTER 17

1. Nikos Kazantzakis, THE LAST TEMPTATION OF CHRIST, trans. P. A. Bien (New York: Simon and Schuster, 1960), p. 497.
2. Trevor Ravenscroft, THE SPEAR OF DESTINY, op. cit., p. 27.
3. Ibid., pp. 27-28.
4. Kazantzakis, LAST TEMPTATION, p. 500.
5. Ibid., p. 504.
6. Ibid., p. 505.
7. Ferguson, op. cit., (after title page).
8. Ibid., pp. 49, 81n, 102, 106, 383.
9. Kazantzakis, op. cit., p. 505.

The
Antichrist

Chapter 18

A New World Order

Throughout history, one desire has dominated the dreams of men — the desire to have a One-World government. In the 15th century B. C., Egypt was the leading world power. Egyptian influence was felt in every corner of the known world. Then came Assyria with its capital at Nineveh. In the 7th century B. C., Nebuchadnezzar, king of Babylon, carved out an empire which included most of western Asia. About 300 years before Christ, Alexander the Great led his armies as far east as India and for a brief time ruled all of western Asia, northern Africa, and southeastern Europe. At the time of Christ the Caesars had subdued much of the same area to form the mighty Roman Empire.

In more modern times Napoleon plotted world conquest — only to have his dream shattered at Waterloo. In the 20th century Hitler hoped to have the world at his feet. But none of these men ever really conquered the entire world.

These rulers were partially successful, having conquered portions of Europe, northern Africa, and western Asia. But no man has ever conquered every nation on the face of the earth.

Until our generation, the world was not really ready for a universal government. However, in light of the advances made in modern technology, our world does not seem to be as big as it used to be. A missile can now reach any part of the globe in less than 30 minutes. Television and radio provide instant communication. The problems of one country become the problems of every country in the world. Every major event in some far-flung country of the world finds its reverberations affecting the rest of the world. Men and nations can no longer live in isolation.

During World War I steps were taken to form the League of Nations, an international body dedicated to the prevention of war. However, it was unsuccessful. The United States was not ready for such a role in world affairs. The idea of world government seemed unnecessary for a country so far away across the ocean from the problems of Europe and Asia.

But the earth was growing smaller and America's isolation could not last for long. In 1941, the United States was again drawn into a world war. The attack on Pearl Harbor marked the end of America's isolation in the midst of a shrinking world.

By the end of World War II, a frightening new dimension had been added to the prospects for world government. Awesome new weapons were developed. The atomic bomb changed the complexion of world politics. No nation could ever be safe again. The destructive capabilities of war had increased to a degree never before considered possible. Nuclear destruction threatened not only military forces, but entire cities and civilian populations.

Today, it is possible to destroy the entire world in only a

matter of hours. The superpowers have stockpiled enough explosive material to equal 300 pounds of TNT for each person on the planet. No wonder many of the world's political leaders feel that the time has come for a new international organization.

The United Nations was born in 1946. Its ultimate desire was to save the world from atomic destruction. At first, it included only a few nations. However, the United Nations soon grew to include most of the nations in the world. With the admission of Red China almost all of the nations have become a part of this international structure.

But the United Nations lacks the power to prevent war. During its history, its weaknesses have been demonstrated again and again. Its failure to solve conflicts in Southeast Asia, Africa, and Central America and its continued inability to prevent flare-ups in the Middle East has demonstrated that the United Nations is not the final answer. Some stronger form of world government seems to be the only hope for a world which can easily destroy itself.

Without such a government, the problems facing the world would be unsolvable. Nuclear war, overpopulation, starvation, pollution, and economic instability are problems that cannot be solved without world government. The United Nations, the Common Market and the World Bank represent only the beginning of a quest for some solution to the world's increasing problems.

Many international leaders and intellectuals believe that a strong and effective world government is the only hope for the survival of man on this planet. As these attitudes are increasingly expressed in our time it is important to ask what the Bible has to say on the subject. As a matter of fact, the prophets anticipated such a state of affairs.

For example, the prophet Daniel described a series of future developments which would attempt to bring the entire world under the dominion of a single man. Daniel predicted with accuracy the progression of preceding world empires which would eventually bring about such a plan.

The first world empire described by Daniel was that of Babylon which conquered Jerusalem when Daniel was a child. As a prophet during the Babylonian exile, Daniel gave a list of all the world empires that would rise and fall before the Second Coming of Christ. His prophecy offers a complete outline of the history of world empires written before those empires came into existence. This outline is so important to the understanding of history that Jesus referred to Daniel while giving His predictions of end-time events.

Daniel's outline of world empires included the Babylonian, the Medo-Persian, the Greek, and the Roman empires. Daniel also anticipated a final stage of the Roman empire for the last days. It is this final world empire and its diabolical dictator that will push the world toward Armageddon. In that day world empires built by conquest will be forever ended. Governments created by men will be replaced by the kingdom of Christ on earth.

Daniel described the fourth world empire:

"After this I saw in the night visions, and behold a fourth beast, dreadful and terrible, and strong exceedingly; and it had great iron teeth: it devoured and brake in pieces, and stamped the residue with the feet of it: and it was diverse from all the beasts that were before it; and it had ten horns" (Daniel 7:7).

The prophecy refers to Rome. In the first century B.C., the Roman army crushed all opposition and extended the iron rule of the caesars over all of southern Europe, western Asia, and northern Africa.

A final form of the Roman empire is destined to emerge

when the leaders of ten European nations form a new confederacy. Daniel's vision involved a beast symbolically representing the Roman Empire with the ten horns of that beast representing ten kings yet to arise on the stage of world history. The interpretation of the prophecy was directly given to Daniel:

"Thus he said, The fourth beast shall be the fourth kingdom upon earth, which shall be diverse from all kingdoms, and shall devour the whole earth, and shall tread it down, and break it in pieces."

"And the ten horns out of this kingdom are ten kings that shall arise: and another shall rise after them; and he shall be diverse from the first, and he shall subdue three kings" (Daniel 7:23-24).

Rome's rise to power along with its decline and fall are now ancient history. But the final phase of that fourth kingdom is reserved for the last days. This has led students of biblical prophecy to expect a new concentration of power to emerge in the Mediterranean world. According to the Bible, this fourth world empire will be revived as a final prelude to Armageddon and the Second Coming of Christ.

The first movements toward a revival of the fourth empire are in today's headlines, and the dreams of international power and wealth again focuses on the Middle East. Twelve strong nations have emerged in an alliance of political and economic power. It may be the beginning of that predicted revival of the Roman Empire. The stage may be set for the emergence of a new world dictator known in the Bible as *"antichrist."*

It is believed that the new world dictator will first reveal himself in the role of a peacemaker in the Middle East. Daniel describes the coming of the antichrist as a *"little horn"*:

"I considered the horns, and, behold, there came up among

them another little horn, before whom there were three of the first horns plucked up by the roots: and, behold, in this horn were eyes like the eyes of man, and a mouth speaking great things" (Daniel 7:8).

The word "horn" is used to describe this new world leader because, in Daniel's day, a king wore a crown which consisted of a number of horns. The protruding spikelets on the top of the crown were referred to in ancient times as horns. So the little horn which emerges from the group of ten horns represents a world leader who will emerge in the midst of a ten-nation confederation seeking to rule the world.

In the process of his emergence, three of the ten nations will be destroyed. The others will yield their authority to the antichrist. He will negotiate a peace treaty between Israel and the Middle Eastern Arab countries to cover a period of seven years. However, in the midst of that seven-year peace treaty, the antichrist himself will break the covenant.

The scripture also predicts that the world ruler will have absolute control over the economy. No one will be able to buy or sell without his permission. Today, with the advent of modern computers, for the first time in history such a thing is possible!

"And he shall speak great words against the most High, and shall wear out the saints of the most High, and think to change times and laws: and they shall be given into his hand until a time and times and the dividing of time" (Daniel 7:25).

The word *"time"* is believed to refer to one year, and the word *"times"* is believed to refer to two years — for a total of three. Then the words *"dividing of time"* is thought to refer to one-half year — making a grand total of three and one-half years, *"a time and times and the dividing of time."* This verse coincides with the three and one-half year Great Tribulation period — the last half of the seven-year Tribulation. It also coincides with the 42 months and the 1,260 days of the book of Revelation.

"But the court which is without the temple leave out, and measure it not; for it is given unto the Gentiles: and the holy city shall they tread under foot forty and two months.

"And I will give power unto my two witnesses, and they shall prophesy a thousand two hundred and threescore days, clothed in sackcloth" (Revelation 11:2-3).

The period of 42 months or 1260 days totals three and one-half years. During this time, the antichrist will make his final bid for world power. Daniel's prophecy provides the key to the drama.

Jesus identified this man as the final military conqueror who would invade Jerusalem and desecrate the Temple. Jesus said:

"When ye therefore shall see the abomination of desolation, spoken of by Daniel the prophet, stand in the holy place, (whoso readeth, let him understand:) Then let them which be in Judea flee into the mountains" (Matthew 24:15).

Our Savior's reference to this event added another important piece to the prophetic puzzle. Daniel wrote:

"And he shall confirm the covenant with many for one week: and in the midst of the week he shall cause the sacrifice and the oblation to cease, and for the overspreading of abominations he shall make it desolate, even until the consummation, and that determined shall be poured upon the desolate" (Daniel 9:27).

In this verse Daniel described a covenant (perhaps a peace treaty) which will be made with Israel and negotiated by the antichrist. Daniel said the covenant would be for one week. In the original language the verse refers to a period of seven years. One day equals one year in Daniel's prophetic time-table. In the midst of the week (or seven-year period) he will cause the sacrifice to cease.

In other words, in the middle of this seven-year period, right at the three and one-half year point, the antichrist will move into Jerusalem, will take over the government, will execute Israel's political leader and religious leader, and will attempt to set up his world government using Jerusalem as his new world capital.

Prophets throughout the Bible have described the last years before the Second Coming of Christ as a time of great trouble. Jesus described the time in this manner:

"For then shall be great tribulation, such as was not since the beginning of the world to this time, no, nor ever shall be.

And except those days should be shortened, there should no flesh be saved" (Matthew 24:21-22).

Writing the book of Revelation, John also describes the hour of this coming world dictator:

"And it was given unto him to make war with the saints, and to overcome them: and power was given him over all kindreds, and tongues, and nations" (Revelation 13:7).

Satan's man of destiny will have 42 months of power as world dictator. During his rule, God will pour out His wrath upon a wicked, Christ-rejecting world. The prophetic calendar has been announced for centuries; the die is cast; the Middle East will return to the center of the international stage.

The leaders of the European confederacy will revive the power lost by the fall of Rome. The future world dictator will await the right moment to upset three of those nations and seize control of the ten-nation alliance.

For three and a half years he will masquerade as a prince of peace. For the next three and a half years he will use satanic wonders and power to declare himself God and ruthlessly crush all opposition. Near the end of that period the nations of the world will field their armies to challenge him. Gripped in a dramatic world war, the armies will converge to begin the suicidal Battle of Armageddon.

It is most significant that in our 20th century there is more than just a need for world government. The tools for establishing such a government are now in our hands.

For a world government to work would require rapid communication. Today, the electronic media, especially the use of television by way of satellite, would be a tremendous tool in the hands of the world dictator who needs instant communication with the entire earth.

A workable world government would also require rapid transportation. Today, men and arms can be transported to any part of the world in comparatively few hours, something that was impossible in any previous generation.

Missile warfare would also be a tremendous tool in the hands of any world ruler. Missiles can be fired to any spot in the world in less than 30 minutes. A world dictator with nuclear missiles at his disposal could threaten any portion of the world, blackmailing it into submission with the threat of extinction. No previous ruler in the history of the world had such fearful weapons to enforce his rule.

The Scripture also predicts that the world ruler will have absolute control over the economy. No one will be able to buy or sell without his permission. Today, with the advent of modern computers, for the first time in history this would be possible.

A world government could keep financial accounts of all the businesses in the world controlling the purchases and sales and compiling an infinite amount of information about every individual in a day when individuals in the United States are being reduced to a Social Security number as their ultimate identification. Computers using a number system could compile any information necessary to maintain worldwide economic control.

Our world today continues to be plagued by problems — problems that seem unsolvable without world government. There are more wars and rumors of wars in the world today than ever before. Armed conflicts in Southeast Asia; Angola, Chad, Ethiopia, Mozambique, and South Africa on the continent of Africa; El Salvador and Nicaragua in Central America; the recent Iran-Iraq war in the Middle East; as well as the ongoing, constant turmoil between Israel and the Palestinians; all prove the necessity for strong world leadership.

The increasing availability of nuclear weapons, the propaganda power of the world media, and the blackmail power of international economic agreements now make it possible for a world dictator to seize control of the world in a way that would have been impossible in any previous generation.

The necessary ingredients for world government are present for the first time in the history of civilization. The time may not be far away when the Scriptures which predicted such a government (written long before one was possible), will have their accurate and complete fulfillment.

Chapter 19

The Man from Hell

During the coming Tribulation, the political power of this world will be invested into the hands of one man. Perhaps he will be the hero of the Battle of Gog and Magog and will be credited with saving the world from the communist menace. His power and influence will continue to build throughout the first half of the Tribulation Period until he has control of the world's economy. During the last half of the Tribulation, however, he will lead the world into its most devastating period of history. The Bible calls him *"antichrist."*

The term *"antichrist"* is found in two small books of the New Testament — I and II John. In his first epistle, John wrote:

"...as ye have heard that antichrist shall come, even now are there many antichrists" (I John 2:18).

Out of seven times the term is recorded in the first and

second epistles of John, this is the primary one which refers to that future man of sin. *"As ye have heard that antichrist shall come."*

The prefix "anti," according to ancient Greek, means to "substitute for" or "in place of." This meaning speaks of the antichrist as a person who will "take the place of" Christ. The term "anti" also refers to "one who is against." The future antichrist will not only be a world leader who will substitute himself for Christ, but will also stand opposed to the Son of God.

In the Bible, the antichrist has been described in various symbolic terms. Daniel described him as a *"little horn."* John, the Revelator called him a *"beast."* And Paul, in II Thessalonians, described him as the *"son of perdition."* Let's consider those three basic designations for the antichrist.

The term *"little horn"* is used first in Daniel 7. In his vision, Daniel saw four beasts rise up out of the sea of humanity. They represent those nations whose power and influence shape the course of world history. The fourth animal is not identified, but is described as *"exceedingly strong."* I think it represents the Revived Roman Empire.

The term *"little horn,"* used in Daniel 7, is an apparent reference to the future antichrist. In chapter 8, Daniel again used the term *"little horn."* That time, however, he was describing Antiochus Epiphanes, the king of Syria.

This passage presents Daniel's second vision. Once again animals are seen, but this time there are only two — a two-horned ram and a one-horned goat. The ram, according to verse 20, represented Medo-Persia, and the goat, according to verse 21, represented the empire of Greece under the leadership of Alexander the Great.

In the vision, the horn of the goat was broken and, in its place, four horns arose. Prophetically, this represented the death of Alexander the Great and the division of the Greek Empire into four provinces headed up by the four generals of his army:

"Therefore the he goat waxed very great: and when he was strong, the great horn was broken; and for it came up four notable ones toward the four winds of heaven.

"And out of one of them came forth a little horn, which waxed exceeding great, toward the south, and toward the east, and toward the pleasant land" (Daniel 8:8-9).

According to verse 8, when the goat had become victorious, his great horn was broken, symbolizing the death of Alexander. He died in the city of Babylon at the young age of 33 after sweeping all the way to India.

Following this, four notable horns grew in its place. This symbolizes the division of Alexander's vast holdings into four parts under the control of his four generals. It is from one of these divisions that a *"little horn"* arose. According to Flavius Josephus, a first-century Jewish historian, this little horn represented Antiochus Epiphanes, a descendant of Seleucus Nicator, one of Alexander's four generals who achieved rule over the Syria division. [1] It should be noted, however, that even though Antiochus Epiphanes ruled the Syrian division, he was not Syrian. He was Greek. He was, therefore, as shown in our earlier study on the Spartans and Trojans, possibly from the tribe of Dan.

It was Antiochus Epiphanes who stormed the city of Jerusalem in 168 B.C. and sacrificed a pig upon the brazen altar, thus committing an historic "abomination of desolation." [2] In light of this fact, the reason Daniel used the same term, little horn, becomes obvious. Antiochus Epiphanes was another type of the antichrist. Though he was not that final, future man of sin, he was at least a partial fulfillment of the prophecy giving future generations the privilege of studying the exploits of

Antiochus Epiphanes, and from them profile the coming antichrist.

By designating the Syrian (Greek) general, Antiochus Epiphanes, as a little horn, Daniel was predicting the character and deeds of the future antichrist. Those who would live after the period of Antiochus Epiphanes could know the general pattern of the future antichrist by studying the life and deeds of the former *"little horn."*

For instance, the future antichrist will have the same interests as Antiochus Epiphanes in changing the religious beliefs and practices of the Jews. This is also suggested in Daniel 9:27 when he causes *"the sacrifice and the oblation to cease"* on the day he commits the abomination of desolation. In Daniel's vision, Gabriel referred to the seven-year Tribulation Period as the 70th *"week"* in which the antichrist, that future little horn, will break his covenant with the Jews:

"And he shall confirm the covenant with many for one week: and in the midst of the week he shall cause the sacrifice and the oblation to cease, and for the overspreading of abominations he shall make it desolate, even until the consummation, and that determined shall be poured upon the desolate" (Daniel 9:27).

According to this verse, another future abomination of desolation is on the agenda. The future little horn will desecrate the restored Jewish sanctuary, stop the sacrifices, and claim to be the one for whom it was built.

Finally, in Daniel 11:36-39, the exploits of the little horn are once again described. Daniel departed from his description of Antiochus Epiphanes in verses 21-35 and began to speak prophetically of that future man of sin in verses 36-38:

"And the king shall do according to his will; and he shall exalt himself, and magnify himself above every god, and shall speak marvelous things against the God of gods, and shall

prosper till the indignation be accomplished: for that that is determined shall be done.

"Neither shall he regard the God of his fathers, nor the desire of women, nor regard any god: for he shall magnify himself above all.

"But in his estate shall he honour the God of forces: and a god whom his fathers knew not shall he honour with gold, and silver, and with precious stones, and pleasant things" (Daniel 11:36-38).

In verse 36, the antichrist is said to *"magnify himself above every god"* and to *"speak marvelous things"* against the true God. In verse 37, he is said to turn from the god of his fathers, which leads many to believe he will be of Israelite descent. Neither will he regard the *"desire of women,"* an ancient term referring to the Messiah. It was the desire of every Jewish mother to bear the Messiah. Christ was the *"desire of women."* In verse 38, he is said to honor *"the god of forces."* Perhaps this refers to a powerful, satanic influence during the days of the Tribulation.

According to verse 45, he will enter the Tabernacle of David and will declare himself to be the Jewish Messiah. He will sit in the Temple of God showing himself that he is God. Verse 45, in fact, describes his takeover of the city of Jerusalem:

"And he shall plant the tabernacles of his palace between the seas in the glorious holy mountain; yet he shall come to his end, and none shall help him" (Daniel 11:45).

These verses were written by the prophet Daniel to describe the future antichrist. Since the term *"antichrist"* did not exist in the days of Daniel, a colloquialism was used, befitting the generation in which Daniel lived. That future man of sin was called the *"little horn."*

In the book of Revelation, however, the antichrist is described in an altogether different manner. There, he is called a *"beast."* The term is used most frequently in Revelation 13 where he is described at some length. In that chapter, there are two beasts described by John. The first beast rises up out of the sea, which most consider to be the sea of humanity or the nations. The second beast rises up out of the earth, symbolic of the land of Israel.

The first beast (out of the sea) represents the ten-nation Revived Roman Empire. In fact, John compares it to Daniel's vision described in Daniel 7. This first beast is a composite of the creatures seen by Daniel, including the ten horns upon its seven heads. The beast out of the earth seems to represent the false prophet or the antichrist. He is one who looks like a lamb, but talks like a dragon:

"And I beheld another beast coming up out of the earth; and he had two horns like a lamb, and he spake as a dragon" (Revelation 13:11).

If the beast out of the earth represents the antichrist, there are certain characteristics we should note. First of all, it appears that he will be a descendant of the children of Israel. His rising *"out of the earth"* may have reference to his being from the lineage of Abraham. The tribe of Dan (according to the Rabbis) is considered to be a missing tribe. This "lost tribe" of Israel could produce the antichrist. Rabbinic scholars speculated upon this possibility some 150 years before the birth of Christ. If this beast is a descendant of the tribe of Dan, he would meet the requirement of having come from Israel.

The two characteristics, listed in verse 11, represent the two meanings of the prefix "anti." As a *"lamb,"* he represents a substitute for Jesus Christ, and as a *"dragon,"* he represents one who is opposed to Christ. The word "anti" comes from a root word with two meanings — "in place of," and "against."

The New Scofield Reference Bible notes that many identify the beast *"out of the sea"* as the antichrist, and the beast *"out*

of the earth" as a false prophet. However, some do not necessarily see both an antichrist and a false prophet in the two
beasts. In other verses (Revelation 16:13, 19:20, and 20:10)
the term, *"beast"* is maintained as a symbolic description
while the term, "false prophet" is faithfully rendered as a
mortal person. I see only one prominent world leader during
the coming Tribulation Period, the antichrist himself. The
New Scofield Reference Bible indicates that if "the beast
coming up out of the earth is the antichrist, he is the same as
the false prophet " of Revelation 16:13, 19:20, and 20:10.³ In
Revelation 13:11 the *"false prophet"* is also described as a
beast. Some think that the beast *"out of the sea"* represents not
one man but ten men — leaders of those ten nations which
confederate to establish the "Revived Roman Empire." Their
confederation will constitute a loosely knit world government.

Many prophetic scholars interpret the first beast, *"out of the
sea"* to be the political ruler, the dictator of the revived Roman
Empire — namely, the antichrist. They believe the second
beast, *"out of the earth"* to be the religious leader of the world,
the one referred to as the false prophet. ⁴

Nevertheless, the beast *"out of the earth"* will perform
miracles as credentials of his authority and will lead the world
to worship, or give allegiance to the first beast and the one-
world political system. In verses 16-18, he will demand that
people receive the "Mark of the Beast" in their right hand or
forehead as he implements his new world economic system.

The third term used for the antichrist is found in II Thessalonians 2. He is referred to as the *"son of perdition."* In verse
3, the apostle Paul wrote that the future *"son of perdition"* and
"man of sin" will make his appearance at the beginning of the
Tribulation. In fact, his appearance will be one sign that this
period has begun. In verse 4, Paul wrote that he will oppose

and exalt himself above all that is called God, or that is
worshiped. This statement is quite similar to that which was
written in Daniel 11:37. Paul, however, adds that *"he, as God,
will sit in the Temple of God, showing himself that he is God."*
Apparently, the antichrist will be bold enough to take a seat in
the sacred building, as if he were the god for whom it had been
built.

In verses 6 and 7, Paul indicated that a certain power has
been present down through history to prevent the antichrist
from appearing sooner:

*"And now ye know what withholdeth that he might be
revealed in his time.*

*For the mystery of iniquity doth already work: only he who
now letteth will let until he be taken out of the way"* (II
Thessalonians 2:6-7).

The word *"let,"* in verse 7, is an old English word meaning
"hinder." Down through the centuries, something has hin-
dered the antichrist from making his appearance. One day,
however, that hindrance will be removed. It is generally
believed that the power which hinders is the Holy Spirit in believers. We will be taken out of the way when the trumpet
sounds and the shout comes from heaven to rapture all
Christians out of this world into heaven.

*"And then shall that Wicked be revealed, whom the Lord
shall consume with the Spirit of His mouth, and shall destroy
with the brightness of His coming"* (II Thessalonians 2:8).

In this verse, the antichrist is called "Wicked," with a capital
W! But Paul is quick to write that the Lord shall consume him
with the *"Spirit of His mouth, and shall destroy him with the
brightness of His coming."*

The antichrist — was called by Daniel, *"a little horn"*; was
called by John, *"a beast"*; and was called by Paul, *"Wicked,"
"man of sin,"* and *"the son of perdition."*

Chapter Notes

CHAPTER 19

1. Josephus, op. cit., Antiquities, Book X, Chapter XI, par. 7, p. 227.
2. Ibid.
3. THE NEW SCOFIELD REFERENCE BIBLE, C.I. Scofield, ed., (New York: Oxford University Press, 1967), notes on Revelation 13:11.
4. M.R. DeHaan, REVELATION (Grand Rapids, MI: Zondervan, 1966), p. 210.

The Tower of Magdala at the Rennes-le-Chateau in southern France.

Chapter 20

Looking for a Superstar!

The world is looking for a man who can solve the problems of our planet. That elusive dream of a world without war, poverty, and disease has always been just beyond our reach. Most politicians are perplexed — overwhelmed by the magnitude of the problem. They are convinced that the dilemma cannot be solved by committees or systems, be it democracy or socialism. Most believe they can only be solved by a man — a superhuman superstar!

A European statesman once said, "Give us a man who can solve the problems of our world, and we will follow him — even if he be the devil himself!" He was voicing the opinion of many of our world leaders — not because they wish to serve the devil, but because they think mankind is on the brink of disaster.

The late Dag Hammarskjold, Secretary General of the

United Nations, once said, "We have tried so hard and have failed so miserably. Our problems are beyond us." The weariness of war, the differences of ideologies, the uneasiness of our economy, the influx of inflation — all of these things are pressing upon Mr. Average Citizen until he does not know which way to turn. "Give us a man!" is the cry across our nation and around the world. So eager is humankind to have a superstar problem-solver, they will choose the wrong man.

Consider what the Bible has to say about his person and his work. First of all, just as Jesus Christ had a genealogy, so also must the antichrist be of a particular lineage, and the Bible does not leave us in the dark in this regard.

Daniel wrote, *"Neither shall he regard the God of his fathers"* (Daniel 11:37). That statement leads me to believe that the antichrist will be from a similar background as Christ. Perhaps the antichrist will also be from the lineage of Abraham. The antichrist may be of Israelite origin. I have offered a previous study on the "lost" tribe of Dan, in Chapter 6, and have considered the possibility that the future world leader could be from that tribe. Let's review Genesis 49. This scripture gives us an account of the dying Jacob and his last words.

"Gather yourselves together, that I may tell you that which shall befall you in the last days" (Genesis 49:1).

It is here that the aged Jacob looked into the far future — to the last days, and told each son what should befall him and his offspring during that time. For example, he said of Judah:

"Judah, thou art he whom thy brethren shall praise: thy hand shall be in the neck of thine enemies; thy father's children shall bow down before thee.

"Judah is a lion's whelp: from the prey ...

"The sceptre shall not depart from Judah, nor a lawgiver from between his feet, until Shiloh come; and unto him shall

the gathering of the people be" (Genesis 49:8-10).

How perfect is the prophecy! For indeed, Judah has been the leading nation among the 12 tribes throughout the centuries! In fact, every Israeli today bears the name of Judah; he is commonly called a "Jew." Prophecies of each of the 12 sons are listed in these verses, but there is one in particular which should be considered:

"Dan shall judge his people, as one of the tribes of Israel.

"Dan shall be a serpent by the way, an adder in the path, that biteth the horse heels, so that his rider shall fall backward" (Genesis 49:16-17).

The dying Jacob prophesied that the tribe of Dan would bring judgment upon the other tribes. He would be a *"serpent by the way, an adder in the path."* It is here that we can see the trail of the serpent — satan! So wicked was the tribe of Dan that it was eliminated from the tribes listed in Revelation 7. In the Garden of Eden, God told Eve about the coming Redeemer and His conflict with the serpent:

"And I will put enmity between thee and the woman, and between thy seed and her seed; it shall bruise thy head, and thou shalt bruise his heel" (Genesis 3:15).

This scripture refers to the *"seed"* of the serpent. The term implies a direct lineage through which the antichrist will come. At Calvary, the prophecy of the bruised heel was fulfilled. However, there is another side to the story which is yet to come to pass — Christ *"... shall bruise thy head."*

There are some theologians who believe that the future Master-ruler of the world will be a resurrected Judas Iscariot. There are others who believe he will be born of a harlot, opposite to Jesus Christ, who was born of a virgin. Some believe he will be born without a human father, the son of the devil, just as Jesus was born the Son of God. Such movies as "Demon Seed," "Rosemary's Baby," and "The Omen" lend further credibility to that speculation.

Revelation 13 gives a prophecy of his rise to world prominence. Whether his power will be supernatural or simply political, no one knows. A list of the fantastic feats, attributed to the antichrist, can be produced today through our modern means of technology.

According to Daniel 7, the antichrist will rise to power during the days of a political confederation. He will be asked to aid a group of ten European nations, who together will attempt to establish a loosely-knit world government. There are three main areas he will seek to develop: a One-World monetary system, a One-World political system, and a One-World religion.

He will convert all the currencies of the world into one currency and will attempt to make it mandatory for all people to receive a mark in their right hand or in their forehead in order to be able to buy or sell.

His One-World religion will reach its peak when he declares himself to be god. That will occur when he enters the future Jewish Sanctuary and sets up his throne in the Holy of Holies in the middle of the Tribulation Period.

He will rise to power on a platform of peace. It is my opinion that the Battle of Gog and Magog may be the catalyst upon which he rises to power. After the defeat of Russia, he will be hailed as a great peacemaker and will be considered the savior of the human race.

The first three and one-half years of his rule will be characterized with peace and a semblance of prosperity. It will be a false peace, however, with a continual number of problems arising within the bureaucracy. With the Soviet Union destroyed at the beginning of the Tribulation Period, all of the countries which have fallen to communism will be set free — free, that is, to serve the victor, Mr. 666!

In the middle of the Tribulation, he will seek to make Jerusalem his world capital. He will commit the "abomination of desolation," setting up his throne in the Temple and claiming to be God. He will demand that all people throughout the world receive the "Mark of the Beast" in their right hands or in their foreheads in order to be able to buy or sell. It is my opinion that about this time the nations of the world will rebel against his authoritarian dictatorship. They will begin to prepare their armies for the last great battle, Armageddon.

During the last three and one-half years of the Tribulation Period, referred to in the Bible as the "Great Tribulation," there will be colossal natural disasters in addition to the problems of political upheaval. This, in itself, will create panic throughout the world. Various governments will become disenchanted with the rule of the antichrist. The whole world will then turn against him and will amass their armies for war.

Once again, the world will blame the Jews for their problems. Armageddon will be a final attempted genocide of the Jews. The armies of the world will converge upon Israel for the most devastating battle of history. If the war were allowed to continue without the intervention of Jesus Christ, there would be no flesh saved. What a mess man will make when he tries to establish a world government without God!

In the height of the battle, the sun will be turned into darkness and the moon shall not give her light. The earth and the heavens will be shaken. The mountains will crumble, and the islands will be moved out of their places.

Suddenly, Jesus Christ will appear in the heavens. He will come to the aid of Israel (though certainly not to the aid of the antichrist), and he will put down the armies of the world.

"I saw heaven opened, and behold a white horse; and he that sat upon him was called Faithful and True, and in righteousness he doth judge and make war. His eyes were as a flame of

fire, and on his head were many crowns; and he had a name written that no man knew, but he himself. And he was clothed in a vesture dipped in blood: and his name is called The Word of God" (Revelation 19:11-13).

Jesus Christ will throw the antichrist into hell:

"And the beast was taken, and with him the false prophet that wrought miracles before him, with which he deceived them that had received the mark of the beast, and them that worshiped his image. These both were cast alive into a lake of fire burning with brimstone" (Revelation 19:20).

Christ, the victor, will judge the nations, set up His glorious kingdom and rule over the earth for a thousand years!

In this book I have attempted to explain Bible prophecies regarding these last days. I have tried to paint a scenario that I believe will fulfill the Scriptures concerning the present status of the world and the men who desire to control it. I believe I have made a good case for the student of Bible prophecy to now be able to identify with current events. I trust that all who are faithfully looking for the appearance of our Lord, will prayerfully consider this possible source for the antichrist.

I have laid the groundwork which may connect the future leader of the world with the royal families of Europe. I also have shown that certain esoteric groups are attempting to establish a One-World order and a One-World religion. Though these so-called "guardians of the Grail" did not intend to reveal their "secret," I believe they have. Furthermore, they are moving full-steam ahead to produce that future world leader — the man from hell!

The antichrist will be perhaps the greatest intellectual, the greatest politician, the greatest statesman, and the greatest economist who ever lived! But when he usurps the throne of God and gives his allegiance to satan, he will become the greatest fool!

Chapter 21

The Last Crusade

The timing for the release of the movie INDIANA JONES AND THE LAST CRUSADE may well have been by divine appointment. We learned of its release after the manuscript had been completed. I had wondered how people were going to understand the "Grail" terminology. I could imagine someone seeing the title in a bookstore and asking the question, "what's a grail?"

Now that the movie has been released, my problem is solved! Everyone now knows about the legend of the grail!

There are a few points about the movie which I would like for you to consider. For example, the title "THE LAST CRUSADE" refers back to the FIRST crusade in 1099 when Godfroi de Bouillon drove the Moslems out of Jerusalem and established a Crusader kingdom. Godfroi declined the crown, but his brother Baudouin became the "King of Jerusalem" upon Godfroi's death in 1100.

I believe the real LAST crusade will occur when the heir to the title "King of Jerusalem" tries to reclaim his throne. That should take place in the midst of the Tribulation Period and is called in Matthew 24:15, the *"abomination of desolation."*

In the movie, Nazi involvement in the quest for the Grail lends more truth than fiction. Adolf Hitler was indeed an adept of the Grail along with the Thule Society, an esoteric group of Grail students which evolved into the Nazi party.

At the end of the movie, Sean Connery was asked what he learned when he found the Grail? His reply was, "Illumination." In this book, we have discussed the so-called Secret Doctrine of illuminism. We have a chapter on the Illuminati. The concept involves the opening of the mind's eye — the All Seeing Eye!

Finally, the story ends in Petra, a city carved out of the mountains of southern Jordan. The city was once the capital of the Edomite empire. There, the encounter with the Grail takes place.

Well, in the real LAST crusade, the remnant of Israel will flee from the abomination of desolation and head for the wilderness area of Petra. Most students of prophecy agree that Petra will be the place where the Jewish remnant will be safe for the concluding days of the Tribulation Period. Isaiah 16:1-4 describes the occasion. *"Send ye the lamb to the ruler of the land from Sela (Petra) ... unto the mount of the daughter of Zion ... hide the outcasts ... Let mine outcasts dwell with thee ... from the face of the spoiler ..."*

Petra may well be the place where the remnant of God's Chosen People will have their encounter with the one who held the cup on the night before His crucifixion and said, *"This is my blood of the New Testament"* (Matthew 26:28). The producers of the movie may be more right than they realized!

A Final Word with You

The subject matter of this book, I realize, will presumably be more acceptable to Christians who believe in a premillennial return of Christ, than to Christians with a different eschatological outlook, or to non-Christians in general. At the same time, I know that the content herein has tremendous interest among secular readers as well. Those interested in history, especially a conspiratorial view of history, may feel they have discovered more evidence to support their theory. It is my hope and prayer that I have helped to inspire some non-believers to review their priorities and accept Jesus Christ as Savior before it is too late!

If you are a Christian, then I am glad you have read this book! This information should have provided you with a realization of the shortness of time we have left before the Lord begins His final countdown to Armageddon! May I urge you, dear Christian, to win as many people to Christ as you can while there is time.

I believe that Christians will not be forced to endure the wrath of God's judgment. We will be "raptured" to meet our Lord in the air at some point prior to the beginning of that dreadful time. Perhaps this book can be used before that great event to help some who need to turn their life over to Jesus Christ. After the Rapture, some, hopefully, will use this book as a means to understand what is taking place and learn how they can escape those events.

To you who have not yet accepted Jesus Christ as personal Savior, may I urge you to turn to Him right now.

Simply bow your head and pray. Repent of your sins and receive Jesus Christ as your personal Savior. God will forgive your sins and give you eternal life.

Your prayer could be as simple as this example:

Dear Lord, I know I am a sinner. Please forgive me for my sins. Come into my heart and life and save my soul. I pray in Jesus' name. Amen.

If you now receive Christ, may I invite you to call my office toll-free, 1-800-245-5577, Monday-Friday, 9 A.M.- 5 P.M. (Central Time), and let me know of your decision.

May God bless you,

J. R. Church

About the Author . . .

J. R. Church obtained his formal education in theology at Tennessee Temple University, Chattanooga, Tennessee. In 1962 he received his B. A. degree with a major in Bible and a minor in history. His love for history gave him insight into God's great "Plan of the Ages" and has prompted him to pursue his present field of prophetic research.

He has been preaching the Gospel since childhood. Converted at age seven, he set out with one main goal in life — to win others to Jesus Christ.

J. R. was led to receive Christ by the teacher of a Child Evangelism class, Mrs. Pauline Click. From her class in those early years came several ministers and missionaries. He delivered his first sermon at age seven. By the time he was in the fifth grade, he was winning scores of children with his "Wordless Book." Mrs. Click also encouraged him to memorize over 1,200 Bible verses. It was during those early years that God moved upon his heart to dedicate his life to the Gospel ministry. Both he and his twin brother, Terry, were baptized together, arm in arm, at age 10.

J. R. and his wife, Linda, have been married 31 years. They have two children, a daughter, Terri, and a son, Jerry, Jr. He pastored in Texas for 17 years. During the 1970's his interest turned toward prophetic research and television as a means of sharing his studies with others.

In 1979 he moved his family to Oklahoma City. J. R. felt he could be more centrally located for the ministry God had laid before him.

Over the years he has developed the ministry, PROPHECY IN THE NEWS, and has traveled across America many times lecturing on the subject of prophecy. He has hosted several tour groups to Israel and the Middle East. His panoramic film presentations have been a delight to thousands.

J. R. has authored several books on prophetic subjects. His book, HIDDEN PROPHECIES IN THE PSALMS, has become a "Best Seller" across America and has warmed the hearts of those who also look for the "Blessed Hope" of the Second Coming of Christ. Over 100,000 books have been distributed, not only in the United States, but in other countries as well. It has been translated into other languages for distribution in South Korea, the Far East, Finland, Europe and Israel. It is also distributed in Great Britain, Australia, New Zealand, and other English-speaking nations.

The ministry publishes a monthly tabloid on prophetic research as well as a syndicated television broadcast which airs across the country and by satellite network to the entire Western Hemisphere. J. R. is convinced that Jesus Christ will return soon, perhaps in his lifetime.

Though he is not a date-setter, he feels that the return of the Jews to their Promised Land is the great fulfillment which has ushered in a series of events predicted to lead to Armageddon. The rise of an atheistic political regime in the Soviet Union with its awesome military power sets the stage for the predicted Battle of Gog and Magog.

He is convinced that the only hope for this sin-cursed world lies in salvation through faith in Jesus Christ. The return of the Son of God will bring true peace and prosperity to a warring humankind. There really is a utopia in the future — not through government, but through God!

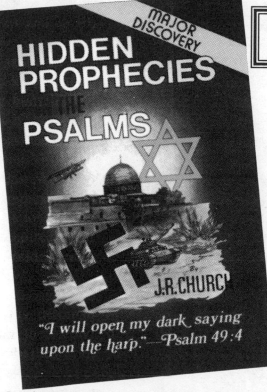